The Olympic Crisis

The Olympic Crisis
Sport, Politics and the Moral Order

John Hoberman

Aristide D. Caratzas, Publisher
New Rochelle, New York
1986

Acknowledgements

The author wishes to acknowledge two special contributions to this book. My editor, Marybeth Sollins, labored over two versions of the manuscript with a steadfastness and care I will long appreciate. The reader, unlike the writer, can scarcely imagine what he owes her. My wife, Louisa generously postponed work on her own book to accelerate this one. I only hope it was worth the wait. Finally, I wish to thank the University Research Institute of the University of Texas at Austin for its support of this work, and Kathleen Lewis for preparing the index.

Published by
Aristide D. Caratzas, Publisher
Caratzas Publishing Co., Inc.
PO Box 210 (481 Main Street)
New Rochelle, NY 10802

Library of Congress Cataloging in Publication Data

Hoberman, John M. (John Milton), 1944-
   The Olympic crisis.

   Bibliography: p.
   Includes index.
   1. Olympic games—History. 2. Sports and state.
I. Title.
GV721.5.H576 1984   796.4'8'09   84-17007
ISBN 0-89241-224-0
ISBN 0-89241-225-9 (pbk.)

Photo Credits
The following organizations have permitted the use of photographs in this publication: The Bettmann Archive, figs. 3, 4; Wide World Photos, figs. 7, 8, 10-16, 18-20; LIFE Magazine, © Time, Inc., fig. 17.

For Anatoly Shcharansky,
imprisoned before the Moscow Olympiad

Contents

Preface 1

I. **Sport and the Moral Order**
Sport and International Morality 5
The Moscow Olympiad and the Helsinki Accords 7
Pre-Olympic Repression 11
How Sport Distorts Political Life 14
The Sport Boycott and the Morals of the Left 16
Boycotting "Culture": Is Sport Different? 22

II. **"Playing the Chameleon": The Moral Bankruptcy
of the Olympic Movement**
Amoral Universalism 29
Pierre De Coubertin: The Career of a Sportive Internationalist 33
Carl Diem: *Olympiadenker in dürftiger Zeit* 45
Avery Brundage: The International Sportsman as
Fellow-Traveler 50
The Converts: Communism and the Olympic Movement 57

III. **The Moscow Olympiad in Political Context**
The American Boycott and the Soviet Response 65
The Dissidents and the Boycott 69
The Moscow Olympiad as Totalitarian Spectacle 71
Could the Olympics Have Changed Soviet Society? 76

IV. **The Critique of Olympia**
Introduction: Olympic Sport as a Modernism 81
The Founder's Critique of Olympia 85
The Fascist Critique of Olympia 88
The Neo-Marxist Critique of Olympia 106
Olympism, Communism, Art and Technology 113
Conclusion: The Defense of Olympia 118

Epilogue
The Olympic Crisis of 1984 127

Footnotes 135

Bibliography 157

Index 163

List of Illustrations

1. Pierre de Coubertin. From *Die Olympischen Spiele 1936*, I, illustration facing page 49.

2. Organizing Committee of first modern Olympiad. From *Die Olympischen Spiele 1936*, I, fig. 120, p. 86.

3. German womens' Olympic gymnastics team. Undated photo. The Bettmann Archive.

4. Cheerleaders. Los Angeles 1932. The Bettmann Archive.

5. Medallion by Hugo Ballin. Los Angeles 1932. From *The Games of the X Olympiad Los Angeles 1932. Official Report,* 1932.

6. Carl Diem. From *Die Olympischen Spiele 1936*, I, fig. 120, p. 86.

7. Opening ceremonies. Berlin 1936.

8. Sign forbidding Jews to enter Olympic Village. Garmisch-Partenkirchen 1935/6.

9. Avery Brundage. From *Die Olympischen Spiele 1936*, I, fig. 172, p. 127.

10. The Olympic flame. Olympia 1952.

11. The Olympic torch. Finland 1952.

12. Portrait of Stalin at Olympic training camp. Helsinki 1952.

13. Injured athlete. Melbourne 1956.

14. Helmeted soldier. Mexico City 1968.

15. Striking students in Main Square. Mexico City 1968.

16. The arrest of a student. Mexico City 1968.

17. Armed policeman dressed as athlete. Munich 1972.

18. Moscow 1980. Rehearsal of opening ceremony. Soviet dancers and gymnasts form a human tower. Wide World Photos. Moscow 1980.

19. Moscow 1980. Brezhnev and Lord Killanin view opening ceremony of Summer Games. Wide World Photos.

20. Misha bear. Moscow 1980.

1. Baron Pierre de Coubertin.

2. Meeting of the Organizing Committee of the first modern Olympiad, Athens 1896. Coubertin is second from left.

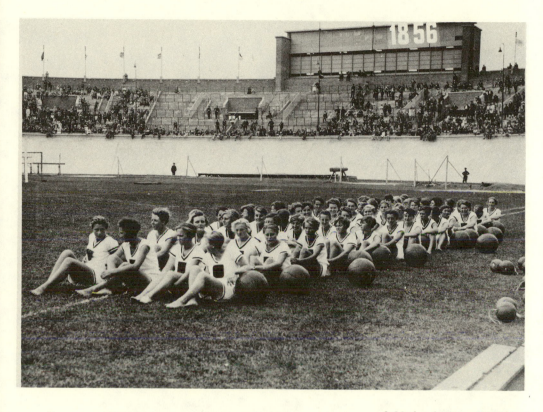

3. Undated photo. German
womens' Olympic gymnastics
team. The Bettmann Archive.

4. Los Angeles 1932. Cheer-leaders. The Bettmann Archive.

5. Los Angeles
1932. The
medallion by
Hugo Ballin is
raised into
position.

6. Carl Diem: General Secretary of the Organizing Committee for the XI Olympiad held in Berlin 1936.

7. Berlin 1936. Opening ceremonies. Wide World Photos.

8. Jews forbidden entry to the Olympic Village at Garmisch-Partenkirchen. Winter Olympics, 1936. Wide World Photos.

9 Avery Brundage: President of the United States Olympic Committee 1936.

10. Olympia 1952.
The Olympic
flame begins its
journey to
Helsinki. Wide
World Photos.

11. Finland 1952.
The Olympic torch
arrives in Finland.
Torchbearer passes
a Laplander and
his dwelling. Wide
World Photos.

12. Helsinki 1952.
A portrait of Stalin
hangs beneath the
hammer and sickle
motif at the
Olympic training
camp for Soviet
and Iron Curtain-
country athletes.
Wide World
Photos.

13. Melbourne
1956. Athlete
injured in fight
during water polo
match between
Russia and
Hungary. Wide
World Photos.

14. Mexico City 1968. Helmeted soldier at cycling track. The Mexican Army provided protection at many Olympic venues. Wide World Photos.

15. Mexico City 1968. Striking students in Main Square in front of Palacio Nacional where troops, riot police, and paratroopers had dispersed them earlier. Light tanks are in center background; police in right foreground. Wide World Photos.

16. Mexico City 1968. Riot police and police agents subdue a student during riots. Students had demanded removal of the police chief and the riot troops' commander for brutality to pro-Castro demonstrators. Wide World Photos.

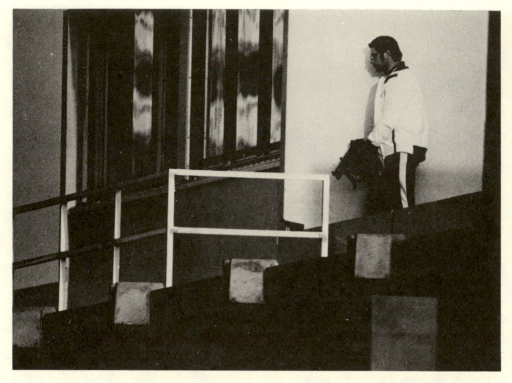

17. Munich 1972. Armed
policeman dressed as
athlete. Co Rentmaster,
LIFE Magazine © Time, Inc.

18. Moscow 1980. Rehearsal of opening ceremony. Soviet dancers and gymnasts form a human tower. Wide World Photos.

19. Moscow 1980
Brezhnev and Lord
Killanin view
opening ceremony
of the Summer
Games. Wide
World Photos.

20. Moscow 1980.
Misha bear,
mascot of 1980
Games, dwarfs
two policemen
outside the
Olympic Village.
Wide World
Photos.

Preface

On March 3, 1980, as the American-led Boycott of the Moscow Olympiad was gaining momentum, ten British gold medalists of past Olympiads released "an open letter to the world." "Boycotting Moscow," their statement read, "would be to make an essentially political statement in a way that will destroy the entire basis of sport enshrined in our society and culture."[1] This was by no means the only prediction of catastrophe. On January 25, a columnist for *Die Zeit* had forecast the end of the Olympic Games,[2] and almost simultaneously the president of Mexico lamented that the boycott proposal had "shattered" the Olympic movement.[3]

These predictions were wrong. In the wake of the Moscow boycott, and on the eve of the 1984 Los Angeles Games, we are about to witness yet another resurrection of this celebrated—and maligned—international movement. What is striking about these prophecies of doom is that they represent a global concern for an institution whose history remains largely concealed from its enormous audience. The very fact of its survival makes it clear that the Olympic movement has benefited from a sentimental dispensation which has encouraged its defenders and frustrated its critics. As both a critic and a defender, I acknowledge this sentimental aura even as I attempt to dispel it.

But the Olympic movement does not just overcome its history; it has also demonstrated a prodigious ability to forget it. The worst crime in Olympic history, the Tlatelolco massacre of October 2, 1968, carried out by the Mexican government to guarantee "Olympic peace," remains unknown to the vast majority of well-informed people. Even the leading figures of the Olympic movement remain poorly understood.

The Olympic movement, directed by the International Olympic Committee (IOC), must be studied as an international institution which some political observers have judged to be a very effective one. "If anywhere in the world a true international body is operating," the Sovietologist Henry Morton wrote in 1963, "it is this small group of men beholden to no one, whose sovereignty is upheld neither by wealth nor by armies but by a powerful ideal that has so far withstood all reorganization by nationalistic interests. Its efficacy is the envy of other world organizations that have found themselves denied freedom of action for the international good by the selfishness of individual countries."[4]

Until relatively recently this was the conventional interpretation of the status of the IOC, and it contains an important element of truth. The Olympic movement has represented an impressive victory for internationalist principles during a violently nationalistic century. At the same time, however, its sovereignty is largely an illusion; its automony and immunity to political pressure have been overrated. In fact, it has preserved a questionable "independence" by collaborating with political power, only rarely by resisting it.

The Olympic crisis is permanent and is rooted in both the procedure and the core doctrine of the IOC. Since the Games are sited on a rotational basis, they are exposed to an endless variety of political conditions. Guaranteeing public order is a major task at every Olympiad, and it has become practical to assign Olympic festivals to the most repressive societies. Even relatively liberal societies have succumbed to the temptation to abridge civil liberties on behalf of international sport festivals. Prior to the XII Commonwealth Games (1982) held in Brisbane, Australia, a Commonwealth Games Act was rushed through the Queensland State Parliament, making it a crime to disrupt the Games in any way. (This legislation was aimed in particular at demonstrations on behalf of the aborigines.[5]) A month later, in November, Prime Minister Indira Gandhi opened the Ninth Asian Games in New Delhi, where 20,000 security forces were under orders to shoot on sight anyone disrupting the sporting event.[6]

The 1988 Olympic Games have been assigned to Seoul, South Korea, currently a military dictatorship under the leadership of General Chun Doo Hwan, who assumed power in 1980 by means of a coup d'état. Chun's term in office under the present constitution runs until 1988 and it is unclear whether he will permit a free election of a successor.[7] South Korea has not experienced a peaceful transfer of power since 1945; 1988 should be an interesting Olympic year.

The core doctrine of the Olympic movement is what I have called "amoral universalism," which strives for global participation at all costs, even sacrificing rudimentary moral standards. The IOC has promoted its pseudo-ethical ideal of "sportsmanship" by employing a pseudo-religious jargon.

The moral poverty of the Olympic movement can be illuminated by comparing it to another international organization, the World Psychiatric Association. In the Olympic movement, which may be called "non-dialogical," international exchange takes the form of sporting encounters. These, however amicable or inspiring, do not possess the power of discourse. An athletic event takes its place in a long series of similar events; it does not constitute one element of a more complex dialogical process. The "understanding" made possible by dialogue and the "understanding" achieved at a sports festival are very different. Such "non-dialogical" internationalism, lacking the capacity or even a motive for adopting moral standards, will of necessity take on the standards of its political environment. In the words of its founder, Pierre de Coubertin, the Olympic movement must "play the chameleon." The consensus universalis is never ruptured as a matter of principle.

In the World Psychiatric Association, which exemplifies "dialogical" internationalism, the universal character of the organization is subordinate to moral principles. Universalism is not regarded as the highest institutional value. At its 1977 meeting in Hawaii, this group voted to condemn "the systematic abuse of psychiatry for political purposes in the U.S.S.R." In February 1983, five months before a W.P.A. convention that had been expected to debate American and British resolutions to suspend or expel the Soviet Union on these grounds, the Soviets withdrew from the organization. The president of Britain's Royal College of Psychiatry said he thought the Soviets had left because they "would have found it difficult to cope with the possibility of a humiliating defeat in the full glare of public debate."[8] In June 1983, the Czechoslovak Psychiatric Society joined the Soviets in withdrawing from the W.P.A.[9]

This crisis elicited contradictory reactions among the organization's members. Just prior to the Soviet withdrawal, the American psychiatrist Walter Reich commented:

> Taking away Soviet psychiatry's right to speak before the world by removing it from the World Psychiatric Association might be no great loss for civilization; it could be argued that the Russians have forfeited that right by their record of psychiatric abuse. But removing them from the world body would also take away their duty to listen—to attend meetings, to hear criticisms, to be asked about this dissident or that, and to receive visitors, such as myself, who might ask them fundamental questions about their habits, beliefs and perceptions.[10]

3

This universalist position differs from that of the IOC in that it offers a specific agenda to justify the preservation of an organization's global character. This agenda is, in a word, the systematic pursuit of discourse.

But the pursuit of discourse can fail. And prolonged failure can turn the pursuit into a caricature of itself. In the wake of the Soviet and Czech withdrawals, Dr. Harold M. Visotsky, chairman of the American Psychiatric Association's International Committee on the Abuse of Psychiatry and Psychiatrists, stated: "We can't have a scientific body without ethics. It would have been unconscionable if we had refused to look at these abuses."[11] This is a position the IOC has never taken.

It is the moral sententiousness and smugness of the IOC and its acolytes which makes this an apt comparison. An organization which has sought—and been granted—the blessings of the Vatican[12] has forfeited any exemption from judgment of its ethics. The gap between the IOC's pretensions and its performance is too wide to ignore. Indeed, the International Olympic Committee has shown itself to be the most self-confident and least self-reflective of institutions. For this reason, the Olympic movement requires historians who can examine its career without prejudice and in a larger context than that of the movement itself.

Sport's political problems derive from the twofold moral burden borne by the international sport festival in general, and by the Olympic festival in particular. First, the sport festival confers prestige—and, implicitly, a kind of moral legitimacy—on its host. For enormous numbers of people, the sports festival is a genuine expression of the fellowship of man. Second, the sport festival removes participants, at least symbolically, from that "real" world of deadly conflict and moral transgression in which innocence is always at risk. It is the power to spread this innocence and "good will"—virtue in its public, disembodied, and anonymous form—which makes the sport festival an appealing vehicle for political propaganda.

I . Sport and the Moral Order

1. Sport and International Morality

As the Olympic movement entered the political crisis of 1980, the prevailing view was that an innocent international culture had once again fallen victim to political forces which had overrun a tragically vulnerable territory. Strictly speaking, this view is correct. In a harshly politicized world, sport is a virtually weightless force, outranked by the more tangible goals of political, economic, and military interests.

From Mexico City to Los Angeles, five successive Olympiads have been tarnished by political scandals, two of them involving mass murders. Why, then, sport's reputation for innocence? "There is inherent in sport," a West German sociologist has written, "the outline of a utopia, what generally should be but is not, for which we should not cease to strive. Perhaps this is the deeper basis for its power to fascinate."[1] It is the utopian dimension of sport, as much as the political forces which seek to exploit it, which accounts for the survival of the Olympic movement.

Imperiling its survival are the decline of this utopianism and the appearance of critical voices. But this crisis is not only the result of political intervention; there is inherent in global sport, and in the Olympic movement in particular, a moral vacuum from which political crises derive.

Moral claims can occasionally outweigh the claims of sport. This is the basis of the campaign against apartheid in South Africa; it was the basis of the African boycott of the Montreal Olympiad of 1976. It is the moral status of sport that has challenged a global public's infatuation with the best-known international organization after the United Nations—itself the sponsor of sport boycotts as an anti-apartheid strategy.[2]

The most familiar moral problem affecting international sport concerns the location of a sports festival—a state may be deemed unfit to hold a sports meet on account of internal repression or foreign aggression. If the Berlin Olympiad of 1936 is an example of the first, then the Moscow Olympiad of 1980 is an example of the second—or perhaps an example of both.

The first sport boycott of quasi-international character occurred in 420 B.C. when Sparta, the most powerful of the Greek states, was barred from the religious rites and the athletic games at Olympia for its failure to pay a fine after breaking the Olympic truce. A subsequent boycott resulted from the murder of an athlete while he was on his way to the Isthmian Games.[3] Such actions demonstrate a greater moral fastidiousness in this area than is practiced by most modern states.

In an address titled "The Boycott as a Sanction of International Law," made in Washington on April 27, 1933, Professor Charles Cheney Hyde of Columbia University defined a boycott as "conduct whereby two or more States combine to interfere with the economic or political freedom of another, as by cutting off trade with its territory."[4] This analysis of the boycott, offered less than three months after Hitler's seizure of power, and after the commencement of a Jewish boycott directed against Germany,[5] emphasizes the gravity of such measures and the need to prove that a breach of international law has actually occurred. The speaker warns that "the group may in fact set loose against that State a vast and harm-producing force regardless of the absence of proof that it has violated a single international obligation."[6]

The idea of an Olympic boycott is particularly disturbing because it appears to represent a crisis of international ideals. An American boycott of the Moscow Olympics, the New York Times stated,

> might well spell the end of the Olympics that the world has known since 1952, when Soviet athletes first competed. Future Games would be forever plagued by political storms; they would not soon again be universal. Many would say, so what? The Olympic ideals of nonpolitical and amateur competition have long since been dishonored by ideological and commercial exploitation. But there is a wider perspective, in which the Olympics are not merely games but one thread in a web of international arrangements that transcend frontiers and celebrate the fraternity of peoples. In this sense, at least, the Olympics are worth saving.[7]

While the Olympic Games are the most glamorous thread in this international web, they are not the most important. There is a hierarchy of international contacts which is often forgotten when the Olympic movement is being considered. An unjustifiable boycott, from the standpoint of an internationalist, is one which denies an adversary, not expert athletes, but expert physicians—a depth to which the world order has not yet sunk.

There is no question that the the theatrical qualities of the Games, and the mystical sentiments they inspire, have given rise to a spectacular overestimation of their value to the cohesion of the world community. As a result, Olympic internationalism has been charged with a salvational mission for which it is unsuited. The idea that the Olympic movement has been an important vehicle of moral influence from its inception is an illusion which has thrived for nearly a century (see chapter 2).

The paradox is that sport has become an emblem of the moral order precisely because it does not call for moral actions. It is universally acceptable because it does not make judgments. Indeed, far from being an ally of ethics, modern sport is better interpreted as one of its antagonists. The idealism of the sporting internationalists has failed in situation after situation in which sportsmen (and the officials who manage them) have ignored, avoided, or repudiated ethical standards.

The very ease with which the Communist states have embraced Olympic idealism (since Stalin's abrupt change of policy in 1951—see below) suggests its lack of ethical content as much as its reconciling powers. With a hollow camaraderie, all sides agree that sport is a kind of "humanism," an activity which improves mankind. But it is a humanism that expresses itself in a carefully guarded international code of platitudes analogous to the highly abstract language of diplomats.

This code is a language in which Olympic officials and Communist functionaries feel supremely comfortable. Formulas like "the Olympic spirit" or "the humane ideals of sport" are examples of language-by-committee, the point of which is to mitigate conflicts. But such language also serves as a screen behind which the voice of conscience is sacrificed to the myth of global consensus. Respectability recommends itself, and for many years it has been unfashionable to inquire into the ethical stature of this consensus. The content of "the Olympic spirit" was not at issue; what people debated was the chances of its survival.

The Olympic jargon is a universal propaganda, one that is aimed in all directions. It is a language the world chants to itself, and it is time we better understood the origins and functions of this curious ritual.

2. The Moscow Olympiad and the Helsinki Accords

From the beginning of its campaign to host the world at the 1980 Olympic Games, the Soviet Union insisted that it had a "moral right" to stage this athletic festival.[8] When this goal was finally achieved in 1974, a Soviet journalist proclaimed that "the choice of Moscow can only be viewed as a vote of confidence in the first socialist state, which is conducting a foreign policy of peace that is fully in tune with the times."[9] In 1979, a Soviet commentator described the Moscow Games as an expression of the spirit of the 1975 Helsinki accords.[10]

Even before the Soviet invasion of Afghanistan and the exile of Andrei Sakharov to the "closed" city of Gorky had scandalized the West and provoked a boycott campaign against the Moscow Olympiad, these claims struck an odd note. Aside from the question of their truth, such statements invited controversy by associating international sport with the moral obligations of the state and the related issue of human rights. An examination of what the Soviets actually meant can tell us a great deal about the differences of perspective which separate the political cultures of East and West.

What did B. Bazunov mean by Moscow's "moral right" to hold the Games?

> What other town can stand comparison with Moscow as regards the quantity of sporting accommodation that has as much modern equipment and is sufficiently comfortable? Moscow has long been renowned as a repository of national and world culture. It has considerable experience as a centre of international tourism. The Soviet capital's healthy environment—clean air, unpolluted waters and abundant greenery—makes it a very suitable sporting venue. Muscovite hospitality is world-famous.
>
> By and large, these arguments are universally acknowledged. The moral right of the Soviet capital to hold the games is obvious . . .[11]

By Western standards, this argument assumes a very peculiar definition of "moral right." Yet behind its official bonhomie we may reconstruct three important themes.

First, the Games represent a certain kind of political and cultural legitimacy: "The Moscow Olympics are meant to be a monument to the Soviets' self-esteem, an extravaganza of self-congratulation that in a way betrays their profound insecurities."[12] All nations, the Soviets are saying, have a "moral right" to the sort of international stature that has been withheld from the socialist states by a hostile "bourgeois" world order, of which the Olympic movement was for many years a despised symbol in the U.S.S.R. Ironically, sport festivals now tend to be a preoccupation of underdeveloped nations. As President Mobuto Sese Seko of Zaire declared on the morning of the championship boxing match between George Foreman and Muhammad Ali in September 1974, the bout and the music festival which was to precede it "defy those who said Zaire could not organize such events."[13]

Second, the assertion that the Moscow Games express the spirit of the Helsinki accords gives the Soviets' claim to a "moral right" yet another dimension. It suggests that the Games will somehow express the theme of "human rights." As a matter of fact, paragraph (g) of "Basket Three" of the Helsinki declaration supports at least part of the Soviet argument:

> *Sport.* In order to expand existing links and cooperation in the field of sport the participating states will encourage contacts and exchanges of this kind, including sports meetings and competitions of all sorts, on the basis of the established international rules, regulations and practice.[14]

Sport, by its inclusion in "Basket Three," became an internationally recognized "human right" comparable to "Contracts and Regular Meetings on the Basis of Family Ties," "Reunification of Families," "Marriage between Citizens of Different States," "Travel for Personal or Professional Reasons," "Meetings among Young People," and so on. It may, in fact, have been the only "human right" the Soviet authorities had any intention of honoring, and its exceptional status in this regard should tell us something about whether sport as a "human right" can be taken seriously outside the Socialist bloc.

As I will argue below, sport is *not* comparable to the fundamental human rights. It should be added that the willingness of the Western democracies to define sport as an unqualified good is a major concession to Soviet and East German ideologists, who have a vested interest in equating the limited world of sport with culture itself.

From the Soviet viewpoint, the fundamental human right is the right to physical survival and well-being. The signing of the Helsinki accords elicited, for example, the following Soviet comment: "For the nations of Europe this unprecedented event buttressed the hope of securing for themselves and future generations that most important of human rights—the right to life, to peace and peaceful international cooperation."[15] It may well be that this emphasis derives in part from the catastrophic losses the Soviet Union sustained during the Second World War. In addition, given Soviet cultural and ideological xenophobia, sport's mute and virtually nonconceptual form of expression constitutes an ideal medium for contact with the outside world.

It may be noted that the Soviets define "humanism" with some very specific restraints in mind:

> Humanism is an inalienable aspect of the Marxist philosophy. However, Marxist proletarian humanism is a qualitatively new and higher phase compared with the humanistic ideas and theories of the past. Briefly speaking, the essence of the revolution accomplished by Marx and Engels in humanistic views is that humanism was placed on the solid foundation of science, and its principles were given a real content and became a militant weapon of the proletariat's struggle for emancipation.[16]

Humanism has become a "science," but one which requires strict supervision:

However, in some cases this humanism is speciously interpreted and turned into its opposite—into liberal reconciliation with violators of the norms of the socialist community: idlers, bodgers, irresponsible people, exponents of morals and psychology alien to us.[17]

Mass sport in the Socialist style, in addition to being the foundation of the developmental "pyramid" which produces the elite, is a mass hygienism. It is the only way for a state to dramatize the otherwise mundane concerns of public health. Virtually all Socialist states have an excellent record in this area dating back to the early Bolshevik years in the Soviet Union. Sport—and its hygienic benefits—is literally a constitutional right in the Soviet Union, East Germany, and North Korea. Sport is also viewed as emotionally hygienic, and is considered a means for the development of self-discipline, strength of will, and other non-intellectual character traits.

One aspect of the Soviets' ideological strategy is to confuse hygienic rights with human rights, and sport serves this strategy like no other activity. As soon as "hygiene" is expanded to mean "social hygiene," and the state assigns itself the role of physician to the body politic, then totalitarian controls for every aspect of social life—from the arts to official soccer strategy—are inevitable.

In fact, in the longstanding Soviet campaign against religion, one argument has been that religion is simply unhealthy: "Certain religious practices are seen as directly endangering the health of parishioners, e.g., prolonged fasting, frenzied prayer, baptism by immersion, overindulgence at religious celebrations, or contact with stagnant holy water." This sort of hygienic concern is entirely consistent with the following passage from one Soviet criminal code, which makes it illegal to organize or direct a group "whose activity, carried on under the guise of preaching religious beliefs and performing religious ceremonies, is connected with causing harm to citizens' health, or with any other infringement of the person or right of the citizens, or with inducing citizens to refuse social activity or the performance of civic duties, or with drawing minors into such a group."[18]

In any totalitarian state, "health" is an ideological condition as well as an organic one, and it will be noted that the legal doctrine just cited assumes that religious activities endanger both ideological and physical well-being. Sport, on the other hand, represents a perfect fusion of the ideological and organic forms of health, and it is no accident that in the Socialist block sport is sometimes used as an anti-religious prophylactic. Both Soviet and Polish officials have scheduled sporting events against religious observances in order to dissuade young people from developing religious feelings.[19] The Soviets, unlike Pope Pius XII, do not associate sport with undefined "spiritual boons."[20]

For Communist social planners, the sport mentality is a predictable, uncritical mentality. That is why Western acquiescence to the sentimental notion that sport is a "human right" represents a substantial concession to political regimes that aspire to limit and channel the life of the mind.

Third, implicit in the claim that the Soviet Union had a "moral right" to host the Olympic Games is the philosophical basis of the Olympic movement itself. The fundamental principle of the Olympic ideology is a global universalism which, it is hoped, will bind a diverse membership of decent nations into a world community. This is certainly the sense of Pierre de Coubertin's writings on the subject. In the next chapter, I will offer a critical history of the Olympic "idea" in order to demonstrate why it could not survive twentieth-century ideological conflicts intact. At this point,

9

it suffices to say that the Soviet Union joined the Olympic movement—after denouncing it for years—for essentially the same reasons it participated in the Helsinki conference: it wanted legitimacy in international circles. It joined in order to take advantage of the principle of universalism, the moral implications of which have never been taken seriously by the International Olympic Committee or its founder Coubertin.

By joining the movement, the Russians achieved, in a formal sense, a certain kind of moral parity with the rest of the world, since it is assumed that a deep interest in sport presupposes wholesome instincts. This, at any rate, is the fiction on which international sport jargon has rested for years. In both 1951 and 1975, Soviet ideologists discerned an opportunity to change international norms by adding their voice to an Establishment which had been dominated by liberal-democratic Western societies. Thus they gained a foothold in a virtually global culture.

What is more, they seized the opportunity to turn the Olympic motto of *citius, altius, fortius* into an absolute performance principle which has, inevitably, become the reigning doctrine of world sport. In this philosophy the Soviet bloc excels, if only because the tangible goals of any sporting performance are so one-dimensional in scope. Olympic-style sport has become a matter of mobilization, and the Communist states are mobilized for sport in a way Western societies are not.

Naively, Senator Edward Kennedy has publicly accepted the Communist thesis that sport superiority signifies the superiority of the political culture which spawns it. "Adolf Hitler's vaunted Aryans were bested by the Americans in 1936," one cultural official wrote in the *New York Times*. "History often repeats itself. Can Americans not do as well in 1980?"[21] The real question is—should it matter?

Do the Soviets accept the idea of an international sport culture "in the spirit of the Helsinki accords"? In December 1962, with a fine flourish of calculated naiveté, the mayor of West Berlin, Willy Brandt, proposed that the 1968 Olympiad be held in Berlin. The staging of this festival would, of course, require the dismantling of the Berlin Wall. Walter Ulbricht, *Der Spiegel* reports, "destroyed this illusion with a harsh *Nein*."[22]

Has Soviet-bloc sport policy advanced beyond this point during the last two decades? One answer emerged from the European Sport Conference held in October 1979, in Berchtesgaden. This summit meeting of sport chieftains eventually assumed the form of a tug-of-war between Eastern and Western mentalities. The chief concern of the Communist states turned out to be uncontrolled border crossings. East German athletes and trainers, in particular, constantly escape to the West, and are supposedly subjected to "inducements to commit treason" in their native country. "Treason" may well refer to the divulging of state-sponsored high-performance sport research, which is considered a state secret and sometimes denied even to the Russians. Manfred Ewald, the head of the East German state sport establishment, emphasized the theme of control to the point of complaining that the European Cup soccer tournament was tinged with an element of anarchy by virtue of the fact that initial opponents were chosen by lot! The principal aim of the Soviet and East German delegations was to ensure that East-West Sport contacts would continue to be confined to an elite class of athletes. So much for the "competitions of all sorts" specified by the Helsinki document.

A former senator from West Berlin proposed that international sport contacts be extended throughout "all levels of competition and age classes"—an idea which is in keeping with the domestic sport cultures of the Communist states, but which presents unacceptable perils to regimes which fear the consequences of large-scale exchanges. Ewald, one of the most powerful men in the GDR, summed up the impasse by accusing journalists of "poisoning the atmosphere" and thereby blocking wider sport contacts between eastern and western Europe.[23]

This was an edifying spectacle, and one which confirms the view that, for the purposes of "international understanding," the Socialist bloc defines an athlete as a person who possesses a highly technical skill combined with will power, and who therefore embodies nothing except performance with reference to an objective goal. Here is one more reason for the Soviets to embrace the Olympic Games, which are akin to a conference of technocrats whose "mutual understanding" is likely to be channeled along predictable and ideologically innocuous lines. Complete absorption in sport signifies the decline of the ideal of the traditional amateur's determination to integrate sport into a responsible and well-balanced life. The repudiation of "amateur" idealism represents in effect a significant approach to the Marxist doctrine which holds that play and leisure do not differ essentially from labor, and that they, too, are subject to the overall ideological mobilization which characterizes, at least theoretically, a "total" society.

11

Today sport is the one international culture which is developing in accordance with a Communist model. "The Communist countries will dominate the medals because they have organization and a system," John Walker, an Olympic champion from New Zealand, declared a year and a half before the scheduled Moscow Games.[24] He spoke, not as a cultural critic, but with an envy laced with contempt for the less militant, less scientific sport cultures of the non-Communist world. In this sense, the ethos of the sport mobilization initiated by Stalin in the mid-1930s has become a global standard.

3. Pre-Olympic Repression

The Olympic Games and the World Cup soccer tournament are the world's great sport holidays. "A holiday," Freud wrote in *Totem and Taboo* (1913), "is a permitted, or rather a prescribed, excess, a solemn violation of a prohibition. People do not commit the excesses which at all times have characterized holidays as a result of an order to be in a holiday mood, but because in the very nature of a holiday there is excess; the holiday mood is brought about by the release of what is otherwise forbidden."[25] "We know," the founder of the modern Olympic movement wrote, that sport "tends inevitably toward excess, and that is its essence, its indelible mark."[26]

Muscovites, too, an American journalist reported in January 1980, had been looking forward to their Olympiad as "a fiesta." But what sort of fiesta could Soviet authorities permit? For how does a society bent on preventing at all costs the internationalization of its population conduct a cosmopolitan festival without giving up controls which are likely to rob the festival of its spontaneous dimension?

This is a problem even for an authoritarian government which rules over a relatively cosmopolitan citizenry. Prior to the World Cup soccer championship held in Buenos Aires in June 1978,

> the Argentine authorities found themselves faced with a dilemma . . . how could they institute relatively relaxed security measures which would give the impression of a country back to normal after a period of chaos without risking serious incidents?

How could they maintain such measures without confirming the 'prejudices' of observers from the world over and yet heading off possible violence? The military mind prevailed, and uniforms and rifles have been visible everywhere.[27]

In the end, the lesson of Argentina was that nationalistic sport hysteria is rarely compatible with a visible apparatus of repression. The Argentine sport fiesta produced a potentially embarrassing, yet ineffectual, kind of protest which grew out of the euphoria of victory itself. On the day after Argentina won its great final-round victory, a gray and rainy Monday, two thousand youths assembled before the presidential palace and chanted: "Mr. President, we don't want to work today!"—before breaking into the national anthem. Later that evening, the government issued the following press release: "Lieutenant General Videla left his desk and proceeded to the entrance at Calle Balcarce 50, where he met with the young people. Having done so, he stated: 'The government feels an obligation to the future which you represent. I thank you for coming here. It is a reason for pride.' "

This demonstration was, in effect, a response to a proclamation issued by the Ministry of Public Information the day before the championship game: "These events should inspire us, not only to participate in spontaneous demonstrations of joy, but also to return to work, which is another expression of joy. Argentines will show up at their places of work with enthusiasm and the consciousness of victory, spurred on by their capacity to accomplish great things, and with confidence in our own powers."[28] For General Videla, who the next day would weep for joy at the trophy presentation, such exuberance threatened to become too much of a good thing.

There was in 1980 no chance that the Soviet regime would face risks comparable to those taken by the Argentine generals. The dissident trials held in Moscow during the summer of 1978 marked the beginning of a two-year campaign to purge Moscow of all potentially disruptive elements. As early as July of that year one journalist was predicting the worst: "Moscow must be cleaned out before 1980 of all elements who could alone, or through their contacts with thousands of Western visitors, provoke demonstrations hostile to the Soviet regime. By condemning Mr. Slepak and Mrs. Nudel, Soviet authorities were just laying the groundwork for future operations of this type on a much larger scale."[29]

This prediction was confirmed by many press reports. In January 1980 the Swedish *Dagens Nyheter* reported: "Since 1979 Moscow's local authorities have for week after week been purging the capital of all dissidents as well as overeager religious types, black-market operators and criminals. All of this in order to empty the city of those individuals whom the authorities deem to be 'disruptive' prior to and during the Olympic Games."[30]

In June 1978 "Czechoslovakia went through a dress rehearsal of this type of operation at the request of Soviet authorities. Prague was purged of its dissidents for the duration of Leonid Brezhnev's visit. The operation was a complete success and there was no incident to mar the stay of the illustrious Soviet guest."[31] In July 1979 one of the principal planners of the liberalization policies of Alexander Dubček, the Czechoslovak leader deposed by the Soviet Union in August 1968, pointed out that the detention of ten leading members of the Charter 77 human rights group was part of the same strategy: "they're trying to get all of this unpleasantness out of the way before next year when the Moscow Olympics and the Madrid conference reviewing the Helsinki human rights agreement focus attention again on Eastern Europe."[32]

Dagens Nyheter also reported that the isolation of Andrei Sakharov, which was probably occasioned by his support of President Carter's Olympic boycott appeal in an interview with ABC-TV, would end only after the Games.[33] As of this writing (1984), he remains in preventive detention in Gorky.

The prospect of incarcerated dissidents and the planned evacuation of children from the Moscow area prior to the Olympiad (to shield them from ideological contamination by foreigners)[34] raised serious questions about the Soviets' conception of a festival. Historically, one object of a festival has been to display cultural differences in an atmosphere of mutual acceptance. This is an aesthetic matter as much as a moral or political one; civil repression violates the very style of a festival. It must be noted that a festival is not the same thing as anarchy. Pierre de Coubertin, founder of the Olympic movement, wrote that the Games should be anything but "a kind of chaotic and vulgar fair."[35] Every festival partakes of a tension between discipline and spontaneity, between form and the dissolution of form. But it is one thing to plan Olympic amenities to the last detail, and quite another to attempt to dictate the scope of normal human contacts, a project in which the KGB had been engaged for three years prior to the Games.[36] As Freud points out, there is a dimension of the festival experience which lies beyond good and evil, but its excess is that of instinct, not of the state.

Pre-Olympic repression is not a Soviet innovation. "How can you bring yourself to threaten the whole Olympic movement?" a Soviet sports official exclaimed early in 1980 as the boycott tide began to swell. "We saw students shot down in the streets before the Mexico City Olympics, but we stayed . . . And now you're going to walk away from the Olympics because we sent troops to help a neighbor whose house was being broken into?"[37] However implausible the explanation of Soviet intervention in Afghanistan, the reference to the Tlatelolco massacre of October 2, 1968, was appropriate. The famous Mexican essayist and poet Octavio Paz has provided an account of these events in *The Other Mexico: Critique of the Pyramid* (1972):

> Near the end of September [1968] the army occupied the University and the Polytechnical Institute. This action was so widely criticized that the troops withdrew from both institutions. There was a breathing spell. The students, full of hope, gathered for a meeting—not a demonstration—in the Plaza of Tlatelolco on the second of October. At the end of the meeting, when those attending it were about to leave, the plaza was surrounded by the army and the killing began. A few hours later it was all over. How many died? No newspaper in Mexico dared to print the number of deaths. Here is the figure that the English newspaper, *The Guardian*, after a careful investigation, considered the most probable: 325. Thousands must have been injured, thousands must have been arrested. The second of October, 1968, put an end to the student movement. It also ended an epoch in the history of Mexico.[38]

What were the origins of this great political crime?

> In order to gain international recognition of its transformation into a modern or semi-modern country, Mexico requested, and was granted, the designation of its capital as the site of the 1968 Olympic Games. The organizers of the Games not only passed the test successfully, they even added an original program to that of the sports events, a program underlining the pacific, noncompetitive nature of the Mexican Olympics: exhibits of international art; concerts, plays, and dance presentations by

orchestras and companies from all over the world; an international meeting of poets; and other events of a similar nature. But, in the context of the student revolt and the repression that ensued, these celebrations seemed nothing but gaudy gestures designed to hide the realities of a country stirred and terrified by governmental violence. Thus, at the very moment in which the Mexican government was receiving international recognition for forty years of political stability and economic progress, a swash of blood dispelled the official optimism and caused every citizen to doubt the meaning of that progress.[39]

For some reason, this greatest of Olympic calamities has remained the least discussed and the least censured. In an editorial published on January 8, 1980, the *New York Times* offered the following historical judgment: "All this flood-lighting of the Olympic stage encouraged a student uprising in Mexico City and the massacre of Israeli athletes by Palestinians in Munich four years later."[40] The fact that the death toll of the "uprising" was thirty times that of the "massacre" had still not sunk in.[41]

4. How Sport Distorts Political Life

As suggested above, the moral—not to mention historical—significance of the pre-Olympic massacre of 1968 is grotesquely disproportionate to the role it has come to play in public consciousness. "The students," K.S. Karol wrote in *Guerillas in Power* (1970), "their ranks decimated by repression on so vast a scale, were confident that the Tlatelolco massacre would cause an outcry throughout the world. Jean-Paul Sartre and Bertrand Russell called for a boycott of the Olympic Games. Had there been such a thing as a world conscience, every civilized country would have heeded their appeal, would have shown its abhorrence of a government that used such vicious methods against students on the eve of a great festival of sport and youth. But the appeal fell on deaf ears in the West, in the East, and most surprising of all, in Havana."[42] What these students found, in effect, was a global silence, the effects of which can be observed to this day. They might also have noted that, when faced with the prospect of renouncing the gratification provided by the Olympic spectacle, the "world conscience" became quiescent.

"The party of the football fans," *Der Spiegel* remarked during the World Cup year of 1974, "is as strong as it is amorphous. It nominates no candidates and still manages to influence politics at the local and national levels—in other countries even more so than in the Federal Republic. The football party, which is truly a mass party, is ubiquitous, to be found wherever stadiums and floodlights, subsidies for the local team or privileges for football-favorites are at stake."[43] If anything, this description is not comprehensive enough. For the "sport party"—as the survivors of Tlatelolco discovered—is actually a global one which has affected the moral order, almost always at the expense of ethical standards.

The world of sport has given rise to more bizarre, violent, aberrant, and even criminal behavior than its faithful public is disposed to recall. Its overlap with the world of politics has often resulted in a kind of amoral freak show, which fascinates because of the element of absurdity which is inherent in the spectacle of its grotesquely inverted priorities.

The worlds of sport and politics coexist, and either realm may impinge upon the other in a destructive manner. Politics, for example, may introduce atrocity into the domain of sport. During the Second World War a German commander occupying Kiev authorized a soccer game between Russian prisoners-of-war and a squad which represented the Luftwaffe. When the prisoners had thoroughly injured Nazi honor by defeating their (undoubtedly better-fed) opponents by a score of 5-3, the German commander had four of them shot. A granite monument to these fallen warriors still stands in Kiev.[44]

A less vicious travesty of the concept of sportsmanship occurred during the first East German soccer championship in 1950. The game—at which Walter Ulbricht himself was present—was between a team considered by the ruling Socialist Unity Party as representative of "bourgeois" sport and a team promoted by the Party as a standard bearer of "socialist football." The referee, a Party member, controlled the course of the game by sabotaging "bourgeois" offensives with offside calls and by awarding penalty kicks to the "socialists," who eventually won by a score of 5-1. Ulbricht and other Party officials in attendance had to be saved from the crowd by police.[45]

In addition to the comedy of sportsmanship violated, sport offers the comedy of sportsmanship absurdly triumphant. During the Nigerian civil war of the early 1970s, the general who was waging genocidal war on the secessionist Ibo province of Biafra made a point of having two Ibos placed on the national soccer team.[46] There is also the comedy of sportsmanship righteously suspended. After a European Cup soccer match between Holland and West Germany, during which the Dutch players employed a flagrant and illegal degree of violence, the president of the Dutch club explained, "the Germans have not absolved themselves of crimes committed during the Nazi period."[47] Yet another comic variant is sportsmanship which has been forcibly reacquired. After a soccer match held in Poland in 1961 between the national team and that of the Soviet Union had been punctuated by ugly scenes, Polish sportswriters convened a special conference to subject themselves to Socialist self-criticism and to confess that they were responsible for having produced "a chauvinistic climate."[48]

Finally, there is sportsmanship so cynically violated as to require an apology from the chief of state. During a 1969 World Cup match played in Buenos Aires between Argentina and an Italian club, some of the Argentine players ran amok, seriously injuring two of the Italians. After the Italians had, nevertheless, won the game, Argentine police broke into the room where they were passing around the champagne-filled trophy and arrested the victors' best player (who at the age of eighteen, had emigrated to Europe) for evasion of military service. In the wake of public outcry, the Argentine president, Juan Ongania, apologized, declaring that Argentina's reputation had been "compromised around the world." Three of the Argentines were suspended and sentenced to thirty days in prison. They were reinstated after Ongania's overthrow in 1970.[49]

There are many such anecdotes. It is well known that a soccer game helped to ignite the 1969 war between Honduras and El Salvador, and less well known that another soccer game once occasioned the breaking of diplomatic relations between Uruguay and Argentina.[50] All of these incidents have a comic effect because "fairness" is expect to reign in the world of sport, which in fact mimics the struggle for political power.

Less comic are those instances where the power of sport has literally frightened politicians into a state of paralysis. "As a leader in the Third World movement," one journalist pointed out in 1980, "with close political ties to many countries in Africa, Jamaica would have been expected to join the 1976 [Olympic] walkout. But by boycotting, it would have forfeited [Donald] Quarrie's chances for a gold medal, and Quarrie was arguably more popular in his homeland than Michael Manley, the Prime Minister. To have denied Quarrie that opportunity could have shaken an already unstable government, a fact acknowledged by Jamaican political and sports officials."[51]

In 1978, the *Frankfurter Rundschau* reported that Dutch politicians who had been paying lip service to the idea of boycotting that year's World Cup soccer championships in Argentina because of that country's gross human rights violations, were finally unwilling to put such a plan into effect: "For the politicians an important factor is the fear that they might alienate voters; they do not want to burn their fingers in the holy football fire." While expressing sympathy with the idea of a boycott, the Dutch Prime Minister, Andries van Agt, "did not, however, want to take a general position against participating in sporting events in countries having undemocratic governments, but rather wished to judge each case on its merits."[52] Perhaps he had forgotten that in 1956, Holland had been one of only three countries (the others being Spain and Switzerland) to boycott the Melbourne Olympiad to protest the Soviet invasion of Hungary.

But the most disturbing report associated with the 1978 World Cup came from Amnesty International, that Argentina may have been spared condemnation by the United Nations Human Rights Commission because it was playing host to the World Cup.[53]

If the world had boycotted Hitler's Olympics, the course of history might have been different,[54] asserted Rolf Pauls, the West German NATO representative, during the initial phase of the 1980 Olympic crisis. Implicit in Pauls' thesis is the idea that it was in the power of the Olympic movement to assist in the formation of that "world conscience" which competes so poorly with the appeal of sport. Pauls also assumes that the Olympic movement actually helped to preserve the moral vacuum within which the Berlin Games took place.

As of February 1980, this argument had appeared in a West German court of law, offered by a defense attorney for a former Nazi officer accused of aiding in the murder of 73,000 Jews in a concentration camp. The lawyer argued that his client—the mayor of a small Bavarian village before his conviction—"never had a chance to step back and analyze the Nazi regime but saw for himself 'how the whole world had applauded the [Nazi] system at the 1936 summer Olympics in Berlin'."[55]

This is a pathetic alibi, but one which demonstrates how sport can deform the moral order. Once again conscience is pitted against the appeal of sport, and the courtroom argument holds that it is somehow natural for men to suppress the former so that they may succumb to the latter.

5. The Sport Boycott and the Morals of the Left

An international moral standard for sport has been proposed at the governmental level in connection with events other than the Olympic Games. In November 1977, the official Cuban press agency announced that Cuba would not participate in an international baseball tournament in Nicaragua because the selection of that country as the tournament site represented "the most brutal negation of the very principles that sports events should uphold," because Nicaragua did not meet "minimum conditions of moral order that every sports event should have." It added that Nicaragua was "the current setting of bloody repression."[56]

This sort of proclamation—from any government—was long overdue. It is well known that Fidel Castro takes a personal interest in baseball, and it is certain that the decision to boycott such a tournament bore his imprimatur. But the Cuban appeal on behalf of "minimum conditions of moral order" for sport was diminished by the fact that it was not made ten years earlier. For the Fidel Castro who found Nicaraguan conditions so intolerable in 1977 had not, for some reason, considered the pre-Olympic slaughter in Mexico City a "brutal negation of the very principles that sports should uphold."

The Cubans who in March 1968 had decided to withdraw from the Olympic games in protest against the expected presence of South Africa, saw no reason to make a similar gesture after the Tlatelolco massacre, no reason to demonstrate their solidarity with the thousands of young Mexicans who were being detained in Mexican prisons for allegedly participating in a Castroist plot and for deliberately provoking the peaceful Mexican army. On October 19, 1968, the Cuban athletes filed past Gustavo Diaz Ordaz, just like their comrades from Eastern Europe. The Soviet prime minister, Kosygin, sent the Mexican president warm wishes for the success of the great Olympiad.[57]

The modern concept of the sport boycott has its origins on the political left, in the series of Workers' Olympiads sponsored by the (European) Socialist Workers' Sports International (SASI) during the 1920s and 1930s. These events were held even after Hitler had destroyed its strongest (German) branch shortly after his accession to power in 1933. "Organized as a counter to the chauvinistic tendencies of the more well-known modern Olympic games and as an expression of international working class solidarity, the first of these grand events was held at Prague in 1921. In sharp contrast to the Olympics in Antwerp (1920) and Paris (1924) where the 'losers' in the Great War were prohibited from participating, the Prague Games featured competition between worker athletes from erstwhile enemy nations."[58] This kind of reconciliation was achieved, of course, by viewing the worker-athlete as a world citizen. As the Germans workers' sport leader Fritz Wildung put it in 1925, the exclusion of Germany and Russia from the 1924 Paris Games was justified neither "from the standpoint of the sportsman nor from that of the international citizen."[59] An authentic international movement could rightfully claim to have nullified the national chauvinist element otherwise endemic to international sport, and the results were impressive. According to one historian, the Second Olympiad, held in Austria in 1931, offered "a display . . . that compared favourably or better with the 1932 Olympics in Lake Placid and Los Angeles."[60]

Representing only one aspect of a highly developed "workers' culture,"[61] the Worker's Olympiads were a "boycott" phenomenon that expressed not the sporadic humanitarian impulses of an age of atrocity, but the specific ideals of an international movement. Socialist workers' sport, unlike Soviet sport, was a genuine humanism which emphasized the welfare of the athlete over the caliber of his performance. It offered an intellectually honest critique of sport[62] even as it sought recruits for the movement—a virtually unique example of political integrity in the history of sport. It should also be emphasized that the workers' sport movement had come into existence for defensive reasons, as a response to the exclusion of workers on class

17

grounds from the "bourgeois" sports clubs of late 19th-century Europe. How important was this sport culture, given its life span of only forty years?

The Workers' Olympiad represented, in fact, an amazing achievement—the first and only alternative sport festival ever to challenge the Olympic movement on its own ground. What is more, the workers' movement was the first sport culture ever to take both moral and political principles seriously. Its attempt to schedule a counter-Olympics in Barcelona against the Berlin games of 1936, aborted by Franco's seizure of power that year, may be seen as the real initiation of sport into the sphere of international morality.

With the transition from "workers' sport" to Stalinist sport during the 1930s, much of the ethical and humanitarian content of left-wing sport culture was sacrificed to a cult of productivity analogous to the forced industrialization of the Soviet economy. Stalin's version of the Workers' Olympiads was a series of World Youth Festivals which failed as a counter-Olympic boycott strategy, and in 1951 the Soviet Union applied for membership to the International Olympic Committee. (Avery Brundage's account of his negotiations with the Russians appears in Chapter 2.) The Soviets' eagerness to join the Olympic movement may be measured against the company they were now willing to keep. When they demanded the ouster of "Fascist Spain" from the Olympic movement as a condition for their participation, their protest was obvious posturing and was not taken seriously.[63] Another new colleague, the head of the West German National Olympic Committee, Karl Ritter von Halt, was none other than Hitler's last *Reichssportführer* and a member of the SA.[64] When the Winter Olympic Games were held in Oslo in 1952, the Norwegians would not even let him into the country—the first time any nation had dared to boycott a member of the IOC.

In 1951 the East German sport establishment had also begun to make compromises. When Walter Ulbricht issued his directive in favor of "Germans around one table," East German sport officials found themselves across the table from an ex-bicycle racer named Manfred von Brauchitsch, a former storm trooper and adviser to Albert Speer's Ministry for Armaments and War Production. Von Brauchitsch, however, turned out to be an agreeably flexible political personality, whose constant principle seems to have been an unlimited devotion to the world of sport. After a number of visits to the GDR as a sport diplomat, von Brauchitsch took over the leadership of the East German Motor Sport Association, a position he lost after wrecking an East Berlin bar in a drunken rage. Back in the Federal Republic, he presided over a West German committee making preparations for the Communist World Youth Festivals. Brought up twice on charges of high treason by the West German public prosecutor's office, von Brauchitsch was conveyed back to the East in 1954, where the Socialist Unity Party eventually made him president of the "Society for the Promotion of the Olympic Idea in the GDR.[65]

The Soviet Union has kept the idea of the moral-ideological boycott alive by applying it where it would least affect Soviet sport prestige—against the racist government of South Africa. For the past two decades it has hounded the South Africans at every turn within the International Olympic Committee and in other sports federations.[66] In March 1968, after thirty-nine Third World nations had announced plans to boycott the Mexico City Games because of the IOC's refusal to ban South Africa, the Soviet National Olympic Committee issued the following statement: "If the I.O.C. refuses to convene an emergency session and insists on its decision about South Africa, the USSR OC will be impelled to reconsider the question of the participation of Soviet sportsmen in the Summer Olympics of 1968."[67] The exiled South African sport activist who had been pressing Soviet officials for a boycott commitment "later admitted that he believed the lure of potential gold medals in Mexico would have ultimately kept the Russians in the Olympics. While he was convinced of this, he knew that keeping the threat of a Soviet boycott alive was almost as important to the outcome on South Africa."[68]

On September 26, 1973, a soccer game took place in Moscow's Lenin Stadium. It was not announced in *Pravda,* and Soviet television broadcast instead a local ice hockey game. Fewer than half of the spectators normally attending such a match were present. In the course of the game itself, neither side scored a goal. There was good reason for keeping a publicity vacuum around this sporting contest, which was attended in large measure by people who had been mustered to the stadium by Party organizers.[69] For this game matched the Soviet national team against that of Chile where, on September 11, a group of right-wing military officers had overthrown the constitutionally elected government of the Marxist president, Salvador Allende. They had murdered him and his aides and then had begun a campaign of torture and killing aimed at exterminating the Chilean Left. The junta had also turned the National Stadium in Santiago into a concentration camp, where the torture and machine-gunning of political prisoners was to become a routine.

It was a routine which could not go on indefinitely in the National Stadium, however, for there were other uses to which it was to be put. On November 21, the Chileans were scheduled to host the Russians on these grounds in order to repair the indecisive result of the silent match in Moscow. But as it turned out, this rematch was not to be. For in the course of the two weeks following the tied match in Lenin Stadium, something resembling a conscience had apparently developed in Moscow. This conscience finally spoke on October 12: the Russians, it said, would not play on a field "red with Chilean patriots' blood, transformed into a torture arena and execution site."[70] What was more, it continued, the return match would have to be moved either to Cuba or to Peru, where a left-wing government happened to be in power. The junta—which had actually taken the trouble to announce that it would remove its prisoners from the infamous stadium prior to the game—offered its opponents a compromise: the contest would not have to be played in that particular stadium. The Russians, however, refused: they would not play on the "blood-soaked soil of Chile" at all.[71]

The Soviet demands were directed to the Secretary General of the International Football Association (FIFA), Dr. Helmut Käser, a Zürich lawyer and former colonel in the Swiss army. The Secretary General promptly dispatched himself to Santiago to inspect the disputed stadium. Upon his return he announced: "What we have here is an identification camp, in which a group composed primarily of foreigners is being held in order to clarify their status."[72] It was, in short, a somnambulistic performance worthy of U.S. Olympic officials who, in 1936, had traveled to Berlin and had failed to turn up any irregularities worth mentioning.

At this point FIFA ordered the Russians to play—or else. The Soviets, in turn, pointed to an apparent precedent. Northern Ireland, on account of its civil war, had been permitted to play its qualification rounds in England. FIFA's press secretary, however, begged to differ: "In Northern Ireland the situation was entirely different, since neither the teams nor the spectators could be guaranteed security. But in San-

19

tiago no one need fear for his life any longer."[73] Having reduced the entire controversy to a police matter, FIFA expelled the Russians from the 1974 World Cup. In an open letter, the Soviet Football Association accused FIFA of playing "a dirty game with the fascist junta" and of having trampled on "the humane ideals of sport."[74]

In a booklet prepared for the Moscow Olympics titled "Soviet Sport: Questions and Answers," the Soviet Union's sport boycott policy, alias "sport as an instrument of peace," is illustrated by citing two examples: "When, for instance, Soviet representatives call for the expulsion of the South African and Rhodesian racists from the Olympic movement, this is, of course, a political move. But this is a policy for the sake of peace. . . . When Soviet football players refuse to play a match at the Santiago stadium, where the ground is stained with the blood of Chilean patriots, this is also, of course, politics. It is a policy of struggling . . . against fascist regimes."[75]

As noted above, the Russians' anti-apartheid policy has cost them virtually nothing; even the activist who solicited the appearance of their support for the putative 1968 Olympic boycott assumed that they would eventually sell out the principle of anti-racialism for gold medals. What, then, can we make of the Santiago affair? It is the apparent triumph of principle, an anomaly even more curious since not a single ideological ally of the Soviet Union felt obliged to observe it. When FIFA ordered the East Germans to play Chile in West Berlin—against which they had hitherto observed a sport boycott of fifteen years' duration—the official response from East Berlin was: "No problem." The GDR had, after all, qualified for the World Cup for the first time in its young life. First things first.

In West Germany, a more cynical interpretation of Soviet motives had appeared. Only the winner of two qualifying matches between Chile and the U.S.S.R. would be admitted to World cup competition, and Soviet prospects—given a tied match on their own territory—were not good. Contemplating the return match in Santiago, the Chilean trainer had said: "We're going to shoot the Russians to the moon." Ten days after the coup in Santiago, Soviet soccer officials had met with FIFA's Secretary General Käser; the possibility of Soviet cancellation of the return match "was never so much as mentioned." Three weeks later, the voice of conscience would rumble forth from Moscow. As Der Spiegel put it: "Better martyrs than losers."[76]

While shunning any boycott action, the East Germans took the trouble to weigh in with principled words. When the Soviet Union was ordered to Santiago by FIFA, the chairman of the GDR Football Association wrote its president a letter of protest: "It can be required of no human being to play in a stadium which has been defiled by the blood of noble and courageous people."[77] The German Communist Party had not shown the same scruples in 1936. Hitler had staged an Olympiad in a stadium he would have preferred not to defile with the sweat of Jews and Negroes; yet Werner Seelenbinder, a wrestler and a hero of the workers' sport movement who would eventually die in one of Hitler's prisons, had taken part in these fascist Games. How could it have happened? On the 35th anniversary of his death, readers of the East German party daily were assured that the heroic wrestler had been there "on orders from the Party."[78]

In June 1978, the World Cup of soccer—a global event comparable to the Olympic Games—was held in Buenos Aires. In Europe this was considered controversial due to the Argentine junta's massive human rights violations in its campaign of extermination against anyone or anything which smacked of leftism. "Despite a campaign by European leftists for a boycott by European teams, an exiled leader of the Montoneros, the left-wing Perónist guerilla organization, said that there would be no attempt to disrupt the competition. Such a boycott would be unpopular with the tens of thousands of Argentine fans holding tickets and the millions looking forward to watching television."[79] There was a lugubrious irony in this at once astonishing and rather pathetic confession. Latin American radicalism, which had once produced class-conscious critiques of Donald Duck, was capitulating before soccer's very own version of Disneyland.

But ideological pride was not dead. In Paris, the sole surviving founder of the Montoneros assured an interviewer that "there is no contradiction between the profound desire of the Argentine people to triumph in football and their no less profound desire to overthrow the Videla regime. We are well aware that this does not correspond to the very elaborate ideas circulating in certain leftist circles, particularly in Europe, regarding the relationship between sport and politics. We are not so pretentious as to claim that our position on this subject has universal validity. But we do consider it to be correct in the context of our struggle to return democracy to Argentina." A boycott, he said, would be counter-productive; let the world come and see the real Argentina. What is more: "For the first time in two years, hundreds of thousands of Argentinians have been able to assemble and walk through the streets without fear of repression, and they have been able to affirm their political identity through a certain number of symbols indigenous to our political folklore."[80]

In Eastern Europe, the boycott movement being supported by Jean-Paul Sartre and the "New Philospher" Bernard-Henri Lévy was not even discussed in the press. A brouhaha like the one raised by the Soviets over Santiago in 1973 was non-existent.[81] Before, during, and after the 1978 World Cup the East German party newspaper published only one comment of a social or political nature on the Argentine festival: it wondered whether a country beset by such "great social contradictions" could really afford to put on such an event.[82] In France and Sweden, socialist politicians like François Mitterand[83] and Olof Palme,[84] from whom one might have expected greater militancy, were practicing the politics of non-intervention and lighting incense to the holy autonomy of sport.

There was one leftist in Europe, however, who did come up with an original proposal for Argentina. The *New York Times* had discovered Paul Breitner in 1972: "The newest hero of the West German counterculture is a tall and articulate 20-year-old athlete who has captured a surprising place for the New Left in the most popular and highly paid group in the country—the national soccer team. . . . In widely publicized interviews, the star fullback has bitten the hand that feeds him with his Marxist analysis of professional soccer, its sociology and economy, as well as his negative view of the fans that adulate him and his team."[85] Paul Breitner's soccer itinerary had taken him to Santiago de Chile and Buenos Aires, in whose slums he had found his own political conceptions "confirmed in an eerie way." In 1973, he was waiting for an adoptive child from Vietnam and planning to use his bloated income to found a home for handicapped children.[86]

Paul Breitner did not go to Buenos Aires in 1978 because of his longstanding feud with West German soccer officials, who had not appreciated his radical posturings over the years. What he did do was publish an appeal to his Argentina-bound teammates: "Refuse to shake the General's hand!" He did not support the idea of a boycott. "Whoever demands a boycott must be consistent and require that this position be applied to all international sport relations, because I see no difference between the behavior of the military dictatorship in Argentina and the violations of human rights occurring in the Eastern bloc and elsewhere. But then what will be left of sport?"[87] It turned out, however, that there was another philosophical perspective Paul Breitner had not mentioned in his manifesto. Several years earlier, when asked about the moral issues involved in his playing for a royal club in Franco's Spain, he had replied: "I'm a hardened professional, and for money I will play anywhere."[88]

6. Boycotting "Culture": Is Sport Different?

a. Is Sport an International "Culture"?

In March 1978 the Royal Dutch Football Association expressed alarm over a boycott campaign then being waged in Holland against the World Cup competition scheduled for Buenos Aires in June. "It is being noted with some exasperation," the *Frankfurter Rundschau* reported, "that these questions of conscience are always invoked in connection with sporting events, whereas no one raises any objections when congresses or performances in the areas of science, culture, or the arts are involved."[89]

This argument is inaccurate: the worlds of science, culture, and art often follow the dictates of conscience when faced with moral dilemmas which might require an international boycott strategy. American publishers, for example, made public issues of the Moscow International Book Fairs of 1977 and 1979.[90] A number of American political scientists refused to attend the 1979 meeting of the International Political Science Association held in Moscow because of Soviet treatment of dissidents.[91] In 1978, the Romanian-born French playwright Eugene Ionesco refused to preside at an international writers' conference held in Paris because he did not "wish to preside at a police meeting; the writers sent by the Soviet Union and its satellites are selected by the police."[92] International sport culture differs from the other branches of international "culture" in this important respect: boycotts based on moral reasoning are almost never initiated by sportsmen or their bureaucratic guardians.

Does international sport promote the exchange of ideas? In July 1978 the *Manchester Guardian* looked ahead to the 1980 Moscow Olympiad and asked the following question: "Is it appropriate that the climax of sporting competition should be reached in a capital which outlaws the far more important competition of ideas? It is not, and the national bodies which coordinate Olympic activities should now think seriously about what is implied."[93] The idea that there is a hierarchy of international cultures, and that some are more important than others, is seldom applied to sport, which has long benefited from a special dispensation of sentimental origin. As we shall see below, Soviet bloc ideologists confer on sport a primary, rather than a secondary, cultural significance.

They are also sensitive to criticism regarding the "competition of ideas." In 1977, a commentator for Novosti, the semi-official Soviet news agency, offered the following defense of Russian policy: "Consider the argument about the free movement of people and information. This is a matter of great importance for normalized international relations and for better mutual understanding between peoples. Yet, the West insists that the Soviet Union tries to cut itself and its people off from broad international contacts. . . . Concerning the 'free flow of information' and 'Soviet censorship' it is easy to see by simply scanning our press that we raise no obstacles to the free flow of scientific, technical, international, sports and other information. But neither do we accept what is alien to the interests of our society and contrary to our traditions."[94] As this observer demonstrates, sport is as valuable to the xenophobic mentality as technology. In an age when East German troubadours and mild-mannered Romanian surrealists are presented with one-way passports, sport crosses international frontiers at will.

All international systems, Mussolini wrote, "as history proves, can be blown to the winds when emotional, idealistic and practical movements storm the hearts of peoples." Fascism, he said, "rejects universal concord." As a nationalist, and as a fascist, Mussolini celebrated the fragility of internationalism, whereas the liberal conscience is inclined to protect it. Should this inclination extend to international sport and the "universal" culture of the Olympic movement? This problem requires an assessment of sport's value as culture. What follows is a brief attempt to provide a conceptual framework for such a judgment.

b. Is Sport a Religion?

As we have seen, the Olympic movement has offered itself to the world as an ecumenism, a "religion" of humanity. As such, it is an artificial construct, an international doctrine of "communion" with only shallow roots in the societies which subscribe to it. Its claim to cultural authority is indirect, resting on a Hellenic revivalism of uncertain cultural value. The claim of Carl Diem, organizer of the 1936 Berlin Olympiad, that the modern Games bear "the impress of a holy purpose,"[95] presents us with a profound ambiguity: does the modern festival merely accept passively a holy impression from the past, or does the holy impression illuminate the Olympic festival from within?

In 1933, a more sophisticated cultural conservative, the Dutch historian Johan Huizinga, drew a pessimistic conclusion about Olympic culture in his famous *Homo Ludens*. "In modern social life sport occupies a place alongside and apart from the cultural process. The great competitions in archaic cultures had always formed part of the sacred festivals and were indispensable as health- and happiness-bringing activities. This ritual tie has now been completely severed; sport has become profane, 'unholy' in every way and has no organic connection whatever with the structure of society, least of all when prescribed by the government. The ability of modern social techniques to stage mass demonstrations with the maximum of outward show in the field of athletics does not alter the fact that neither the Olympics nor the organized sports of American universities nor the loudly trumpeted international contests have, in the smallest degree, raised sport to the level of a culture-creating activity."[96]

Huizinga was a rare creature: a devotee of the *ludique* [the play sphere] who was not at the same time its sentimental apologist, and he challenges the Olympic ideologues on historical grounds. A cultural unity has been ruptured, he maintains, and modern sport is unsuited to the task of healing the breach.

The Olympic movement promotes the religious character of "Olympism." Huizinga, too, understood that there is a relationship between play and notions of divinity: "In the form and function of play, itself an independent entity which is senseless and irrational, man's consciousness that he is embedded in a sacred order of things finds its first, highest, and holiest expression. Gradually the significance of a sacred act permeates the playing. Ritual grafts itself upon it; but the primary thing is and remains play."[97]

But Huizinga would never have subscribed to a quasi-religious cult of sport, if only because he was convinced that sport was assuming increasingly degenerate forms. "To what extent does the civilization we live in still develop in play forms? How far does the play-spirit dominate the lives of those who share that civilization? The 19th century, we observed, had lost many of the play-elements so characteristic of former ages. Has this leeway been made up or has it increased?"[98] The answer is that it has increased, and that a major cultural casualty of the decline of "the play-spirit" has been sport. "In the case of sport we have an activity nominally known as play but raised to such a pitch of technical organization and scientific thoroughness that the real play-spirit is threatened with extinction."[99] Unlike the Olympic ideology, Huizinga's cultural criticism cuts across the board, and sport receives no special dispensation. *Homo Ludens* contains only one reference to the Olympic movement, and it suggests disdain; in fact, Huizinga had a far higher opinion of the Boy Scouts.[100]

Huizinga's differences with the Olympic doctrinaires help to clarify the nature of Olympic "religiosity." "With a word whose depth surpasses all understanding," he wrote in 1935, "Plato once called men the playthings of the gods."[101] But Olympic doctrine has nothing in common with this sort of cosmic humility. "To celebrate a festival," Carl Diem writes, "means to cast a collective thought in a visible form. Man demonstrates to himself that he is stronger than fate."[102] What is striking about this quotation from the organizer of the Berlin Olympiad is that it could express an allegiance to Hitler—or to Marx. It celebrates, not a divinity, but man in a state of heroic self-assertion. "Man bows," not before God, but "before the annunciation of his thousandfold kinship." Diem's paganism is apparent in the following passage from "The Olympic Idea":

> The rising of the human spirit above its fate is noteworthy if it occurs only once; the capacity for repetition shows that whatever may later lie in store, the idea of the festival has shown itself stronger than fate.
> The time interval is fixed in the certainty that with such a scale of values the future can and will always be mastered. By so doing one lifts one's relation to fate, and that means to God, into the sphere of solemnity and religion.[103]

Diem's primitive anthropomorphism turns God into "fate," thereby making the human situation an apparently sportive one: fate, after all, is an opponent with whom one can wrestle. Equally revealing is Diem's association of religion and "solemnity"— ceremony, a mood, the hush of sacred groves, and a piety built on luxuriating in emotional effects. Above all, Diem has no sense of human imperfection, or of necessary self-restraints.

It is not surprising that Communism and "Olympism" have enjoyed such a philosophically congenial coexistence. Both rescue man from the doctrine of original sin; both are optimistic; both have use for a cult of the body. Huizinga, on the other hand, was a Christian philosopher and had an immunity to ceremonial hocus-pocus. Huizinga knew very well that there is a profound link between sport and ritual, which "has all the formal and essential characteristics of play." Like play, liturgy is "pointless but significant."[104] But the religious function of liturgy is to establish a relationship with a transcendent Being. Diem settles for a relationship to another order of experience, that of sport.

For Huizinga, ritual "transports the participants to another world." For the Olympic faithful, the new world is a world of stirring emotions and delicious feelings of universal brotherhood. Thus the Olympic doctrine is finally narcissistic: man's worship of the emotions stirred up by the perfected body and the euphoria of communion.

c. Is Sport a Fine Art?

In one of his lectures on art, Hegel offered his students a parable of sterile athleticism from the ancient world. "A man had taught himself to throw lentils through a small opening without missing. He displayed this skill of his before Alexander, and Alexander presented him with a bushel of lentils as a reward for his frivolous and meaningless art."[105]

Hegel's sarcasm constitutes a judgment of great cultural import: art, religion, and philosophy are the content of absolute spirit or mind, but physical dexterity is not. But modern sport has found many apologists anxious to compare and even equate it with art.

"Sport," Charles de Gaulle once said, "like science and art, disregards borders. Its rules and structures are universal . . ."[106] This is the classic argument on behalf of the proposition that sport is the sixth fine art; it is also a doctrine which has been given quasi-official status by both Olympic and Communist ideologists. In 1970, the Hellenic Olympic Committee published an elaborate defense of the idea "that Sport itself is indeed one of the Fine Arts," and a worthy companion to architecture, sculpture, painting, music, and literature. The author of this treatise, Henri Pouret, adds to the ancient media three modern ones which offer special advantages to the Olympic movement in its quest for global publicity: cinema, radio, and television. "These Fine Arts seem to correspond to Tolstoi's wish that *Art is an appeal for communion among men and it constitutes one of the biggest feasts of Humanity.*" Art, like "the Olympic idea," is conceived as a form of "inspiration."

In "Is Sport an Art?", Henri Pouret supports this idea with nine theses. (1) Sport is an entity: "it creates a closed world with its own space and time." (2) Sport is a gratuitous activity: "its activities are characterized by the absence of any utilitarian purpose." (3) Sport is certainty, offering "a hierarchy of values sanctioned beyond dispute by the final result." (4) Sport is universal: "it is a kind of universal language that is immediately clear to all men." (5) Sport is a creator of beauty: "As Pierre Coubertin pointed out, 'Sport produces beauty since it creates the athlete who is a living sculpture'." (6) Sport is a creator of harmony: both athlete and spectator "perceive the harmony which, almost always, accompanies great athletic performance." (7) Sport is a creator of the sublime: "Sport, like the Arts, is a constant search for the sublime, the will to be first, to break a record, to excel . . . " (8) Sport is a creator of drama: "Like theater, Sport in its fields conveys to us a recognition of the fragility of our aspirations or the satisfaction of victory." (9) "Like all other arts, Sport is an apotheosis of the 'sensory'."[107]

Pouret offers three major arguments. First, sport is universal: "Like music, painting and sculpture, athletic activity is directly understood by all men on earth: it is a kind of universal language that is immediately clear to all men. Due to this universality, sport is capable of bringing the souls of men together in communion, thus demonstrating the virtue attributed by Tolstoi to each one of the Fine Arts." Universality, however, is only as significant as the articulated meanings it conveys; it is a formal characteristic which does not address the question of content.

Second, Pouret asserts that sportive beauty resides "in the revelation of man's possibilities through the euphoric recognition of health in the athlete and through the viewing of [the] perfect human specimen . . . " The representative human being, in other words, is that "specimen" once termed by Leo Lowenthal "the morally insensate body-beautiful ideal of the racial hero."[108] Such an argument forces the human image down to the level of kitsch; "the euphoric recognition of health" is thin soil for the growth of art.

Third, sport is a form of theater. Even Bertolt Brecht, hungering for an emotionally involved audience, seems to have been tempted by this notion in 1926.[109] But sport has no room for thoughts of human imperfection (except the failure of will), death, or any pathos more complex than that which may accompany the temporary disappointments of competition. Sport offers a style which is naturally suited to what Jean Genet once called "the clear simplicity of manliness."[110] It offers an intense experience on its own terms; but it is an impoverished context in which to ask the fundamental question of art and philosophy: "What is man?"

This point requires emphasis because Communist ideologues too have conferred upon sport the cultural status and the emotional content of art. In East Germany, artists, writers, musicians and filmmakers are officially admonished to demonstrate in their works the "beauty and optimism, the joy of life and competitive drive which are inherent in sport." Artistic works should help as many people as possible find "the way to sport."[111] An art attaché of the East German National Olympic Committee has written hopefully of "a question raised by composers who would like to solve the problem of creating music specifically intended for sport and adjusted both the the the laws of music and to the sequence of bodily movements and exercises. . . ."[112] The Polish sport sociologist Andrzej Wohl has argued that sport is virtually an art form: "In its competitive form sport becomes an art of the widest range and attraction. It becomes a way of knowing the world. Just as an imaginary scene in the theater or on the screen conveys truths about life to the viewer in an imaginary form (if only as movement), the experiences and impressions of a genuine struggle, which is passionately experienced at first hand and then discussed and commented on for a long time. . . . The simplicity of the sportive drama is not, however, synonymous with poverty of expression, of the emotions, or of its content. Because of the generally recognized rules of play, the contemporary sporting event has become a well-composed unity which enchants through its logic, measurability, and form, through its technical and tactical perfection, sweeping one along through the drama of its tension, the exertion of will and the striving for victory. From the standpoint of aesthetics, too, the contemporary sporting performance is not far behind theatrical performances."[113] Here Marxist aesthetics shows its didacticism; art has become an edifying emotional force which emphasizes excitement at the expense of subtlety.

d. Does Sport Have Conceptual Content?

It is "a special property of muscles," Yukio Mishima wrote, "that they [feed] the imaginations of others while remaining totally devoid of imagination themselves . . ."[114] What, then, do athletic movements have to offer the imaginations of others? They do not constitute, as dance movements do, a symbolic language of the emotions. The expressive repertory of athletic movements comprises two major themes: physical *beauty* and *force* of muscle or will. As Huizinga points out: "In play the beauty of the human body in motion reaches its zenith. In its more developed forms it is saturated with rhythm and harmony, the noblest gifts of aesthetic perfection known to man. Many and close are the links that connect play with beauty."

But Huizinga refuses to equate play and art: "All the same, we cannot say that beauty is inherent in play as such; so we must leave it at that: play is a function of the living, but is not susceptible of exact definition either logically, biologically, or aesthetically." What is more, Huizinga describes play as an absolutely non-conceptual phenomenon: "The play-concept must always remain distinct from all the other forms of thought in which we express the structure of mental and social life."[115] Play is antithetical to the systematic life of the mind.

Sport symbolizes force. A triumphant athlete can stand for the triumph of a race or an ideology. Mass gymnastics display the force of the body politic. As Susan Sontag has pointed out: "The rendering of movement in grandiose and rigid patterns is another element [which fascist and communist art have] in common, for such choreography rehearses the very unity of the polity. Hence, mass athletic demonstrations, a choreography and display of bodies, are a valued acitivity in all totalitarian countries."[116]

These totalitarian cultures have ascribed to sport meanings determined by their political and ideological requirements. Even as it cultivated a profound anti-intellectualism, Nazi sport ideology insisted that sport should be politically articulate. "The body," one Nazi philosopher wrote, "is a political entity (*ein Politicum*)." Another Nazi sport theorist complains of the "intellectual emptiness" (*Gedankenlosigkeit*) of sport. Sport should point beyond itself, but instead it has been made "to anxiously avoid fundamental ideas of pedagogical or political significance."[117]

Like the Nazis, Communist ideologists reject the idea of "unpolitical sport." Styles of play, for example, can be assigned ideological meanings. "The Russians," a Danish journalist reported in 1973, "have changed their ideology in ice hockey: they are trying to create individualists. In contrast to the past, when they trained primarily in passing, now they are practicing dribbling. . . . The collective form of ice hockey, where everyone helped everyone else in each situation is just a memory. The players who triumphed in Moscow are no longer socialists but upper-class types who have the right to take initiatives on their own."[118]

"Dogmatic collectivism" has also impeded the progress of East German soccer, since dribbling, running, and feinting with the ball were once considered forms of egocentricity alien to socialism.[119] When an Albanian basketball team played the Chinese in Peking in 1971, "the Albanians were reported as having given, in their play, attractive evidence of the spiritual world picture created by Comrade Enver Hoxha, the Mao Tse-tung of Albania."[120]

Does sport have conceptual content? In this symbolic domain, meaning is in the eye of the beholder. Even under the best circumstances (a pre-conditioned audience), the "grammar" of sportive language is confined to the three major "parts of speech": physical beauty, force of will, and ideological truth. Major elements of human experience such as reflection, doubt, irony, anxiety, and pathos must be omitted. Claims that sport is a branch of "culture" should be judged in this light.

II. "Playing the Chameleon": The Moral Bankruptcy of the Olympic Movement

1. Amoral Universalism

The moral reputation of the Olympic movement is one of the public relations phenomena of this century. There are several reasons for its success. First, the International Olympic Committee has managed to effect the global canonization of the movement's founder, Baron Pierre de Coubertin (1863-1937), whose career and ideas are addressed later in this chapter. Second, sport in general benefits from a presumption of innocence; Olympic officials are quick to promote "Olympism" as a form of moral hygiene which can be applied efficiently to large numbers of people. Third, there is the moral effluvium with which the Olympic movement in particular has always surrounded itself, a claim to virtue which has been endorsed by high representatives of the Catholic Church.[1] Finally, the Olympic movement meets a deeply rooted human need to experience the fellowship of reconciliation—or a convincing substitute. It may be noted that the dream of a harmonious mankind has produced a large number of political eccentrics, ranging in type from Rudolf Hess to Dag Hammarskjöld, and a few famous traitors as well. As we shall see, the IOC has been incubating political eccentricity along these lines since its earliest days.

But the Olympic movement has never possessed an *ethic*. It does have a code of sportsmanship and international understanding which has found eager subscribers of every political stripe precisely on account of its obvious and banal character. But how, one might ask, has the amorality of the Olympic ideology come to be? Didn't the movement's patron saint, Coubertin, provide a sound moral doctrine for his disciples in the IOC? He did not; in fact, his *Olympic Memoirs* congratulates the IOC on having "played the chameleon"[2] in order to reduce its own political vulnerability. As one former associate put it, Coubertin "was willing to make concessions in writing and in action to anyone . . . as long as the Games continued."[3]

The foundation of the Olympic movement is what Coubertin called "the fundamental principle of universality."[4] In the 1975 *Olympic Rules, By-Laws and Instructions*, this idea is given an up-to-date and highminded tone: "No discrimination in [the Games] is allowed against any country or person on grounds of race, religion or politics."[5] What this has meant in practice is that the IOC has turned a blind eye to any sort of political crime committed by a member of the Olympic movement. In

September 1978, the president of the IOC, Lord Killanin, made this clear: "I am not for one moment saying we have any right to tell what governments should do in the interests of their own country . . ."[6] Such a disclaimer is made to preserve the "universality" of the movement. What is thereby forgotten is that another side of universality is the failure to discriminate.

The anti-discrimination clause of Rule 3 of the 1975 "Fundamental Principles" is an antidote to racist policies; though it was not until May 1970 that the Republic of South Africa, due to outside pressure on the IOC, was finally expelled from the Olympics, an action its IOC delegate denounced as "illegal and immoral"—that is to say, anti-universal. But this action should not be taken for anything more than it was intended to be, namely, the preservation of the movement's pluralism *for its own sake.* Coubertin himself was a cheerful colonialist whose views on race were typical of his era. An understanding of the Olympic movement requires that this sort of toleration not be mistaken for a genuine fraternalism based on ethics.

Sport has an impressive reputation as a guarantor of morals. Nadejda Lekarska, the Romanian author of *Essays and Studies on Olympic Problems* (1973), like many before her, views sport as a kind of moral prophylactic, especially for young girls.[7] And several modern popes have offered public endorsements of sport.[8] In February 1978 Pope Paul VI stated: "We are firmly convinced that the serious practice of sports activities and competitions, carried out in the spirit of the universally recognized ethical principles, will constitute a valid contribution to stemming that process of dehumanisation in social living, the alarming signs of which are by now only too clear to all far-sighted spirits. In fact, does not athletic commitment perhaps provide an effective antidote to the idleness, laxity and soft living which usually constitute the most fertile ground for the sad proliferation for all sorts of vice?"[9] This kind of cautionary hygienism represents the homely ethics of reflexive self-censorship. But both authors have grand ideals in mind. The Romanian enthusiast talks of "Olympic ethical principles" and the "solid humanitarian traditions" of the Olympic movement;[10] and the pontiff of "universally recognised ethical principles." But to what extent can one take seriously the "ethical principles" of the Olympic movement?

"The aims of the Olympic movement," Rule 1 states, "are to promote the development of those fine physical and moral qualities which are the basis of amateur sport . . . " Rule 24G states that the members of the National Olympic Committee shall be "men of good standing, of upright character . . . "[11] These stipulations, and the anti-discrimination clause, constitute the entire "ethics" of the Olympic charter. Lord Killanin, the former president of the IOC has, however, attempted to convey the impression that the charter can be construed as a "human rights" document as well: "It is essential to protect the freedom of the individual in regard to any form of discrimination, whether racial, political or religious, and the duty of governments to assist."[12] That this was sophistry became evident when, two months later, the same official insisted that he would not dream of dictating norms to a sovereign government. This, in fact, is the basic contradiction of the Olympic movement: it claims to be international, but relinquishes moral authority to national governments.

This policy can accommodate atrocity, such as the pre-Olympic slaughter in Mexico City, or just farce. "We wish to do good to the human being, the person," Lord Killanin has said, "by creating the complete human, physically and mentally, but not by creating some artificial robot."[13] But events have overtaken Olympic idealism, leaving the IOC to preside over what it chooses to call an "evolution" of its vision.[14]

"Olympism," in short, has betrayed the cultural conservatism which gave it birth and in which it could have found a moral foundation.

The most prominent culturally conservative institution which supports the Olympic movement as a moral crusade is the Vatican. In April 1978 the Holy See sent its own delegation to the second conference of European sport ministers and submitted a document which began: "The Church—all Churches—have always considered sport as a school where the highest human and social values are taught . . ."[15] But Coubertin knew that fifteen hundred years of mind-body dualism and mortification of the flesh had left the Church openly hostile to the cult of the body as late as the end of the 19th century. Indeed, Coubertin's transformation of sport into a form of moral rearmament reversed the momentum of centuries. The Church, as he pointed out,[16] had at first seen the Olympic cult as a return of paganism—which it certainly was. More recently, the Head of the Vatican Library went out of his way to put in a good word for the paganism associated with the Olympic Games: "Thus paganism, even in its mistaken concepts, could pride itself in the possession of a few glimmers of light."[17]

In 1962, the eightieth and final year of his life, Dr. Carl Diem,[18] the organizer of Hitler's Berlin Olympiad and one of Coubertin's collaborators in the movement, published an essay titled "The Olympic Idea as Moral Challenge." Diem's meditation, like much of the prose from the Olympic inner circle, is devotional literature. Its focus—and the real source of the Olympic movement's doctrine—is the ancient Hellenic world. Of the "Olympic Academy" of antiquity Diem wrote: "They taught laws of humanity here, which were not only binding on all Greeks, but attractive to them. They taught laws of justice, valid for all contestants, laws of unselfishness and contempt for shallow profit, laws of solemn observance which bound together a whole people and other contemporaries into a cultural unity. Is there not here an achievement of astounding moral force?"

Although Diem declares that the modern Games still bear "the impress of a holy purpose," his emphasis is on the "religious instinct" of the ancient Games. He admits the modern Olympic movement has seen "the decline of idealism," but Diem believes that "nothing remains in this situation but to 'make the best of it' and to trust to the inner health of the Olympic Idea."[19]

The "moral force" of the Olympic movement is actually a twofold ethos composed of neo-pagan and neo-Christian doctrines. Neither of these has anything to do with the individual conscience or the capacity to distinguish good from evil. As a neo-pagan doctrine, "Olympism" celebrates the cult of the body and its public display. Diem writes: "Where sport takes place in natural surroundings it generates a shared romanticism, a romanticism fearless and delighting in action. Where it calls only for athletic achievement, there is a ruthless collective urge to perfection." Diem had seen the "ruthless collective urge" come to life in the Nazi Olympiad of 1936 and, like Coubertin,[20] had found it good, since it was only the collective expression of communion which interested him. For this reason, Diem believed the fundamental human experience is the festival: "To celebrate a festival means to cast a collective thought in a visible form. Man demonstrates thereby his free will and his artistic power. He proves to himself that he is stronger than fate."[21]

As a neo-Christian doctrine, "Olympism" is a cult of reconciliation. In the celebration of the festival, "Man bows before the annunciation of his thousandfold kinship. It is a moment that takes one's breath away when in the Olympic Games the

teams from nearly a hundred nations enter the stadium."[22] This doctrine of reconciliation is as inspirational as fundamentalism. Small wonder that Coubertin was fascinated by religious revivalism in America,[23] which became one more model for
Olympic pageantry. In this sense, Coubertin may be seen as Elmer Gantry's more
sophisticated French cousin.[24]

Coubertin did not grapple with ethical issues. Instead, he saw them as problems in
public relations. Participation in the Olympic movement, for example, has func-
tioned as a *de facto* index of international respectability since 1920. Note how
Coubertin addresses this issue in his *Olympic Memoirs*: "Good sense suggested that it
would be imprudent for the German teams to show themselves in the Olympic
stadium before 1924. On the other hand, to solemnly proclaim any sort of ostracism,
even in the wake of the conflict which had just drenched Europe in blood, would
amount to a rending of the Olympic constitution which had heretofore proved so
resistant; and a dangerous precedent might well result."[25] Right and wrong are not at
issue; there is only "good sense" and the Olympic constitution.

Jean Meynaud has described the lame subterfuge to which the IOC had recourse
in order to deal with the issue of German readmission to the 1920 Antwerp Games: it
simply had the Belgian national committee send out invitations, excluding Germany
as well as other nations, thus permitting the IOC to claim it had not violated its own
principle of universality. The same strategy was used to exclude Germany and Japan
from the 1948 London Games.[26] Somewhat more courageously, and in accordance
with his own, much more explicit principle of amoral universalism, Avery Brundage
demanded the immediate readmission of Germany even before the Second World
War had ended.

Amoral universalism substitutes sportsmanship for ethics. But sportsmanship is
actually a mere etiquette for the strong, the select community of potential victors,
and "Olympism" is a ministry to the healthy. As a form of "positive thinking" it represents not ethics, but the flight from conscience, its suffering, and its doubt.

The three major figures of the Olympic movement, Pierre de Coubertin, Carl
Diem, and Avery Brundage, have all been proponents of amoral universalism. In
practice, fealty to Coubertin has meant sacrificing all other principles to ensuring the
eternal recurrence of the Games, and his two principal inheritors have never
doubted, showering the founder with accolades. To Diem, Coubertin appears, like
Christ, as the prophesied Redeemer: "Coubertin had to come. He it was who
transformed the fundamental conceptions of antiquity, clothing them in a guise suit-
able to the new age and lending them the nobility of a loftier spiritual content."[27]
Diem called Coubertin a "true humanist," "a creative spirit," and—not least—a
friend of German music who had demonstrated thereby another sort of universality
of spirit.[28] Brundage called Coubertin "the prophet" of "a modern, exciting, virile,
dynamic religion," referring in his autobiography to a "conversion" to "Coubertin's
religion."[29]

These three men, of whom Coubertin (1896-1925) and Brundage (1952-1972)
served long terms as President of the IOC, constitute the great triumvirate of modern
Olympic history. More recently, there has emerged a fourth pillar of this community
which, judging by sheer athletic performance, is now the most successful one: the
Socialist bloc, whose conversion to Olympism has been ardent and unswerving. The
remaining sections of this chapter attempt to explain the doctrines and motives of
Coubertin and his most important successors, East and West.

2. Pierre de Coubertin: The Career of a Sportive Internationalist

a. Democracy and Social Equilibrium

"A merciful history," Carl Diem wrote, "offered us Coubertin, who was at the same time philosopher and teacher, historical researcher and psychologist, a teacher and a researcher in gymnastics and in sport. He was a talented speaker and a fluent writer, a tireless and inspiring campaigner for a new education for the human race. But above all he was a moral prophet, nay more, a model and a teacher of morality. He gave an example of self-sacrifice, even to the sacrifice of his fortune. This he did with a deliberate artistocratic pride, when it was needed."[30]

Coubertin the "moral prophet" must be understood both as a representative of his social class (the nobility) and an exemplary citizen and social theorist of the French Third Republic. For Coubertin was less a moral prophet than a social engineer. His goal was to ease political conflict on two levels: first, class conflict within the French body politic and, second, conflict between nations. "Cooperation in sport," he wrote in his *Sport Pedagogy*, "diminishes the importance of social distinctions." "The essential thing is that bourgeois youth and proletarian youth drink from the same fountain of muscular joy," a shared experience which will make possible *la bonne humeur sociale*.[31] In international relations, sport is the special point from which the brotherhood of man is visible to all. "Sport," Coubertin writes, "is the possession of all the peoples of the world. . . . It is a sign of singular superiority when an institution can simultaneously take the form of a deep social manifestation and still spread across the surface of the globe."[32]

For all his fame as the founder of an international movement, Coubertin was at first interested in revitalizing French society and in preserving its domestic tranquility. To a certain extent, the focus of his interests changed over the years. Early in his career as an Olympic activist, around the turn of the century, his writings are preoccupied with preserving the equilibrium of "modern" individuals and societies. By 1931, with the publication of his *Olympic Memoirs*, his outlook is directed more toward preserving the influence and autonomy of the IOC, even to the point of disregarding the significance of titanic political struggles: "Whatever it may be, this diffusion of sport among the manual laborers is an undeniable proof of the survival of Olympism, no matter how the struggle for global power being waged by totally opposed social doctrines may turn out."[33] For Coubertin, the survival of the Olympic movement is more important than the ideological cleavage of the world. And this despite his own nationalism and aristocratic distaste for Marxism and for the revolutionary impulse.[34]

Coubertin's strategy for resolving the conflict between his nationalist and internationalist impulses was to blur the difference, and propose the therapy of sport for everyone. Traumatized, as was his entire generation, by the military disaster of the Franco-Prussian war, Coubertin offered a healthful prescription: "sports can provide the virile formula on which the health of the State can be founded."[35] But as an internationalist, Coubertin offers sport to the world: "Modern man inhabits the center of a civilization whose increasingly agitated character weakens him even as it overexcites him. Happily, he finds in sporting exercise an antidote which strengthens him and calms him down simultaneously." And again: "At the present hour, anger is everywhere in the world: it disturbs both the family hearth and social institutions; it endangers both the tranquility of the individual and the public peace. But sport is the greatest "pacifier" [*apaiseur*] there is."[36] The function of sport, then, is to lower the socio-political temperature while raising the psychic temperature of the sportsman, when this is appropriate.

"Pierre de Coubertin," Eugen Weber has written, "was born in his parents' *hôtel* in Paris, rue Oudinot, half-way between the École Militaire and the parish church in St. François-Xavier. The family was wealthy, ultramontane, and legitimist. The mother, a Mirville, was pious, elegant, busy; the father, Charles-Louis, Baron Fredy de Coubertin, a mediocre if fashionable academic painter."[37] Coubertin, a devoted biographer maintains, was "a royalist and a Catholic as were his parents, but not in the same manner."[38] Quite so, for it was precisely the distance he put between himself and his family's political and religious heritage that made possible his career as a social activist.[39] Past alliances, Weber points out, "related Pierre to most of the noble Faubourg. Yet he felt little sympathy for what he called 'the cretins of the Faubourg Saint-Germain'. Too many of his peers (like his own father) had opted out of the world around them. And in return the world ignored them. No longer resented or persecuted, the nobility was left to itself and to the public's occasional surprise that it continued to exist."[40]

The young Coubertin, on the other hand, had no intention of resigning himself to such historical obscurity. The strategy he used to avoid it was by no means unique. In late nineteenth-century France, as Theodore Zeldin notes, "the nobles learnt how to extract what they really wanted from the republic. They learnt to become magnates of a new sort in a pseudo-egalitarian society."[41] Coubertin used sport as a vehicle for promoting *his* pseudo-egalitarianism. In what follows we shall see how Coubertin discarded the aristocratic political and religious views of his parents, and how he managed to integrate conservative class interests into a modern ideology of sport which persists to this day.

"Coubertin," Weber comments, "*was* a reactionary figure, albeit an enlightened one," who "had jettisoned the . . . conservative tradition in which he had been born, retaining only the internationalist and pacifist aspects along with the code of honor."[42] Weber's depiction of Coubertin as an "enlightened reactionary" nicely captures the element of contradiction which pervades his doctrine of sport. In France this contradiction has been interpreted in two ways by right-wingers who are still interested in Coubertin. On the one hand, he is credited with having possessed "the genius to harmonize every contradiction" and the wisdom to have rejected both Right and Left, both "reactionaries and demagogues."[43] On the other hand, he is described as an aristocrat who called for democracy and a pacifist who managed to unleash furious rivalries among nations. Paul Werrie remarks: "The least one can say is that the *rénovateur* of the Olympic Games and the prophet of modern sport was fertile with paradoxes."[44]

Coubertin's "paradoxical" formulations represent his own efforts to adapt reactionary instincts to certain features of an emerging mass society he deemed both undesirable and irreversible. "The tendency today," he wrote at the turn of the century, "is toward a total culture. It is not just democracy which is pushing in this direction, but especially the transformation of labor, the industrial character of the epoch, the almighty goddess Activity who already reigns uncontested."[45] But Coubertin was willing to swim with the current. And though he had elected to ride the modern "democratic" tide for his own ends, we should bear in mind the shallowness of his allegiance to it. That as canny an observer as Werrie should take Coubertin for a democrat and pacifist demonstrates the degree to which his reputation has benefited from the diverse character of his recorded opinions and the selectivity applied to them by later generations.

Coubertin was a "democrat" who listed "the triumph of democracy" as one of four innovations (*faits nouveaux*) history would have been better off without;[46] and he was a "pacifist" who referred to antimilitarism as "a form of neurosis, a kind of weapons phobia, infantile and pitiful," adding: "To curse war is no longer the way to diminish its frequency. Only the strong and those who favor force are qualified to preach serenity, inaction and—if necessary—retreat."[47]

It is apparent that Coubertin permitted himself conceptual liberties which obscure his views on a number of issues. He could proclaim the vanity of futurist hopes to create the world anew, call for the reconstruction of civilization in accordance with Greek or Roman models, while simultaneously declaring that "the next society will be altruistic or it will not exist at all: it will be necessary to choose between that and chaos . . ."[48] The grandiosity and confusion of these notions bear witness to the utopian element in Coubertin's thought.

The contradictions in Coubertin's ideology are seen most clearly in two of his major themes: the nature of democracy and the search for social and psychological equilibrium in an increasingly feverish civilization. Coubertin's endorsement of "democracy" should be viewed against his distaste for revolution, for the "evangelist Karl Marx," and for socialism, which he saw as unlettered and, worst of all, as hostile to *l'enseignement superieur* [higher education],[49] the mission he saw as the basis of his life's work. Democracy, he writes, is a "natural and durable phenomenon. That it is accompanied here and there by a few violent crises does not give its adversaries the right—as it is certainly their wish—to attribute to it a revolutionary character."[50]

But what does he really want? Coubertin finds two aspects of democracy especially attractive. First, it offers the prospect of social harmony and a minimum of political instablity; Coubertin believes that cooperation in sport is "a kind of preparatory school for democracy."[51] A football team, for example, is "the most perfect prototype of human cooperation."[52] Second, Coubertin sees education as "the program of action for modern democracy,"[53] and in a sense its justification. It will form "a basis for general culture . . . accessible to all and capable of indefinite development,"[54] and an important feature of this "general culture" is its affinity for the ethos of sport. Democracy is charged with the task of providing egalitarian conditions on a mass scale which make possible the selection of an "aristocracy of sport,"[55] for birth and wealth are meaningless in this meritocracy.

Eugen Weber suggests that "to the current elitism of the contemporary upper classes, Coubertin opposed another brand of elitism, more in tune with the times because more activist, more competitive, and also ,at least apparently ,more open and accessible."[56] It is poignant to hear the voice of Charles Maurras raised in protest, albeit indirect, against the cheerful rough-and-tumble of Coubertin's "democratic" ethos: "But it is by no means certain," Maurras writes, "that justice insists upon competition in all things, nor that everything in life should be competitive. There is nothing to prove, either, that the weaknesses exposed on the race track do not find compensation elsewhere and that, in the final analysis, the champion's shield, the prize winner's diploma ,the riband of the prime steer should be the only criteria upon which to classify humanity."[57] As we shall see, Maurras' attendance at the 1896

Athens Olympiad convinced him that international athletic competition was both distasteful and a failed internationalism.[58]

To Coubertin, the ideal democratic citizen's civic education consists of all praxis and no theory. "So," he writes, "the citizen most useful to democracy will not be the one who has been induced to study sociology, or the one to whom the theories of solidarity and mutual responsibility will have been explained, but the one who will enter into active life already having felt drawn to collective efforts. . . ."[59]

Coubertin, like other anti-democratic thinkers of his time, evidently harbored serious doubts about the survival of high culture in a democratic age. "Democracy," he writes, "will receive the Guardianship of the Temple without ever having been admitted within to contemplate its contents, this Temple wherein the treasures of Intelligence and Beauty have been collected, the effort of vanished generations, the hope of civilization."[60] In summary, then, Coubertin's publicly proclaimed version of democracy must be seen against his private reservations and non-democratic leanings.

The second major paradox of Coubertin's doctrine concerns his ambivalence toward sport's capacity to function both as a social stimulant and as a tranquilizer. In his own terms, there exists a dynamic relationship between "equilibrium" and "excess." "One point at which sport bears on the social question," he writes, "is its pacifying character. Sport relaxes the coiled springs which have been stretched by anger"—that social plague which Coubertin had identified as the root of all social and political conflict. Elsewhere, he calls for an educational system capable of producing a "collecive calm."[61] Sport is viewed, then, as a tranquilizing therapy on both the individual and social levels. "Precisely because, in the modern world which is emerging, sport can play an eminent role in promoting progress and social rapprochement," Coubertin writes, "we wish it to be purer, more chivalrous, more transparent, more calm."[62] Sport is needed to mitigate what he calls the "intensive character" of a "pulsating and complicated" civilization: "Considering the substantial expenditure of nervous and mental force demanded of people by modern civilization, they need an equivalent dose of muscular force" by way of compensation. "Total repose of the limbs," he continues, "should be extended to the brain. But it is perfectly apparent that the excessive aspect of civilization, in destroying in part its equilibrium, has falsified the relation between [limbs and brain]. Thus it becomes necessary to re-establish this equilibrium artificially . . ."[63]

It turns out, however, that "equilibrium" cannot be an absolute goal. "Far from causing the tendency to excess to spread, [the Olympic Games] restrain it." But, Coubertin adds, "the idea of [wholly] suppressing [the element of] excess is a utopian notion of the anti-sporting types."[64] For there exist sportsmen, "that is to say, of the instinctive kind, active types belonging to a certain category, whom one does not have the right to stop, and whose élan should not be compromised in the name of a principle of equality which has recklessly been pushed to the point of the absurd." One suspects that while Coubertin the "democratic" theorist is promoting equilibrium, the "instinctive" sportsman within feels a certain disdain for this sort of temperance. For "we know," he says, "that [sport] tends inevitably toward excess, and that this is its essence, its indelible mark."[65] Coubertin's instinctive appreciation of "excess" and élan would eventually inspire in him the idea that the Nazi Olympiad of 1936 represented the culmination of his life's work.

b. The Third Republic

Coubertin was an almost perfect representative of the French Third Republic. "You have the epic spirit," Jules Ferry told him in 1889.[66] It was appropriate for Coubertin to seek the benediction of one of the Republic's more memorable presidents, since Coubertin—like so many others of his class and political outlook—managed to be a man of the Republic without being a republican at heart. This attitude was not contradictory, since the Republic had been founded in 1875 by royalists. As Albert Guerard once noted, the Constitution of that year "was inspired by a deep-seated distrust of the masses, which, unless properly curbed, might turn Red; and by an equal distrust of the chief executive, who might have a will of his own and become another Charles X or a new Napoleon III. It was intended to be a *grand bourgeois* regime: at one time it was indeed a Republic of Dukes. With the years it became *petit bourgeois*, even *tout petit bourgeois*, but never democratic."[67]

In 1902, Coubertin published a meditation on the state of the Republic, an essay tinged with the sort of ambivalence that would enable him to assume the mantle of the Great Reconciler: "The Third Republic, studied at a distance, recommends itself by virtue of qualities which had become most indispensable to us but seemed at the same time to be the farthest removed from our temperament: perseverance, consistency, silent and regular labor. For the first time we seemed to know what we wanted and how to achieve it.[68]

But there are also reservations, though expressed with Coubertin's customary tact: "One would have to be quite out of touch with what is happening beyond our borders not to see that the Republic, as a dogma, has lost most of its loyalists. A new form of monarchy has been born, one which responds better to modern ambitions; the old dynasties, in recognizing them, have experienced a renewal of their vigor and their resiliency. At once chief of staff and captain of industry, the sovereign of today sees his subjects returning to him and restoring to him many of the rights they had taken away from his predecessors, as well as initiatives they had appropriated to the profit of their elected representatives. They demand of him, however, a strenuous effort and a constant vigilance, and he is repaid for his cares in popularity and stability. Thrones are no longer at the mercy of the slightest storm."[69]

One notes in this passage the ease with which Coubertin slips into a royalist idiom—the future admirer of Mussolini (a "sovereign" if not a royalist) is already raising his voice.[70] Of equal importance is the responsiveness to "modern ambitions," which he characteristically views as fated developments to which one must submit. Coubertin could always find a silver lining inside the "modern," and this too played a role in the survival of his Olympic vision.

What associated Coubertin with virtually all of the pre-1917 leaders of the Republic was his devotion to social cohesion and keeping the political temperature at a safe level. Hence his admonitions to "calm," "social peace," "equilibrium," and *la bonne humeur sociale*—the consummate Third Republic fantasy. Coubertin was so concerned about "social peace" that in 1911 he devoted an essay to the sociopolitical impact of the automobile on French society, which, for this purpose, he divided into two social classes: those who rode in automobiles and those who had to stand and watch others drive by. It was the feelings of the second group that worried him: "This can give rise to ambition; it will certainly produce envy, and one sure result will be the spread and reinforcement of socialist ideas. The ambition to 'make it' will sometimes germinate in juvenile brains which witness the passage of the machine which symbolizes the dreams of movement and of the unknown which are so dear to youth. It is a stimulant."[71]

On government policy, foreign and domestic, Coubertin stood behind the men of the Republic. "The memory of Jules Ferry," Albert Guerard notes, "is inseparable from three major developments in the eighties, the expansion of popular education, a sharp conflict with the clergy, and the creation of a vast colonial empire."[72]

For Coubertin, "education" was the foundation for virtually everything he did. When he traveled to England or America, his object was to visit universities, to assess the latest developments in producing a vigorous younger generation which, among other things, would never be humiliated on the battlefield. But Coubertin was not merely a conventional pedagogue. He was, rather, an aspiring social engineer for whom French society constituted an enormous classroom in which the lessons of sport would be taught for the good of the Republic. In his fear and loathing of "the crowd," Coubertin very much resembles his contemporary Gustave Le Bon, author of the famous treatise *The Crowd* (1895). Like Le Bon, Coubertin assigned himself the role of advising the leaders of the Republic on mass psychology and its political risks.

The issue of education was one reason that Coubertin and the leaders of the Republic were ambivalent about the Church. When the Republic broke up the clerical monopoly on education, "it declared that education under the state was to be 'lay', or nonsectarian, that is to say, not specifically Catholic. The Church chose to interpret neutrality as hostility and branded the new schools as 'godless'."[73] Due to Coubertin's instinctive aversion to partisanship, his own conflict with the Church was comparatively low key. When he found his Olympic campaign being opposed by clerics who had, quite rightly, detected its pagan element,[74] his approach to the Church was conciliatory. In fact, he need not have worried at all, since the twentieth-century Vatican would soon adopt sport and the Olympic movement as exemplary instruments of moral hygiene.

The struggle for the French educational system represented the antagonistic side of Church-State relations under the Republic. The other side of this relationship was a collaboration made possible by the government's appreciation of religion's role in keeping the social peace. Coubertin's attitude toward religion was in basic accord with the casual utilitarianism of the regime. With his exquisite balance of views, he was, according to one biographer, "against anticlericalism and clericalism," and opposed to "an intolerant and meddlesome state religion." At the same time, however, he was "profoundly marked by the doctrine of Christ."[75]

As I will argue at greater length below, it is doubtful that Coubertin possessed much in the way of genuine piety. But this is easily overlooked by the Olympic movement. To this day, the *Olympic Review* continues to publish the testimonies of popes and cardinals extolling sport as "a natural school for genuine human virtue," and so on.[76]

Coubertin's peculiar religiosity should not be mistaken for Christianity. It was comparable to the doctrine of Jules Ferry, who said that he belonged "to the religion of the Feasts of Humanity." As Theodore Zeldin points out:

> The religion of humanity meant liberty for Ferry because it encouraged the development of 'sociability', which he saw as a growing force in modern society. He meant that the egoism he attributed to Christianity was being replaced by a new outlook with the right of the strongest giving way to the duty of the strongest. Humanity was

now emerging as 'no longer a fallen race, doomed by original sin, dragging itself painfully in a valley of tears, but as a ceaseless cavalcade marching forward towards the light'. He felt himself 'an integral part of this great Being which cannot perish, of this Humanity which is ceaselessly improving' and he believed he 'had conquered his liberty completely, because he was free from the fear of death'. The next stage was to effect 'that fusion of classes which is the aim of democracy'.[77]

There is an authentic Coubertinian element in this sort of visionary language. As Zeldin points out, Ferry preferred the notion of "sociability" to that of "fraternity" because it sounded more scientific. Coubertin, in a similar vein, viewed himself as a kind of sport psychologist who could dispense practical advice. "Sport," he wrote in "Can Sport Stem the Universal Neurosis?" (1913), "is an incomparable psychic instrument and, we may note, a dynamic to which one can profitably appeal in the treatment of many psychoneuroses. For, very often, the psychoneuroses are distinguished by a kind of disappearance of the virile sensibility, and there is nothing like sport to revive and maintain it."[78] Coubertin's promotion of the reconciling "Olympic idea" partakes of the evolutionary optimism inherent in Ferry's "ceaseless cavalcade marching forward towards the light," "this Humanity which is ceaselessly improving." And Coubertin's vision of the "fusion of classes" is, of course, sport culture itself—the youth of all classes drinking from "the fountain of muscular joy."

Coubertin's idea of humanity was not incompatible with colonialism. "Colonies," he wrote in 1902, "are like children: it is relatively easy to bring them into the world; the difficult thing is to raise them properly. They do not grow up by themselves, but need to be taken care of, coddled, and pampered by the mother country; they need constant attention to incubate them, to understand their needs, to foresee their disappointments, to calm their fears."[79] When King Leopold of Belgium asked Coubertin to draw up plans for a "colonial preparatory school," he was only too happy to oblige. But, alas, the project was never to be. Coubertin had proposed a lay institution in which sport would have played an important role. It was finally scuttled, he says, by certain "monastic influences."[80] In 1912, Coubertin published his advice to colonial regimes on how they could best make sport an instrument of administration. It is a great mistake, he says, to assume that a victory by the "dominated race" over the dominating one constitutes a dangerous temptation to rebellion. On the contrary, the example of British India shows that such incidents actually legitimize colonial rule in the eyes of the "winners."[81]

For all his idealism, Coubertin used the word "utopia" as an epithet. In 1902, he saw France threatened by a "senile mixture of complacent utopias and sectarian fanaticism," perversions he no doubt saw as related. Two years later he wrote: "The British factory, in directly preparing the adolescent for the realities of virile existence, kills in the egg the deplorable germ of which our colleges are the incubator: utopia."[82]

Coubertin's disapproval of utopianism reflected the instincts of a born moderate, and it was these instincts which made him a model Republican of his day. It is interesting to see that Leon Gambetta, a founder of the Republic, for a short time its premier, and a man who had supposedly been a radical in his youth, offered an impassioned criticism of utopianism that could have been written by Coubertin himself: "Let us remain on guard against the utopias of those who, dupes of their imagination or backward in their ignorance, believe in a panacea, in a formula which has only to be found to bring about happiness in the world. There is no social remedy, because there is no social question."[83] Even Coubertin did not claim to have a social remedy. "Olympism" could help society, but it was not a panacea.

c. Ethics and Religion

Did Coubertin understand what ethics and morality really are? Could he distinguish them from the reflexive instincts of a chivalric code? The written evidence suggests that he could not. And yet, late in his life, he produced a passage of unusual insight which appears in his *Sport Pedagogy* (1922):

> Every sportsman who is seriously interested in perfecting himself is led to *examine himself* and, as we have already said, to put into practice the γνῶθι σε αυτόν [know thyself] of the Ancients; but his examination remains *physical* if also, at times, *psychical.* It is a long way from here to the moral inspection of conscience; and yet the instrument is the same. It is only the object and the nature of the observations which differ. The mechanism of conscience is that of a tribunal whose intelligent mechanism must be clearly grasped; it rests on the ever-present idea of imperfection. But in sport this idea manifests itself with singular clarity. For what sportsman, after too easy a victory, does not ask himself if he could not have done even better, or who, in the case of a disputed victory, does not seek to ascertain at what moment and why he might have lost. He takes upon himself those inferiorities for which he is accountable and even those for which, he feels, he is not responsible. Both will enrich his experience and thereby prepare for the improvement of his future performances. And indeed, is not all of this transferable to the terrain of morality; and do not such habits of the spirit, applied to moral situations, constitute a progressive instrument of incontestable value?[84]

The mechanism of conscience and the sportsman's striving for perfection are analogous, says Coubertin, but *not* identical. The "examination of conscience—the only true means for the moral perfection of man—finds in sport an experimental garden where habit will easily acquire the necessary gestures."[85] Elsewhere in his writings Coubertin chose to emphasize, not the difference, but the analogy. But one wonders whether he had ever grasped the significance of the difference in the first place.

"The man without remorse," he once wrote, "is a monster."[86] But what is the opposite of the monster? "An army of sportsmen," he wrote in 1912, "will be more humane, more given to pity in the struggle, calmer and more gentle afterwards. There can be no doubt in this regard. The Spanish-American War proves the point; for no one can forget the sublime words of the American commander calming his men as their hurrahs hailed the sinking of a Spanish warship: 'Don't cheer! They are dying!' These words were sporting words, and this morality, which will be, let us hope, the morality of the future, will be greatly aided in its diffusion by sport."[87]

In other words, the "morality of the future" would be something like a military code of honor. Coubertin had nothing but scorn for what he called "humanitarian *naifs*" without virility—one of his favorite terms. He lists "the primary needs of the modern democracies" as follows: nobility of feeling, the cult of disinterestedness and of honor, the chivalric spirit, virile energy, and peace.[89] What must be emphasized is that these do not add up to that ethical feeling or the mercy which, even before it refuses to celebrate the death of the enemy, questions the act of killing itself.

This sort of mercy is what the chivalric code cannot afford; the warrior of noble feeling, after all, requires a death about which he can feel noble. This is the contradiction inherent in every "sportive" morality: the individual is confined to a stylized response to a preordained tragedy for which he takes no responsibility and in which he even finds a kind of grandeur. In this sense, chivalry is a perverse cult of the necessary sacrifice. (It was Hitler who called war "the most powerful and classic expression of life."[90]) Chivalry sacrifices ethics for style. This is why a code of honor—for all its self-discipline—is the merest skeleton of ethics.

The ethical weakness of Coubertin's ideal man is that he is essentially a creature of force. Sport, he says, "must be practiced with fervor, I will even say: with violence. Sport is not physical exercise which is good for everyone on account of its being wise and moderate; sport is the pleasure of the strong, or of those who want to be physically and morally strong. Nothing would kill it more surely than the desire to imprison it within a moderation which is contrary to its essence."[91] Sport inspires the *taste for force,* but a force which is cultivated, shaped, controlled and honestly applied. It is a wholesome taste from which civilization draws more advantages than disadvantages."[92]

Coubertin's preferred doctrine, a species of vitalism, admits little self-reflection or self-doubt: "There is inherent in the sportsman a certain obligation to be *impassible,* an obligation which is extremely educative. A sportsman who permits the slightest contradiction to become visible in himself seems a bit shocking; a sportsman who shows the slightest tendency to suffering is scandalous."[93] These quotations make it clear that, in Coubertin's world, the "virile" style is to be preferred to the doubts, the complexities, and the humbling confessions of conscience. In this sense, he had indeed left the spirit of his parents' Catholicism far behind.

In another sense, however, Coubertin anticipates the attitude of Pius XII, the "Papa degli sportivi," who describes "the steeling of the will" as "the most precious fruit" of competitive sport.[94] In a word, Coubertin tended to confuse ethics with self-control: "Sport is not natural for man: it stands in formal contradiction to the animal law of the 'least effort';" it is "a fruitful constraint."[95] To Coubertin, the demands of sport, like the demands of a divinity, originate outside of man and force him to challenge the limits of his nature.

What was Coubertin's religion? His own definition was elastic enough to embrace "modern patriotism" and peace itself, "a sort of religion whose altars are being tended by an ever-growing number of the faithful."[96] The easy answer is the famous one: "for me, sport was a religion with a church, dogmas, a cult . . . but especially religious feeling . . ."[97] A more adequate assessment can be distilled from his many remarks about the Church, a few of which were critical. Well aware of Christianity's traditional devaluation of the body, Coubertin warned of the dire consequences of forcing "the antagonism between soul and flesh."[98] At his most disapproving, he could go so far as to state that "the Churches, entrenched in their opinions as though in fortresses, have always had too great an interest in isolating themselves and in forgetting what they have been"[99]—a standard Republican critique of the time.

What is striking about Coubertin's concept of religion is that it is virtually indistinguishable from his concept of the Olympic Games. "I am not one of those," he wrote in a letter, "who thinks that humanity can get along without religion. I am taking the word here in its most general sense, *not as belief in a determinate form of divine reality, but as adherence to an ideal of superior life, of the aspiration to perfection. . . ."[100]* "The God in which he never ceased to believe," a (hagiographically inclined) biographer tells us, "is the *agnostos theos,* the 'unknown God' of the Greeks, and the Christians' God of love."[101]

With his penchant for embracing apparently contradictory positions, Coubertin the Christian also found room for Christianity's ancient adversary: "In its basic principle, paganism is precisely the cult of humanity or, better, the cult of the present life. As such, it is indestructible. Its periodic reappearance is, as it were, a necessary phenomenon."[102] Given the pagan character of the ancient Games, it could hardly be otherwise.

In a sense, Coubertin's religion was *ceremony* itself. One gets a perfect sense of this in his reminiscence of the 1920 Antwerp Olympics:

> By holding a public service in the stadium itself, as in Stockholm, before the start of the competitions, we would be forcing the athletes, already grown men, to take part in a religious ceremony that might be displeasing to some. By inviting them, quite outside the Games, to a ceremony in church, we were only associating religion like any other great moral force of mankind with the celebration of the Olympic Games. Then again, it was important that the ceremony should be sufficiently neutral in character to rise above all differences in doctrine. No mass, no priestly address at the altar: the *De Profundis,* a hymn to the memory of the dead of the previous four years, and the *Te Deum,* a hymn of success and hope; lay hymns, they might be called, and ideally suited to beautiful musical interpretations. To which could be added a speech, provided that it was couched in liberal terms. This unusual programme appealed to Cardinal Mercier. The ceremony had a special grandeur about it this time owing to the tragic fact that the list of Olympic dead was terribly long. And all those present came away, I believe, deeply impressed by the words spoken in the Cathedral by the famous prelate in a moving service accompanied by the magnificent music of the choirs and organ.[103]

Coubertin was essentially a revivalist. He predicted that "the current trend toward lowering barriers and multiplying human contacts will produce on the religious plane one of these great movements which is endowed with the awesome power of the tides."[104] And the social engineer in him believed that "for the present and for the immediate future—if not for the distant future, as well—the idea of God will remain the ABC of the architecture of young consciences."[105] Both observations also apply to his Olympic mission, which called upon him to be a healing reconciler who could "lower barriers" and a moralist, an "architect of young consciences."

d. The Berlin Olympiad (1936)

"Coubertin," his admiring biographer Marie-Thérèse Eyquem has written, "would never disavow the Olympic symphony, in spite of the false notes of Berlin. No human work is perfect, not even those which hold themselves to be divine. The Church has had its heresies, its schisms, its inquisition."[106] The meaning of the Berlin Olympiad of 1936 is still being debated,[107] but Coubertin's statements are either unknown or ignored. The following remarks, made in the course of an interview during the 1936 Games, were exactly what Carl Diem and Goebbels' propagandists wanted to hear:

> What? "Disfigured" Games? The Olympic idea sacrificed to propaganda? That is entirely false! The imposing success of the Berlin Games has served the Olympic ideal magnificently. The French, who alone or almost alone have been playing the

Cassandras, commit the greatest injustice by not understanding or by not wanting to understand. It is necessary that the Olympic idea be spread abroad, and that we have the wisdom to fear neither passion nor excess, which create the necessary fever and enthusiasm. To seek to adapt sport to a regime of obligatory moderation would be to pursue a utopia.

There was once at Olympia a sacred enclosure, the Altis, which was reserved for consecrated athletes; an entire collective life throbbed around it. Even with the natural deficiencies which modern life imposes on us, this is what happened at Berlin. In the name of what sort of rigorism are we to condemn it?

It is good that each nation of the world be granted the honor of putting on the Games and of celebrating them in its own manner, in accordance with its own creative powers and by its own means. In France they are disturbed by the fact that the Games of 1936 were illuminated by a Hitlerian force and discipline. How could it have been otherwise?[108]

43

In a letter addressed to the French sporting paper L'Auto several days after these remarks had been delivered, the interviewer states that Coubertin "offers his congratulations to Mr. Hitler, whom he salutes as one of the great constructive spirits of the age, for having preserved the Olympic ideal from distortion and for having served it magnificently."[109]

In 1982 the West German sport historian Hans Joachim Teichler further documented Coubertin's collaboration with the Nazi propaganda campaign on behalf of the Berlin Games. The Germans, including Carl Diem, courted the old man assiduously and played upon his sense of being unappreciated outside of Germany ("Only France has forgotten me"). Coubertin responded with statements useful to the Nazis' campaign against the international boycott which threatened the success of their Olympiad. In a letter dated March 17, 1937, Coubertin thanked Hitler for his attentions and looked forward to a German visit he did not live to make. The point is not that Coubertin was a Nazi; he was not. It is rather that, as Teichler puts it: "He did not criticize—he cooperated."[110]

Coubertin did not attend the "Nazi Olympics." Instead, a recording of his message of welcome was played over loudspeakers to the assembled multitude during the opening ceremony.[111]

Did Coubertin understand the significance of the Berlin festival? After a conversation with Coubertin in August 1933, Diem reported that the former was "well informed about sports and politics in Germany" and that he greeted the "upheaval in Germany as the sign of a turning point in history which all peoples would finally understand in the not too distant future." What is more: "He expects the Olympic Games in Berlin to be a major cultural event."[112] It is possible, of course, that Coubertin spoke these words and meant them. As we have seen, he was poorly equipped to resist the temptations of the festival spirit. But Diem, as Arnd Krüger points out, cannot be considered a reliable source; his account may have been intended to further promote the Olympic cause or to enhance his own status as an intermediary between Coubertin and the upcoming Olympiad in Berlin.[113]

In a memorial essay on Coubertin published in 1941, Diem states that Coubertin's wholehearted endorsement of the Berlin Games had appeared, "as a response to certain criticisms," in "a French newspaper." He goes on to say that he had been able to confirm this endorsement in the course of a conversation with

Coubertin just after the Games. They had sat, he reports, by Coubertin's writing table in the Olympic Museum at Lausanne as the old man "contemplated with great satisfaction our attempts to give [the event] an artistic shape."[114] We may certainly assume, in conformity with Diem's account, that Coubertin's eyes were fixed on aesthetics rather than politics. The "artistic" dimension of the Games had always captivated him.

We have no way of knowing, however, how clearly those eyes could see at the age of seventy-three. Coubertin had been gradually losing touch with the reality of the modern Olympiad. "The last Olympics Coubertin attended were in Paris in 1924, Games notable for their placidity, joy, the participation of leading artists and poets, and the central place the Baron occupied in them. Coubertin never saw, and so failed to appreciate, the extraordinary transformation the Olympics underwent in the '30s, when they arrived at truly spectacular proportion and were drawn into the center of international political, ideological, and commercial life."[115]

Did Coubertin's attitude toward the sport spectacle change during his lifetime? In 1890, he had preached the virtues of simplicity before a French athletic association: "The applause you earn from the noisy, turbulent crowd will never displease us, my friends, but we will never consent to the transformation of your competitions into a public spectacle. Such approval would serve you very poorly. Too much concern for the theoretical part of the festival would run counter to the requirements of the sport, the true goal would be lost sight of, and the victors would come to believe that they were demigods."[116] Forty years later, judging from the *Olympic Memoirs* (1931), Coubertin's view of the spectacle is quite intact. The "modern democracies" still require "virile energy," but the prospect of "great fairs" (*foires*) is still anathema.[117]

What had changed was that mass ceremony had entered public political life, and Coubertin again shows the adaptability that served him so well. He praises Mussolini and his struggle against an "adverse fate." He also refers to "a gigantic stadium" (*un stade monstre*) being built at Moscow for the next "workers' Olympiad."[118] What is striking is that Coubertin reserves his sarcastic disapproval for the Communists' attempt to appropriate his brainchild simply by affixing to it a new ideological label. He does not denigrate this step toward Olympic gigantism by predicting a vulgar *foire*. The explanation for this lies in the fact that Coubertin's real concern was less the physical scale of a festival than the possibility of disorder. His distaste for the mob (*la foule*) had less to do with its size than its lack of discipline. Here we should recall that Coubertin's definition of the "democratic" citizen in the *Notes on Public Education* (1901) holds that the citizen's real function is not to think but to participate in a "collective effort."[119] Of course Coubertin did not intend to offer a totalitarian formula, but that is what it became.

The man who acclaimed "Hitlerian force and discipline" had once seen through the aestheticism that is awed by spectacular tyranny: "The same people who condemned the crimes of a Cesare Borgia secretly admired the 'superb contours' of his energy."[120] It is unlikely, however, that Coubertin understood himself as well as he understood the secret admirers of Cesare Borgia. Given the choice between the Socratic ideal of self-examination and the Olympic ideal of public celebration of virility, he chose the latter without a qualm. Coubertin's colleague, Carl Diem, concurred in this choice and paid the price in personal disgrace (see below). Coubertin's successor, Avery Brundage, was just as susceptible to the charms of pageantry and just as inclined to grant moral immunity to the festival of the body.

3. Carl Diem: Olympiadenker in dürftiger Zeit

a. Diem and Coubertin

On March 26, 1938, Coubertin's heart, having been "paganly dug out of his corpse,"[121] was buried at the Greek site of ancient Olympia. Present at this bizarre ceremony was the loyal Carl Diem,[122] who had known Coubertin for a quarter century. Neither then nor later would Diem grasp the impact of Coubertin's legacy on his own fate. The Berlin Games, which Diem celebrated in spite of criticism for the rest of his life, were only two years in the past, and he was now looking forward to the 1940 winter Olympiad he hoped to stage at Garmisch-Partenkirchen.[123]

What Diem never fathomed was the significance of his own involvement in a politically tainted festival, and in this sense Diem was the cardinal victim of Coubertin's Olympic doctrine. "What [Coubertin] could never see," his biographer John J. MacAloon has pointed out, "given the nineteenth-century, utilitarian, progressist cast of his mind, was that the dramatization of evil and conflict at the Olympics would prove an essential component of their global triumph."[124] Although endowed with a less "progressist" cast of mind, Diem was as nearsighted as the master himself. To Diem, festivals, as he wrote in 1940, were "a mirror-image of the soul,"[125] and that was enough.

The differences between Coubertin and Diem are largely differences in politics and temperament. While Coubertin was an exemplary citizen of the Third Republic, Diem was an apathetic observer of the Weimar Republic, which served as nothing more than a framework for his activities as Secretary General of the German Commission for Physical Culture (1917-1933) and pro-rector of the German University for Physical Culture in Cologne (1920-1933)—of which he became rector after the war and remained until his death in 1962. The informed political commentary that characterized Coubertin's *Pages d'histoire contemporaine* (1909) is virtually absent from Diem's published articles. Diem's "political" commentaries are, instead, complaints about the Versailles treaty, invocations of the "stab-in-the-back" theory of Germany's defeat in the First World War, and loud encouragements for Hitler's armies.[126] While Coubertin pursued a collaboration with the political world, Diem simply shunned it until he found the Nazis looking over his shoulder. And at that point, as Arnd Krüger notes, he adapted to circumstances.[127]

Coubertin's republicanism implied concerns that Diem did not share. Coubertin's anxieties about "anger" and "the mob" (*la foule*),[128] about the fragile concord on which social peace depends, are genuinely important themes of his program. And Diem would not have disagreed. "Away," he wrote in 1932, "with the empty divisions between rich and poor, between educated and uneducated, worker and bourgeois, peasant and city-dweller, Bavarian and Prussian."[129] But this was as far as Diem pursued the ideal of "a new unity"; he left the rest to the Nazis, from whom he appears to have perceived little danger to his own interests— until the Nazis began to take over the sport bureaucracy in 1933. In 1922, Coubertin had invoked "the law of evolution and the law of patience, the knowledge and acceptance of which constitute the basis of all political wisdom."[130] Diem did not oppose such thinking; he was simply uninterested in social theory to the point where even Coubertin's meliorist generalities failed to arouse him.

The second important difference between Diem and Coubertin derives from the Volkish roots of Diem's thinking (see below). Diem's nationalism incorporates vaguely mystical and racial themes which are peculiar to Germany and which require a German vocabulary Diem had adopted as his own long before it was legitimated, and developed further, by the Nazis. After 1945, Diem's prose takes on a new sobriety, even if vestiges of the old diction remain.

Such differences are, however, subordinated to a shared doctrine of sport and, of course, the Olympic ideology itself. Both Coubertin and Diem considered sport analogous to religious experience. "Sport," Diem wrote in 1924, "is a kind of worship, provided it is practiced for the greater glory of omnipotent Nature, the human body and soul, and for the glory of the Creation which surrounds us . . . " When we perfect the body, "we are crowning the work of the Highest One."[131] Both were devotees of the mass festival as a rite of communion which expresses the deepest human impulses.[132] Both were pedagogical missionaries[133] who went abroad—Coubertin to England, Diem to America—to find athletic inspiration.[134] Both believed in moderation and warned that the pursuit of sport can become a kind of idiocy.[135] "All the Olympic victories in the world," said Diem, "are not worth a single broken life."[136] On the political level, both believed that patriotic—as opposed to chauvinistic—sentiments could coexist happily with internationalist ideals within the framework of the Olympic movement.[137] As for tactics, both subscribed to the principle that Diem, citing Coubertin's example, called "elastic resistance as the best defense."[138] Specifically, this tactical principle has prescribed the compromises that have enabled the Olympic movement to survive, for better or for worse.

Most important, Diem shared with Coubertin the idea that sport is a universal culture, the "common property of mankind."[139] Sport partakes of "something transcendental,"[140] making possible the "global character" (*das Allweltliche*) of the sport festival.[141] It should be noted, however, that Diem's internationalism has strong Teutonic overtones that have no counterpart in Coubertin's writings. Both men insisted on the coexistence of, and on some sort of parity between, national and international interests. But Diem's pre-1945 internationalism is combined with a Volkish longing for German greatness. One result of this was his fantasy of a new global order—and global Games—under the benevolent auspices of the Third Reich.[142] "We Germans," Diem had written in 1926, "feel more universal."[143]

b. Diem and the Volkish Ideology

Diem's apolitical ambitions were characteristic of his cultural ideology: a right-wing Volkish doctrine which by the 1920s had achieved widespread respectability within the Republic it did so much to subvert. "What differentiated the Germany of this period from other nations," George Mosse has written, "was a profound mood, a peculiar view of man and society which seems alien and even demonic to the Western intellect."[144] As Mosse notes, this was a mood the Volkish groups shared with the Nazis, who became the historical beneficiaries of a peculiarly German conservatism which dates from the early years of the nineteenth century.

Volkish thought is based on the idea of the "Volk," which since the late eighteenth century has "signified the union of a group of people with a transcendental 'essence'. This 'essence' . . . was fused to man's innermost nature, and represented the source of his creativity, his depth of feeling, his individuality, and his unity with other members of the Volk ."[145] From this concept of the "Volk" flow the other major doctrinal themes: the preservation of a specifically German racial identity and hostility to the Jew; a nationalism of grandiose dimensions; an aversion to the modern age, to mechanization and industrialization; and a suspicion of reason and intellect.

Diem's writing prior to 1945 is permeated with Volkish themes and a Volkish vocabulary. But how, one might ask, is this sort of nationalism compatible with the internationalist ideals of the Olympic movement Diem served? The answer, as we shall see, is to be found in the profound ambiguity which marks Diem's relationship to Volkish thought. In some cases Diem simply departs from certain Volkish tenets; in others he plays with Volkish vocabulary, using nationalist terms on behalf of a hidden internationalist doctrine—an interesting example of the "elastic resistance" for which he had commended Coubertin. One might add that it was most surely Diem's love of sport that modified his Volkish bent. Let us now examine Diem's record in relation to the four major Volkish themes: race, nationalism, modernity, and the irrational.

There is no evidence that Diem, whose wife was known to have a Jewish ancestor,[146] was an anti-Semite. In 1955, and again in 1960, Diem claimed that even before 1933, the Nazis had castigated him as a "white Jew" because of his internationalist, i.e. Olympic loyalties.[147] And it is worth noting that a list of great German intellects he published in 1927 includes not only the name of Spinoza but also that of Heinrich Heine,[148] the Jewish poet who became a special target of Volkish resentment.[149]

At the same time, however, Diem did occasionally slip into the idiom of Volkish racism. He refers in a vaguely approving way to the Aryan world-view and its belief in human development toward a higher stage of civilization.[150] In a masterfully ambiguous sentence formulated in 1932, he amplifies on the racial question in the following manner: "The mysterious vital values [*Lebenswerte*], which are associated [*gebunden*] with physiology but not conditioned [*bedingt*] by it, are matters of belief."[151] Less ambiguously, he writes in 1941 that "the position of mastery of the superior race" will endure only if it consents, against certain objections, to engage in competitive sport with "more primitive races."[152] Even this passage, however, does not really prove Diem's racism. It may well be another example of "elastic resistance"— in this case the adoption of a racist idiom to promote multi-racial sport.

Diem's Volkish nationalism, which is found throughout his writings, has an elusive quality. "To be German must mean to demand the world for Germany," he wrote in 1925.[153] But this sort of straightforward assertion occurred only rarely in his articles and speeches. His standard rhetorical technique was to use Volkish terminology to undermine the more chauvinistic Volkish norms. "Throughout our people," Diem told an audience in 1923, "there is a longing for a *Führer*."[154] But it quickly becomes apparent that he was referring, not to the heroic figure of the military leader—a Volkish ideal he specifically disavows—but to the cultivation of leadership in that "school of character" which only physical culture can provide.

Though he spoke, as early as 1915, of global sport's drinking in the German spirit,[155] it should be remembered that the very idea of a "world sport movement" was bitterly attacked by Volkish ideologists who, in fact, made Diem a favorite target as well. Diem's persistent coupling of the national and the international put him at the liberal end of the Volkish spectrum. As Mosse points out, "Volkish thought was not necessarily aggressive or racist: it was possible to think in Volkish categories, and yet grant each people its own contribution to humanity, to accept the Volk, not as something that is eternally given, but as a step toward the unification of mankind."[156]

This is what made it possible for Diem to be a Volkish Olympian. "Every nation," he wrote in 1932, "has reason to practice the politics of humanity, because this is the best national policy."[157] In 1936, while in the service of the Nazis, Diem wrote of "racial consciousness with breadth of vision and a global spirit"[158]—a formula which could only offend the Volkish militants. Finally, it should be emphasized that Diem's "liberal" Volkish rhetoric was not invented to deal with the arrival of the Nazis. On the contrary, it was an idiom that came naturally to him and in which he had been speaking for twenty years before the Volkish revolution engulfed him.

Just as Diem's attachment to the multi-cultural world of sport tempered his Volkish nationalism, so it prevented an unambiguously anti-modernist outlook. Diem was strongly influenced by the Volkish hostility to industrialization, the metropolis, and, in his words, the "passive joys which to some extent signify nothing more than a febrile stimulation of the brain: films, revues, magazines, sport" (1927).[159] But modernity is also dynamic. "Our age," Diem wrote a year later, "has a super-charged presence. The accelerated tempo of labor, the turning away from quiet satisfactions, the speeding up of all means of transport and communication, culminating today in radio and tomorrow in television, these are the underlying causes."[160] The silver lining to be found within this development is sport, which directly serves the emerging world-order.

"Sport," Diem wrote in 1927, "is a feature of our age. We cannot imagine the physiognomy of the age of technology and the division of labor without the lines which sport has etched on its face."[161] Sport counteracts the indolence of urban life, it constitutes a "new form of communal life,"[162] and it opposes "the mechanization of existence."[163] Like Coubertin, Diem was an idealist who knew how to accommodate the inevitable. Like it or not, a "homogenization of world culture"[164] was underway, and sport was its healthiest dimension.

The same ambivalence characterizes Diem's view of the relationship between sport and technology. As a Volkish cultural critic, Diem cannot embrace technology; but as a sport doctrinaire, he is forced to grant it a special kind of recognition: "Sport is technology, a refinement of methods and equipment; the very essence of sport implies refinement, that is, the capacity of movement to be 'technologized', and yet it is also a flight out of the wasteland of our technologized age. Sport is a tension between technology and romanticism."[165] Diem's description of sport as "a reaction against technology"[166] is, then, more complex than it seems.

Anti-intellectualism, compounded of contempt for reason and a belief in the irrational and the intuitive, was a prominent feature of Volkish thought, and one which Diem adopted quite unreservedly. "While there is much of the rational in the modern physical culture movement," Diem wrote in 1932, "its real essence [*Lebensodem*] is irrational, mythical, universal, rising out of the fundamental life-forces, whose source is metaphysical, and therefore something beyond, spiritual, divine."[167] He emphasized the importance of "a belief in basic forces, primal forces, rhythm, the mysterious current of life which transcends all knowledge and explanation."[168] Like other Volkish ideologues,[169] Diem substituted the cult of the body for the life of the mind, claiming that "the most original, the most noble, and the finest thoughts flow from a fresh, blossoming bodiliness which has nothing to do with age."[170]

Diem's anti-intellectual rhetorical strategy follows two lines. First, he frequently denigrates "intellectualism," "theory-babblers" (who lost the First World War), "sharp minds," and "one-sided mental activity."[171] Second, he extols the mystery and depth of those interior regions from which an instinctive wisdom flows: "the wellsprings of our humanity," "the depths of the soul," "the region behind the body."[172]

To the Volkish mind, the body is the realm of "inwardness" and, therefore, of racial wisdom.

c. Diem's Doctrine of Amateur Sport

As Richard Mandell has pointed out, Diem "was a middle- and long-distance runner at a time when track events as practiced among the Anglo-Saxons were almost unknown among his countrymen who were quite devoted to gymnastics."[173] The first organized track and field competition in Germany took place in Hamburg in 1880,[174] only two years before Diem's birth. Thus Diem grew up with—and attached himself to—a sport culture that had been transplanted from abroad. As we have seen, it was this sort of cosmopolitanism that diverted him from the path of virulent nationalism and brought him into the Olympic inner circle.

Diem subscribed wholeheartedly to the Olympic doctrine of amateurism and its philosophical basis, which transcends simple fairness (or what Diem calls "justice").[175] For Diem amateurism is nothing less than a philosophy of life prescribing both purity and heroism—the man who virtuously refuses payment avoids the "desacralizing" of his existence. And the intensity of Diem's devotion has a distinctly religious flavor. "In this self-transcendence there is also an element of self-sacrifice," he writes. "The striving for meaning and heroic experience obeys the holy instinct to preserve the species. Sport is an 'excelsior,' a striving to reach the heights of existence."[176] On an equally important if less transcendental plane, the amateur fulfills Diem's ideal of the well-rounded life. "Our social sensibility," he wrote in 1928, "excludes all of the do-nothings and the drones. Today the only person of value is the one who works . . ."[177] Amateurism, in short, is a doctrine of citizenship.

Diem's view of professional sport, on the other hand, recalls his interpretation of modernity: it is not totally undesirable because it is inevitable. Professional sport is "a natural development; all of the human arts are originally free play which is eventually professionalized, and the definition of what constitutes a professional performance will always remain fluid."[178] However fluid it may be, this definition is the basis of a crucial distinction based, not on character, but on one's solemn choice of social role in relation to sport. For the character of the professional sportsman may be as good, or better, than the character of the amateur.[179] But the fundamental social role of the professional is that of the variety artist or circus performer,[180] though he at least has his own code of honor. It is the "pseudo-amateurs or semi-professionals"[181] who arouse Diem's indignation, because they confuse the categories.

d. Diem and the Nazis

"I felt myself to be Hitler's architect," Albert Speer wrote in his memoirs. "Political events did not concern me. My job was merely to provide backdrops for such events."[182] Diem, like the young Speer, was Hitler's festival master, though far less compromised—and far less repentant—than the dramaturge of the Nuremburg rallies. Whether Diem was, as one observer has claimed, "one of those in the silent opposition"[183] is open to question. He was certainly in opposition to Nazi encroachments on his bureaucratic terrain, but this hardly qualifies as ethical sentiment.

A hypothetical defense of Diem must be based on what he did *not* do, and on what others said about him. He did not join in the anti-Semitic chorus—and there were excellent reasons not to do so. As he pointed out to von Halt in April 1935, the campaign against the Jews could only imperil the Berlin Olympiad by inflaming foreign opinion.[184] At the same time, Diem was being attacked by the scurrilous *Völkischer Beobachter* as "an intolerable burden,"[185] and by Edmund Neuendorff, the Nazi leader of the German Gymnastic Association (DT), as unfit to lead German sport into the New Order, largely because of his foreign affinities.[186] When *Reichssportführer* Tschammer und Osten tried to get Diem a professorship at the University of Berlin in 1939, his proposal was rejected.[187]

Diem's record is not, however, one of uncompromising silence. Having been dismissed in May 1933 from all his positions except that of Olympic liaison, Diem was clearly aware of his vulnerability. In June he wrote to Tschammer und Osten: "I have trained many gymnastics and sports personnel who carry in their hearts the ideal that physical culture is practiced not for its own sake but to serve the fatherland."[188] On the one hand, this was opportunism; it was not, however, invented, since Diem had never concealed his nationalism. But it also contradicts Diem's postwar claims that he was simply an un-political man.

Like many who occupied *de facto* political positions during the Nazi period, Diem cultivated a convenient myopia. Five years after Coubertin's candidacy for the 1936 Nobel Peace Prize was rejected, Diem commented that it had gone instead to "the German Communist Ossiewsky [sic]."[189] Carl von Ossietsky, a non-Communist journalist and a man of obvious courage, had been swept up in the wave of arrests which followed the Reichstag fire of February 28, 1933. By 1936, he had been in a concentration camp for three years and was widely regarded as a prisoner of conscience. It does not seem to have occurred to Diem that, given Coubertin's apparent endorsement of Hitler's Olympiad, he had ruled himself out of consideration for a Nobel Prize.[190]

Diem's postwar apologetics for his role in the Berlin Olympiad show few signs of that inner emigration which became, after 1945, a refuge for some deeper and more compromised heads. In a memoir of the Nazi years written in 1955, he states his disapproval of the fact that the Olympiad—"which everyone regarded as [politically] neutral ground"—had provided the Nazis with "undeserved glory."[191] In 1958, he insisted that the 1936 Games had "proceeded in a manner that was wholly unobjectionable from a political standpoint" and had been "a respected oasis."[192] In his *World History of Sport and Physical Culture* (1960), Diem makes the absurd and dishonest claim that it was only after the German collapse that critics had begun to call the Berlin Olympiad a propaganda show[193] —as though Diem had forgotten the boycott campaign against which he had struggled. All in all, Diem was anything but a cunning apologist, if only because he refused to make any apology whatsoever.

Lacking the moral courage to confront his own responsibility, Diem fell back upon an opportunistic reticence that is particularly evident in the 1955 manuscript. "What I myself thought and think about National Socialism is not something I need to say," he wrote; for "who will reproach me if it is the worst about men which my tongue refuses to speak, and if I must fear in many cases my own lack of objectivity."[194] A sophist to the end, Diem eventually found others to carry the flame on his behalf.[195]

4. Avery Brundage:
The International Sportsman as Fellow-Traveler

a. The Olympian

"I owe much to a great many cosmopolitan friendships," Coubertin wrote in his

Olympic Memoirs. "Nor have they been the least bit injurious to the veneration of my own country. But as much as I believe in the value of this sort of cosmopolitanism, the fact remains that one must reject the other kind, that of the simple voyage, which opens the door to all kinds of dangerous misunderstandings and illusions."[196]

Coubertin's observation anticipated the misadventures of Avery Brundage (1887-1975), an Olympic innocent abroad. President of the United States Olympic Committee (1923-1953), vice president of the International Olympic Committee (1929-1952), and president of the IOC for two decades (1952-1972), Brundage was the second and, perhaps, the last giant of the Olympic movement.[197] For nearly the entire time he spent as an official of the movement, he was a controversial and at times an enormously unpopular figure.

The controversies arose from two causes he championed. First, Brundage was the man primarily responsible for American participation in the Berlin Olympics of 1936, a festival which, it is now recognized, stained the Olympic movment. In the course of this campaign, Brundage mounted a sometimes hysterical attack against the opponents of Olympic neutrality: "The bitter feelings engendered, the attempted coercion and intimidation by fair means or foul, the vicious and insidious propaganda which are being used in this campaign largely by individuals who have never learned the lesson of amateur sport and thus do not hesitate to use methods contrary to all codes of sportsmanship, are an indication of what may be expected if religious, racial, class or political issues are allowed to intrude in the council halls of sport where they have no place." Nor did Brundage mince words about who was responsible for much of this "insidious propaganda": "Certain Jews," he wrote, "must now understand that they cannot use these Games as a weapon in their boycott against the Nazis."[198]

The second, and more important, cause of Avery Brundage's martyrdom-by-insult was his rigid defense of amateur standards for sportsmen. In his *Olympic Memoirs*, Coubertin rather cynically dismisses the amateur ideal as outdated.[199] But Brundage, a more consistent cultural conservative, was above compromise and immune to the seductions of modernity for its own sake. "It did not trouble him," Red Smith wrote at his death, "that what he stood for existed mainly in his own mind."[200]

The tragedy of Avery Brundage is that he traded ethics for this idealism, the absolute defense of a cultural style. Like his model Coubertin, he exchanged morality for an Edwardian ethos of sport, sacrificing ethics for the rigidity and the pseudonobility of a code. What he never understood was the profound vulgarity of applying the Olympic outlook to every situation he encountered.

Like every fanatic, Avery Brundage lived in a kind of isolation. But the paradox of this isolation is that it took the form of an idealistic internationalism. I believe that Avery Brundage, the international sportsman and diplomat, can best be understood as a political eccentric. I will argue that his eccentricity grew out of a tension between his sense of isolation and his need to belong to a wider, more cosmopolitan world. In the course of resolving this tension, a homespun native American, dimly aware and resentful of his own parochialism, managed to assume the identity of an internationalist for whom national boundaries, and the limitations they signify, did not exist.

b. The Isolationist

The riddle of Avery Brundage has its origins in the fact of nationality. "I'm a strange sort of beast," he told an interviewer for *The New Yorker.* "I've been called an isolationist, an imperialist, a Nazi, and a Communist. I think of myself as a Taoist. Actually, I'm a hundred-and-ten-percent American and an old-fashioned Republican. People like me haven't had anybody to vote for since Hoover and Coolidge."[201] This self-portrait is charming but deceptive, and reminiscent of another "patriot." Long before he was shot for treason, Vidkun Quisling—who also had internationalist ambitions—claimed to be a hundred-and-ten-percent Norwegian. The point of this comparison is that conspicuous nationalism may well be a prelude to actions which reflect dissatisfaction with the mother country.

One aspect of Avery Brundage's "old-fashioned Republicanism" was isolationism, a position he abandoned only after Pearl Harbor. He was chairman of the Citizens' Keep America Out of War Committee and a prominent member of the America First Committee. "Nowadays," Robert Shaplen wrote in 1960, "he describes himself as a 'partial isolationist', and says he believes that Americans are open to criticism as 'international busybodies' and 'meddlers'. On several occasions in recent years, he has publicly alluded to the six hundred and seventy-seven billion dollars that, he says, it has cost the United States to engage in two World Wars, which, he also says, were futile."[202]

It is clear that Brundage had ambivalent feelings about his native country. On the one hand, he proclaimed his staunch Americanism, on the other, he denounced American intrusiveness. It is also apparent that he liked to think of his political status as somewhat intangible: "I think of myself as a Taoist."

The isolationism was already evident in a pamphlet Brundage published in 1935 to promote American participation in the Berlin Games of 1936: "Ever since the Pilgrim fathers left Europe to brave the perils of stormy seas and savage tribes in a distant wilderness, there have been political and religious disturbances on the other side of the Atlantic. George Washington specifically advised us to refrain from meddling in these foreign affairs. In all the history of the United States, we have disregarded this advice only once—'to make the world safe for Democracy'—and we have not yet recovered from the after effects." And: "The sportsmen of this country will not tolerate the use of clean American sport as a vehicle to transplant Old World hatreds to the United States."[203]

In one sense, there is less isolationism here than meets the eye. Brundage opposed American intervention in foreign affairs when it involved partisanship or moral judgment, as in 1936; in a word, when it involved conflict. But he did favor "foreign affairs" in the form of the Olympic movement's fraternalism. Brundage refused to condemn the Nazis: they had taken on the responsibility for an Olympiad, and for him that was enough. He was, in fact, distressed when called upon to recognize evil for what it was. Avery Brundage's isolationism, then, was more than a foreign policy. It was a symptom of his personal limitations.

c. The Internationalist

Avery Brundage's isolationism was simultaneously a utopian isolationism. For his sort of isolationism really had little to do with the national interest. By accepting the world as it was, he was spared the humiliating, and sometimes enraging, confrontation with moral issues he was not equipped to handle. At the same time, his isolationism was an oblique expression of that kind of idealism, usually thought of as harmless, which seeks to promote moral uplift by holding revival meetings, jamborees, sports festivals, or other eye-catching demonstrations of good fellowship.

The only time one finds Brundage invoking the memory of George Washington is when he is defending the autonomy of the Olympic movement. For Avery Brundage, America was little more than a place to hang his hat. His heart was in utopia.

Brundage became an internationalist by attaching himself to the Olympic legacy, picking up Coubertin's mantle and wearing it for decades with the singlemindedness of the born epigone. He did not pretend to be an original thinker; indeed, his inability to rise above the thoughts of others is among his defining characteristics. Like Coubertin, he was an optimistic revivalist; just after World War II, he predicted a great sports revival in which "people of all nations will turn to the high ideals of amateurism, away from the tragedies of war."[204] Like Coubertin, he felt that women did not belong in the Olympics. Like (the early) Coubertin he was an enemy of "materialism." He was enthusiastic about Coubertin's inclusion of the fine arts in the Olympics: "Some people wonder why fine arts should be in the Olympics. Why shouldn't they be? The Greeks had them."[205] Like Coubertin, he invoked sport as a chastening therapy: "Man is a lazy animal, he does not like work, either mental or physical"; like his mentor, he warned of the deleterious effects of "mental and moral diseases."[206]

Avery Brundage the athletic internationalist assumed a redemptive mission that included both ascetic and ecstatic themes. "Not to develop the latent possibilities of the human body," he wrote in 1919, "is a crime, since it certainly violates the law of nature."[207] Within sport, Brundage himself found the highest form of asceticism known to man: martyrdom. With "bitter pride," he once described the 880-yard heel-and-toe walk as "the closest a man can come to experiencing the pangs of childbirth."[208] Indeed, a well-qualified observer called the young Avery Brundage the greatest athlete he had ever seen. It is likely that Brundage's interpretation of the athlete as an isolated-hero-in-torment influenced him to see sport as an absolute experience, analogous to religion, which had to be protected from contamination at all costs. Later on, Brundage would become an ecstatic revivalist:

> No one who witnessed the Games of the XVII Olympiad in Japan in 1964 and saw the opening parade, when teams from nearly one hundred countries composed of athletes of every race, every color, every creed and religion and of every political affiliation, capitalist, royalist, socialist, communist and fascist, marched in together and then following the same Olympic code of fair play and good sportsmanship engaged in the most strenuous competition without untoward incident, left Tokyo without renewed hope for a happier and more powerful world. Nothing like this has ever happened before.[209]

Brundage fortified his internationalism by developing what he felt was a cosmopolitan sense of the world's diversity, including an international harem featuring women of seven nationalities.[210] He began by collecting souvenirs during his first tour of the Continent in 1912, a hobby which led to one of the finest collections of Oriental art in the world. In 1956, an impressed interviewer reported that Brundage—a man of limited intellect—had long been "fascinated by Greek and Oriental philosophy and religion."[211] In 1958, Brundage treated himself to a display of his own worldly sophistication. In Japan for an IOC meeting, "he was able, he feels, to achieve the perfect synthesis of sports and art that to him represents the true Olympic spirit. He arranged in advance to be met at the airport by four Japanese, two of them Olympic officials and two leading Oriental art experts, and during the next few days he escorted the sportsmen to museums they had never been in and the art specialists to sports they had never seen. 'It was great fun,' says Brundage, 'and when I saw the Emperor afterward and told what a service I had done for Japan, he agreed'."[212]

Olympic internationalism conferred on Brundage the pleasant illusion that he was an omnipotent diplomat. Looking back on an incident at the Berlin Games, where an Olympic official had corrected Hitler on a matter of protocol, he said: "We told Hitler off and got away with it, and that's more than anyone else ever did"—a piece of wishful thinking discredited by his accommodating behavior toward the Nazi regime. Having negotiated a merger of East and West German teams in 1956, he commented: "It wasn't easy, but we did what the United Nations and a lot of politicians couldn't do." In 1957, he made headlines by forcing the United States State Department to let him travel to Bulgaria to attend a meeting of the IOC, thereby achieving, if temporarily, the status of world citizen. In 1960, he was "trying to make peace between both Chinas and both Koreas, whom we hope to get together, like the Germanys."[213]

Brundage saw himself as the Great Reconciler, reassembling broken nations as though he were putting together the pieces of a global puzzle. It was an eccentric fantasy, but a gratifying one based on an imagined ability to confer the gift of mutual intelligibility upon the world's divided peoples. In conformity with this grandiose vision of himself as the indispensable Global Translator, Brundage eventually pursued the dream of universal intelligibility into the realm of the supernatural. "When I retire," he said in 1964, "I want to do something with extrasensory perception. A lot of work needs to be done in that field."[214]

d. The Fellow-Traveler

One day in 1954, Brundage was invited to attend the Day of the Soviet Athlete in Moscow. "I was surprised to receive the invitation," he wrote a year later, "since the Russians were well aware of my views on Communism. I had been denounced frequently as 'an imperialistic reactionary and a shameless capitalist'. Furthermore, I was skeptical of the fantastic records that Russians had been hanging up in all sports, and I was suspicious of Soviet sports policies."[215]

Brundage's attitude toward Communism was actually more ambivalent than this comment would suggest. There is no doubt but that he disapproved of Communism as a doctrine. As a self-made millionaire, he had every reason to do so. But what sort of anti-communist statements did Brundage actually make? Addressing the pro-Nazi American-German Bund as its featured speaker just after the Berlin Olympiad, he declared: "No nation since ancient Greece has displayed a more truly national public interest in the Olympic spirit than you find in Germany. We can learn much from Germany." "We, too, if we wish to preserve our institutions, must stamp out Communism."[216] A year earlier, in his anti-boycott brochure, he had stated: "It should be known that Soviet Russia is not represented in any of the great international sports federations. In 1932, there was a concerted attempt by Communists both here and abroad to wreck the Los Angeles Games. Many of the individuals and organizations active in the present campaign to boycott the Olympics have Communist antecedents. Radicals and Communists must keep their hands off American sport."[217] What is striking about these comments is that they occur in the context of either promoting or defending the Olympic ideal. Like his patriotism, Brundage's hostility to the Left lacked passion—until the Olympic movement was involved.

Brundage was not a visceral anti-communist. He might have become one, but this possibility was pre-empted by his fascination with Olympic internationalism. Coubertin, too, had made strong anti-Marxist statements early in his career. But he, like Brundage, would eventually lose the taste for this sort of rhetoric, because it lacked Olympic cosmopolitanism. As the second great Olympic internationalist, Brundage came to fill perfectly the role of the "simple voyager" Coubertin had foreseen and had done nothing to prevent.

Specifically, Brundage is remembered for the inspection visit to Nazi Germany in 1934 that failed to turn up any grounds for an American boycott. Brundage's pro-German bias may be gauged by the fact that he questioned Jewish sport leaders in the presence of the *Reichssportführer* himself; the lives of these men probably hung on the nature of their answers.[218] Even before he left he had commented: "It is notable that everyone who has visited Germany has reported courteous and hospitable treatment and that the German authorities are fulfilling every pledge made to the International Olympic Committee. The agitation has been carried on entirely by those who haven't been closer to Berlin than Manhattan Island."[219]

Brundage's attitude toward Hitler's Germany had a warmth the Soviet Union could never inspire. But what is forgotten is that he reacted with similar enthusiasm after witnessing a great sports festival in Moscow in 1954. His self-proclaimed conservatism melted noticeably in the presence of mass gymnastics displays, and his subsequent rationalizations on behalf of the Soviet sport system make interesting reading today.

Two years after returning from his visit to Moscow in 1954, he recalled: "When I was in Moscow I witnessed their annual Sports Parade. I never saw anything like it. It lasted for five hours. It was almost frightening." Was this the pageantry of a slave state? "Well, now, we're told that the Communists force participation in sports. But those boys and girls I saw in Moscow. Do you think they were forced to participate? I saw them. Their faces were happy. They weren't being forced. They were having a wonderful time."[220] What had Brundage seen?

> The day of the Soviet Athlete in Moscow last July the eighteenth—the show that I had been specifically invited to attend—far surpassed in magnitude and beauty anything of its kind that I have seen in other parts of the world. The participants were brought from all over the Soviet Union. There were Uzbeks, Tadzhiks, Armenians, Georgians, Kirghiz. They represented trade unions, sport societies, schools and colleges.
>
> Each delegation included from 400 to 3,000 boys and girls. There were some 34,000 all together. First they all paraded around the stadium, and then the field was turned over to one group at a time. They gave mass demonstrations with wands, large balls, ribbons or hoops, followed by special performances. One brought collapsible gymnastic apparatus, and in a trice seventy or eighty horizontal bars had been set up on which gymnasts were doing giant swings to classical music. Another group erected a framework thirty or forty feet high, and the participants, wearing different-colored costumes, draped themselves on it like a living bouquet of beautiful flowers.
>
> Some of the acts were staged against a solid wall of water twenty-five feet high, rising from a series of fountains extending the full length of the stadium. I thought the turf in the center of the field looked extra fine. When I examined it more closely, it proved to be an immense green carpet covering the entire infield. Each delegation had a music director as well as a physical director. It was like something out of The Arabian Nights.[221]

Brundage's attitude toward Soviet sport was ambivalent. On the one hand, he seemed to disapprove: "Is the Russian system better? As much as I was impressed, I can't say that I admire the Soviet sports program. By American standards, it is harsh and severe. It is both Spartan and puritanical. Most of the spirit of fun seems to have been bled from it, and it thrives on regimentation and fierce national pride." This is an oddly sober note coming from a man who had just witnessed "something out of The Arabian Nights." In fact, Brundage favored "regimentation and fierce national pride." He approved of Stalinist sport for the same reasons he had approved of Nazi sport: "Now it is the U.S.S.R. that has adopted mass athletics on a scale never before attempted, except by the Germans in the 1930s, with Hitler's 'Strength Through Joy' program."[222] Both totalitarianisms had heeded the message "we have been preaching." As for the United States: "The trouble is that life in this country is too soft."[223] At the Stockholm Olympiad of 1912, the Czarist athletes "impressed me as being far more interested in having a good time than in winning."[224] The Bolsheviks had eventually taken care of that.

The term "fellow-traveler," once applied to foreign sympathizers of the Soviet Union and Communist China, lost its impact in the 1950s because of indiscriminate usage. It was an unfortunate loss, depriving our political vocabulary of a valuable concept.[225] Generally overlooked is the fact that fellow-traveling has been a right- as well as a left-wing activity. It can even be both; fellow-travelers like George Bernard Shaw and Lincoln Steffens traveled both sides of the fence, admiring Mussolini's methods as well as Lenin's. In this sort of company Avery Brundage is a very small fry, but it is the general category to which he belongs.

Fellow-traveling is an emotional response to a foreign system or charismatic leader. Its most prominent characteristic is an infatuation with the strong and often violent authority figure who wields a chastising and therapeutic force. Mussolini, Hitler, Lenin, Stalin, Mao, Ho Chi Minh, Fidel Castro—all have won the enthusiastic allegiance of foreign sympathizers whose privileged positions permitted them to applaud forceful leadership abroad without having to suffer its domestic consequences. As David Caute points out, Stalin's foreign admirers "heartily welcomed the torments and upheavals inflicted on the Russian peasantry during collectivization, arguing that only by such drastic social engineering could these backward illiterates be herded, feet first, into the modern world."[226]

For Avery Brundage, sport was so important that it legitimized dictatorship. No one who reads Brundage's comments on Hitler's Germany can doubt that he approved of what he saw. And to an extent, the same is true of Russia. His descriptions of the bleakness of Soviet life have a curiously muted tone: "In those countries behind the Iron Curtain, life is grim and sports fills [sic] a vacuum." Or: "Don't you think a boy or a girl in the Uzbek or some Soviet republic in Central Asia wants to go to Moscow? That's a big thing, the biggest thing in their lives. They work hard, they put everything they have into it. After all, they lead a drab, grim life. Sport is a great outlet for them, a great opportunity to express themselves."[227] Like the classic fellow-traveler, Avery Brundage found the suffering of the masses to be redemptive in the end.

Fellow-traveling represents a response to the foreigner and his special significance. Avery Brundage made much of his foreign connections: "I'm dictating letters every day to all parts of the world on questions and problems relating to the Olympics."[228] The foreign dimension of fellow-traveling suggests, in turn, that the psychology of the fellow-traveler is going to be similar in some ways to that of the traitor who is disillusioned with his own society and sees a better one over the horizon. Avery Brundage was not a traitor, but he did experience some of the traitor's temptations. "While professing to be hardened to abuse from his fellow-countrymen," Robert Shaplen commented, "he quite naturally responded warmly to the contrasting treatment often afforded him abroad . . ."[229] In 1972, it was reported that the IOC's refusal to grant Los Angeles the right to hold the 1976 Olympic Games had cost Brundage the Presidential Medal of Freedom. As one observer put it: "It'll be a damn cold day now if Nixon pins anything on Brundage. The man simply shot down his own country."[230]

That may be true. But, one may ask, what of it? For as Brundage himself had pointed out, "in the International Olympic Committee I am not a representative of the U.S. . . . As a member of the committee, my first allegiance is to a principle—the principle of the Olympic movement as stated by the Baron de Coubertin 60 years ago. Members of the committee cannot be pre-instructed by their countries. We are all dedicated to a principle and an idea."[231]

"The Olympic movement today," Brundage said in one speech, "is perhaps the greatest social force in the world."[232] Avery Brundage's eccentricity was his grandiose mission of redemption to a divided mankind. It is a political role which has been claimed by the noble, the villainous, and the paranoid schizophrenic. Brundage brought to this role an absolute fidelity to an Olympic idealism he elevated above all others and whose significance he overestimated.

5. The Converts: Communism and the Olympic Movement

On June 15, 1977, the president of the International Olympic Committee, Lord Killanin, delivered a speech in the 14th-century Great Hall of Charles University in Prague. His address dealt with political and structural problems facing the Olympic Games and was printed in English, French and Czech. But the alteration of one phrase in the printed Czech text and the outright omission of three sentences caused a minor scandal. A Czechoslovak official of the IOC press secretariat blamed difficulties involved in translating from one language to another.

"The official said that the speech had been received in a French version for translation into Czech and had been revised frequently by Killanin with paragraphs moved higher and lower. Perhaps, the official said, something had gone wrong in the rush to print the texts."[233] A comparison of the two texts quickly revealed, however, that this accident had a political logic. "National Olympic committees," the president had stated, "and the individual athletes must be protected from becoming the instrument of government direction." For "government direction" the Czech text had substituted "commercial interests."

The omitted part of the text read as follows: "If [Olympic competitors] find that their governments make [immunity to political or religious discrimination] impossible, then unfortunately it may be that the athletes suffer for some time until the situation is remedied. In the world today there are governments of left, right and center which, for reasons which may be absolutely justifiable to themselves, take actions which in the interests of their own security prevent complete freedom and liberty." The irony of this episode is that the Czechs had found it necessary to censor the IOC's confession of its own impotence when faced with the sort of government which censors. But this was not the stuff of which Olympic crises are made; it was a bruise the "Olympic spirit" would heal overnight. Communism and "Olympism" remained on excellent terms.

It is not difficult to imagine the combination of sympathy and quiet condescension with which politically committed Communist sport functionaries must view their internationally minded colleagues on the International Olympic Committee. "Utopia, or daydreaming," Lenin wrote, "is the product of this lack of independence, this *weakness*. Daydreaming is the lot of the *weak*."[234] Utopian daydreaming, which has been an element of the IOC since its founding, can be seen from a more charitable, but still critical, perspective. Contemplating the prospect of a Moscow Olympiad, *The Economist* of London stated in February 1980: "It is right to put rude pressure on these committees of nice, old, public-spirited men, not because they are unfeeling, but because they now portray Bagehot's description of the worst failing of a bureaucracy. They imagine 'the elaborate machinery of which they form a part, and from which they derive their dignity, to be a grand and achieved result, not a working and changeable instrument. But in a miscellaneous world, there is now one evil and now another'."[235]

As argued in the previous chapter, these "nice, old, public-spirited men" have never considered it their duty to combat the evils that arise in a miscellaneous world, and this is what had made possible their utopianism. This is also what makes such a utopianism "weak"; it has no purpose other than to perpetuate and admire its own "grand and achieved result." Consequently, the IOC is vulnerable to political and ideological ambition, which it will placate rather than challenge on matters of principle. It refuses to be "political."

At the same time, the Communists' contempt for the Olympic idea of "apolitical" sport is almost as old as Soviet communism itself. So from the Soviets' viewpoint, the weak and anachronistic character of the IOC derives from its lack of ideological ambition. They reject, in other words, the very essence of the Olympic doctrine even as they praise it as a foundation for peaceful relations between states.

The Soviet Union applied for, and was granted, membership in the Olympic movement in May 1951. Prior to this date the Soviets had denounced the Olympic Games as a "bourgeois invention" the purpose of which was "to deflect the workers from the class struggle while training them for new imperialist wars." But, once admitted, as Henry Morton writes, "the USSR's former hostility toward the Games melted away. Although there were still 'bourgeois reactionaries' who were out to subvert the Olympic movement harbored in the IOC, the participation of the USSR had negated their influence and had for the first time in the long history of the Games brought to it 'an absolutely new character', transforming it into an active force for peace and friendship between athletes of all nations." Soviet Olympic participation was an expression of Stalin's policy of "peaceful coexistence."[236] Thirty years later, the Moscow Olympiad would be promoted as an expression of the Helsinki Conference on European Security.[237]

In 1955, Avery Brundage recalled the Vienna meeting at which the Soviets had been admitted to the movement: "There was little that could be said or done on the question of state subsidization of the [Soviet] program. Under Olympic rules, national committees must be independent and autonomous. In communist countries, where everything is subservient to the state, no organization can be independent and autonomous."[238] Brundage's assertion that "little could be said or done" about Soviet violations of the Olympic charter was characteristic of the twisted logic he employed when the "fundamental principle of universality" was threatened; the IOC could, of course, have voted not to admit the Soviets unless and until changes were made, but the necessary number of principled votes was not there.

The issue of Soviet membership, he said, provoked "a bitter controversy" between two factions: "There were two points of view at that meeting. One held that the Communists had no concept of either sportsmanship or amateurism, that they couldn't be trusted and that they should be excluded. The other said they will learn and perhaps some good will result if they compete with the rest of the world. And in any event Olympic rules forbid political discrimination. So the Russians were accepted. We thought maybe in the long run it would do some good. Maybe it will."[239]

The negotiations with the Russians had not, however, gone smoothly:

> They said Russian had to be one of the official languages. The board of directors would have to include a Russian. And throw out Fascist Spain. Well, they were told: you may join if you subscribe to the rules. But as for your conditions—about making Russian an official language: no. Not now. About having a Russian on the board: no. Join, and later perhaps someone will be elected. As for Fascist Spain, so called: no. Spain is a member, an old member, a member in good standing. Membership is not based on politics.
>
> They protested: You have an American on the board of the IAAF [International Amateur Athletics Federation], and that would be unfair to Russia. Well, they were told: You're damn lucky to have an American, because he'll lean over backward to be fair. But no more than that. No more than fair.
>
> Well, they joined, and without conditions. When they appeared before the International Olympic Committee in 1951 they said, we have read your rules, we like your rules, we subscribe to your rules. We ask for recognition.[240]

Despite his network of international contacts, Brundage remained a political neophyte and virtually unaware of the importance of ideology. If his loyalties were still with Calvin Coolidge and Herbert Hoover, it was probably because he had not fathomed their successors. This inability to deal with political doctrine as anything but a menace to Olympic harmony restricted his understanding of what Soviet participation would eventually mean for the Olympic movement.

An authoritative Russian view of the International Olympic Committee can be found in the *Great Soviet Encyclopedia*. Its author is Konstantin Andrianov, former vice-president of the IOC and president of the Soviet Olympic Committee. What Andrianov offers is a combination of dessicating objectivity and sober criticism. His first step is to neuter Coubertin politically by referring to him as a "French public figure." "The IOC," he writes, "conducts the Olympic Games and constantly improves them, guides the development of amateur sports, and helps strengthen friendship among the athletes of all countries." The evolution of Olympism, in other words, is following an historically progressive course which socialist influence can only improve: "Upon the initiative of representatives from the socialist countries the IOC has on several occasions considered general problems of international sports ties and the democratization of the Olympic movement.It has taken a stand against political and racial discrimination in sports. . . ."

Rather than attack the IOC's naive utopianism, Andrianov focuses on matters of procedure: "On certain questions the IOC has maintained conservative positions; in particular, it has not abandoned the undemocratic principle of its formation. Prior to

1930, the IOC periodically convoked Olympic Congresses in order to discuss problems of the Olympic movement. (Nine such congresses were held.) Subsequently, for 43 years the IOC strove to maintain its monopolistic role as the movement's governing body by refusing to convene congresses. After urging by the progressive forces of the international sports movement, the Tenth Congress was held in Bulgaria in 1973...."[241]

Every member of the IOC accepts two unwritten rules: first, Coubertin and his basic ideas must remain above criticism; and second, differences of opinion based on ideology must not be argued past the point of propriety. Andrianov's portrait of the IOC, and Soviet Olympic policy in general, demonstrates the Soviets' interest in preserving intramural harmony within the movement. For without it, the Games could not go on, and the scientific sport cultures of the East would find themselves performing in relative obscurity.

On one occasion, however, the Russians came very close to destroying the movement their excellent political manners had helped to preserve. In May 1970, the IOC convened its 69th meeting in Amsterdam to choose the site of the 1976 Games. On May 12, the Soviet press agency Tass cabled a joyous announcement to the world: "Moscow—Host of the 1976 Olympic Games!" Eleven minutes later, this cable was retracted without explanation: Montreal had been selected by a vote of 41 to 28.

The Russians reacted to this decision with a fury unprecedented in the history of the Olympic movement. On the evening of the vote, Tass released a bitter declaration which gave voice to long-smoldering Soviet resentment of ideological discrimination within the movement. "This decision," it stated, "violated elementary logic and common sense, since Moscow, which also sought the role of host to the XXI Olympiad, was able to present clear and irrefutable arguments bearing on sport, economics, and politics. The impression has arisen that many IOC members were motivated, not by considerations about the expansion and strengthening of the Olympic movement, but rather by personal political sympathies and antipathies. For the first time a city from the socialist camp had offered itself as a candidate, and its rejection can only be seen as a blow directed against the Olympic movement and its ideals. One may conclude that there are people in the IOC who consider the putting on of the Olympic Games to be a privilege of the Western countries."

In its June 1970 issue, the Moscow "New Times" threw Olympic etiquette out the window and suddenly recalled with sarcasm the movement's Nazi affiliation, its gerontocracy, and the profaned ideals of Coubertin: "Mr. Brundage has said repeatedly how wonderful the Olympic movement is. Would that half of the energy he put into holding the 1936 Games in the capital of the Third Reich had gone into making sure that this Committee would choose the city most worthy of the honor. The millionaire Brundage is far past 80. He will probably resign his position in the Committee soon to devote himself to some completely new enterprise. Perhaps the Committee, this decrepit and at best useless organ, should simply disappear without a murmur and make way for a corporate body capable of taking action and which really takes the ideals of Coubertin to heart, rather than political and financial machinations garnished with sport."

In February 1971, Sergei Pavlov, Chairman of the Committee for Physical Culture and Sport of the Cabinet Council of the USSR, issued a stark warning: "There is no doubt that the West is misusing sport for political and ideological purposes. There is good reason, therefore, to assume that the Soviet Union will not take part in the 1976

Olympic Games."[242]

Within five months Soviet officials had weighed the idea of attempting to break the IOC and decided it was not worth the risks. In July 1971, the Soviets invited Avery Brundage to attend the Spartakiad of the Peoples of the USSR and, presumably aware of his vulnerability to sport pageantry, broached once again the idea of a Moscow Olympiad, now with 1980 in mind. According to one West German observer, the IOC had by now been traumatized to the point where a second refusal was unthinkable.[243]

Communist treatment of Coubertin and his legacy has been generous, emphasizing his interest in peaceful coexistence between nations, his alleged hostility to militarism, his interest in mass education, and his apparent awakening in 1922 to the future importance of the international proletariat. The irony of Coubertin's official image in East Germany, the most successful of the Eastern bloc sport establishments, is that it has become progressively more bowdlerized since the strict orthodoxy of Walter Ulbricht's early days gave way to a more liberal sort of regime in the wake of Stalin's death and a more secure national identity for the GDR. The only historically competent and intellectually honest portrait of Coubertin I have seen in a Communist publication appeared in an East German theoretical journal in 1953. Its authors were militant Stalinists who simply could not overlook the opportunity to expose as vulnerable a target as the French baron.

By the early 1960s Walter Ulbricht's plans for an intensive and scientifically conducted sport culture were beginning to bear fruit. As the Olympic movement became an increasingly important showcase for the athletes of the GDR, East German interest in exposing the movement's founder diminished accordingly. One also finds that such candor in published accounts varies inversely with the anticipated size of the audience. On the occasion of the third African Games held in Algiers in July 1978, the official Party newspaper *Neues Deutschland* printed a generally accurate description[244] of how Coubertin had tried to initiate African games in the 1920s and how these plans had been frustrated by French and British colonialist policies.[245] It did not mention Coubertin's earlier writings on colonial policy or the fact that his warm reminiscence of Leopold II had been published in 1931.

On the occasion of the 1976 Montreal Games, *Neues Deutschland* published a long paean to "the French humanist Baron de Coubertin." "Coubertin was not one of those swooners over Greek antiquity, but a realistic pedagogue" who had worked for international understanding. The "Olympic idea," it stated, "is part of everyday life in the German Democratic Republic."[246] The 1973 edition of the standard East German *Physical Culture in Germany* (Vol. II) presents "the French scholar" Coubertin in an almost entirely favorable light. He is credited with having risen above the class interests of his bourgeois peers to oppose the militarization of French sport. He is portrayed as a friend of the working class and as a crusader for "the humanistic principles of the amateur movement." Most important, Coubertin is seen as preserving a role for national pride within the international movement—no small matter for a state as hungry for recognition as the GDR. His only limitation, according to the East Germans, had been an inability to appreciate the significance of "the objective contradictions of imperialist development." Coubertin had been nothing less than "a true humanist." But he had not, unfortunately, been a Marxist one.

In 1953, the journal *Theory and Practice of Physical Culture* published a mildly disputacious exchange of learned opinions about Coubertin's ideas and motivations.

Here were observers who had no difficulty recognizing an "enlightened reactionary" when they saw one. "Coubertin," one of them wrote, "was an outspoken bourgeois ideologue, and his fundamental pronouncements contain hopeless contradictions. We should not build up an exaggerated picture of Coubertin's progressive tendencies."[247]

Coubertin never gave up his hostility toward the Left. He remained, as Yves-Pierre Boulongne has put it, "a vehement anti-communard and anti-socialist" all his life. "Socialism," he said, "is a religion, and Marx is its prophet."[248] Coubertin was not the first anti-Marxist to resent communism as a religion which competed with his own. But his interest in creating a truly global sport culture took precedence over his feelings about "the utopia of all-enveloping communism."[249]

Coubertin did not live to see the day when the international communist movement would embrace "Olympism," but there is no question that he would have welcomed the sight. In 1923, Prince Leo Ouroussoff, a former Russian diplomat and a member of the IOC, argued that both Soviet and Russian emigré teams should be permitted to participate in the 1924 Paris Games. "I have always regretted," Coubertin wrote in his *Olympic Memoirs*, "the manner in which his proposal was considered and then rejected for 'administrative' reasons."[250] Coubertin, of course, had practiced the same sort of committee politics; but here was a vision of reunification, however temporary, which appealed to his universalist instincts, even if the potential beneficiaries included the Bolsheviks. In 1926, Coubertin was in touch with the Belgian Jules Devliger, secretary of the Socialist Workers' Sport International. It is clear that he was sincerely interested in forming some sort of liaison, but nothing came of it.[251]

In the *Olympic Memoirs* Coubertin is strikingly blasé about the "Workers' Olympiads," which the socialists advertised as a humane alternative to those of the IOC. In fact, there were two socialist sport festivals competing with the "bourgeois" games: the European socialists' "Workers' Olympiads" held in Prague (1921), Frankfurt (1925), Vienna (1931), and Antwerp (1937); and the Soviet *Spartakiads*, intended as a universal workers' Olympics, the first of which was held in 1928. The two Left sport movements were separated by a gulf of mutual suspicion and ideological hostility.[252] Coubertin's reference to Moscow in the following passage suggests he was thinking of the Soviet games.

"The war of 1914-1918," he writes, "did not disturb [the Games]." (The 1916 Games scheduled for Berlin had, of course, been cancelled.) He continues: "nor is the social revolution affecting them any longer." ("Social revolution" is, apparently, Coubertin's euphemism for the Bolshevik revolution of 1917.) "It is curious to note," he says, "that alongside the 'capitalist' organization there is already a 'proletarian' one. 'Workers' olympiads' have taken place at regular intervals, and not without success. As I write, it seems they are constructing an enormous stadium in Moscow where the next one will be held. They would do well, however, to change the name of this event, which otherwise will demonstrate a lamentable puerility as well as an aspect of revolutionary action which is only too frequent: while there are many institutions which require renovation, they confine themselves to changing names: words in place of acts." Having delivered this caustic observation, Coubertin continues in a more conciliatory vein: "This spreading of sport among the manual workers constitutes an undeniable proof of the survival of Olympism. . . ."[253]

This remark, according to East Germany's premier sport journalist, was Coubertin's answer to those who hoped he would adopt an anti-Soviet position.[254] It is more likely that this was another occasion on which Coubertin could not help applauding his own prophetic powers. And in this instance, his words were more prophetic than he imagined.

Communist spokesmen constantly emphasize the compatibility of their own sport doctrine with that of the Olympic movement, and in a number of important respects they are correct. Despite its international outlook, Communist sport doctrine insists that an athlete is first and foremost a citizen of a specific country. The de-nationalization of the athlete was an important theme of the Workers' Olympiads of the 1920s and 1930s, but today it is considered an aberration. "Sportsmen," a Romanian author claims, "are not and should never be regarded as citizens of the world. They belong by heart and upbringing to their people and country. In spite of the fact that the Olympic Games are primarily competitions between individuals, Coubertin symbolized by flag and anthem the spiritual link between athlete and country, enhancing the respect due to them."[255]

"It is noteworthy," James Riordan has pointed out, "that the Soviet Union has always resisted attempts to downgrade or abolish ritual in the Olympic Games. In an editorial comment on an interview with the late Avery Brundage, criticising his attempts to 'cosmopolitanise' the Olympics by banning the raising of flags and the playing of anthems for winners, *Sovietski Sport* wrote, "One can only hope that certain people . . . will fail in their attempts to revise the Olympic ritual which vividly illustrates the Olympic oath, obliging an athlete to fight on behalf of his country's honor'."[256]

During the 1976 Montreal Games, the International Olympic Committee demonstrated its firm adherence to this principle when it rejected the appeal of James Gilkes, a world-class sprinter from Guyana, who had asked for permission to compete "under the insignia of the International Olympic Committee or any other designation you would deem appropriate." Guyana had withdrawn from the Games in sympathy with the African boycott protesting the presence of New Zealand. Having weighed the matter, the IOC executive board issued this statement: "After studying the problem raised from an ethical, human and legal point of view, the IOC can [only], unfortunately, give a negative reply."[257]

Ironically, the stateless-athlete doctrine was eventually sponsored by the Soviets on behalf of preserving their Olympiad. Only the desperate circumstances brought on by the threatened boycott of the Moscow Games could have led the Soviet Minister of Sport to suggest in February 1980 that American athletes might be permitted to compete without national sponsorship: "They could compete in Moscow without the U.S. flag, on a private basis. This is another decision which is up to the Olympic committee, however."[258]

The most important pact between the Communists and the Olympic movement concerns the tenet of "amateurism." The IOC has elected to disregard the professional character of Socialist bloc "state amateurism," instead criticizing commercialism, which it calls "the entry of merchants into the temple and the diversion of sports competitions from their noble purpose in order to turn them into money-making machines."[259] This critique of commercialism, though ideologically conservative in its origins, is endorsed by all Communist sports officials.

On what grounds do the Communists condemn professional sport? "Ninety percent of the arguments used by Stalinists in their propaganda," Czeslaw Milosz wrote in *The Captive Mind* (1951), "are based on man's injury to man. The appeal to moral indignation is always present in their slogans."[260] Communist sport doctrine and "Olympism" share the view that sport should be both morally and physically *hygienic* and *edifying*. Both reproach the 'degradation' of professional boxing. "The spectacle," writes the president of the Tunisian Olympic Committee, "becomes spectacle for the sake of spectacle, with success as its sole aim. At issue are no longer ethical and aesthetic values wherein it is the effort that counts, but, rather, the market value."[261] Communist theorists, too, perceive a crucial difference between the emotions provoked by a professional bout and the feelings aroused by amateur competition: one is bloodthirsty, the other wholesome.[262]

64   "On a *collective plane*," says the Tunisian, "the impact of Olympism is hardly less important or less noble. If Olympism collectively serves to purify, such is the case because it works to transform the crowds into a mass, the mass into a community and the community into a communion. Communication among men is carried out on the basis of concrete rather than abstract values; men identify themselves with athletics and devote their efforts to it for self-realization. The Olympic spectacle is a gigantic identification process through competition."[263]

In a similar vein, the Polish sport sociologist Andrzej Wohl has argued that sport was a psychological asset to the Soviet Union during the Second World War: "The important thing was that this entertainment attracted people emotionally, made them cooperate with others, to compete, forced them to show stubbornness and doggedness, devotion, physical effort, it squeezed out of every participant in this entertainment a maximum of his motor ability. This is a type of entertainment that teaches to overcome fear, teaches to control oneself, to master one's own body, it teaches discipline."[264]

Both Communism and "Olympism" assume that the emotions of the stadium are wholesome and even creative; neither chooses to dwell on the abundant evidence that mass sport can also give rise to mass degeneration of the emotions, mayhem, and even murder. Both of these sport doctrines are, in fact, forms of naive "positive thinking."

III . The Moscow Olympiad in Political Context

1. The American Boycott and the Soviet Response

On March 15, 1979, a few weeks after the People's Republic of China had sent its troops into neighboring Vietnam, *Sovietski Sport* offered its editorial comment on this act of aggression and its relationship to "the fundamental principles of the Olympic movement":

> The adherence to and development of the sanctified Olympic principles is the most important duty of every country which is or wants to become a member of the Olympic family. China, too, may take its place in the Olympic movement. . . . But in this matter the socialist countries and progressive world opinion take a firm and principled position: China must find its place in the Olympic movement when it has fulfilled the requirements which every country and Olympic organization are expected to meet. But how does China respond to the Olympic requirements? Does the aggressive, bandit-like war China is waging against socialist Vietnam argue for its admission to the Olympic movement? . . . Olympians and all sportsmen know that for the duration of the ancient Olympic Games all acts of war were suspended. . . . Who can be permitted to appear at this festival with blood-soaked hands?[1]

There is no point in dwelling on the irony of this quote. It does, however, serve to illustrate the relationship between *Realpolitik* and the Olympic platitudes that remain the jargon of political discourse about global sport. What must be emphasized is that this idiom serves an important function for the governments that use it; for it is far more practical to take recourse in the language of Olympic idealism than it is to develop a political discourse which genuinely addresses the moral questions which bear on the world of sport.

On January 1, 1980, at a NATO meeting in Brussels, the West German government proposed that the West consider a boycott of the Moscow Olympiad as a response to the Soviet invasion of Afghanistan which had begun several days earlier.[2] On January 4, President Carter publicly mentioned the possibility of an American boycott, thereby initiating a chain of events that eventually culminated in the largest boycott campaign in the history of sport.

The American position, outlined by the President on January 20 in a letter to the president of the U.S. Olympic Committee, was based on the idea of global inter-dependence and security. "We must make clear to the Soviet Union that it cannot trample upon an independent nation and at the same time do business as usual with the rest of the world. We must make clear that it will pay a heavy economic and politi-cal cost for such aggressions." The President defended the use of sport as a political instrument by noting that in the Soviet Union "international sports competition is itself an aspect of Soviet government policy, as is the decision to invade Afghanistan. The head of the Moscow Olympic Organizing Committee is a high Soviet govern-ment official." On these grounds he urged the USOC, and other national Olympic committees, to advise the IOC not to hold the Moscow Olympiad unless Soviet troops were withdrawn from Afghanistan within one month. In the event that no troop withdrawal had taken place, he urged the USOC "to propose that the games either be transferred to another site such as Montreal or to multiple sites, or be can-celled for this year. If the International Olympic Committee rejects such a USOC proposal, I urge the USOC and the Olympic Committees of other like-minded nations not to participate in the Moscow games."[3]

This instructional letter, a virtual *Diktat*, was in itself an irregularity that could not be disguised by the endorsements of the Olympic movement the American Presi-dent had taken the trouble to add. The pretense that the Olympic movement was an autonomous international movement was about to suffer a grievous exposure.

The Olympic movement, European in origin, is more important on the Continent than in the United States. The differing degrees of affiliation with Olympism can be seen in the fact that, while the British and French governments permitted their national Olympic committees to send athletes to Moscow without their endorse-ment, the Carter administration never intended to tolerate such a separation of Olympic church and state.

President Carter, in short, simply disdained, however tacitly, the official inter-nationalism of the IOC—a policy that enjoyed widespread support in the United States. On January 24, the United States House of Representatives voted 386 to 12 to support the President's request that the Games be transferred, cancelled, or boy-cotted in the absence of a Soviet withdrawal from Afghanistan. On January 29, the United States Senate passed a similiar resolution that, like the House vote, did not have the force of law but carried a significant political message to the USOC. The results of a poll published by *Newsweek* on January 28 indicated that 68 percent of the American public favored moving the Games from Moscow, while 22 percent opposed such a transfer. A survey published by *Time* on February 11 concluded that Americans opposed participation by a similar margin of 67 percent to 24 percent.[4]

Not even during the unoffical campaign (1933-36) to boycott the Berlin Olym-piad had the USOC been subjected to such tactics. On January 20, the president of the USOC, Robert J. Kane, asserted defensively that: "Our concern for the national interest is no different from the President's, and obviously he has recognized this."[5] But Carter recognized nothing of the kind; he felt compelled to apply pressure to the USOC that began in earnest on the evening of February 9, when Secretary of State Cyrus R. Vance addressed the eighty-second plenary session of the IOC just prior to the opening of the XIII Winter Olympic Games at Lake Placid, New York.

There were reports that, before his speech, Secretary Vance had been implored by Lord Killanin, president of the IOC, not to make his address a political occasion; but Vance scarcely deviated from a prepared text shown to reporters earlier in the day.

Juan Samaranch, chief IOC protocol officer, Spanish ambassador to the Soviet Union, and Killanin's eventual successor, persuaded the membership not to walk out or demonstrate against the Secretary's remarks.[6]

"Let me make my Government's position clear," Vance stated at the end of his address. "We will oppose the participation of an American team in any Olympic Games in the capital of an invading nation. This position is firm. It reflects the deep convictions of the United States Congress and the American people. To avoid such problems in the future, we support the establishment of a permanent home for the Summer and Winter Olympics. I know that this distinguished body will carefully weigh the issues now before you. By upholding the principles of the Olympics when they are under challenge, we will preserve the meaning of the Olympics for years to come." The members of the International Olympic Committee, among whom were four princes, four generals, two lords, a sheik, a rajah, a knight, a count, a baron, a marquis, a duke, an admiral and a hadji, sat stunned.[7]

Madame Monique Berlioux, the director of the IOC office in Lausanne, pronounced herself "shocked." "We are surprised," said Mr. Samaranch, "to listen to a political speech."[8] "He didn't even take the time," said one unofficial member of the audience, "to be polite." Two months later, on April 12, the USOC, by a vote of 1604 to 797, decided against participation in the Moscow Olympiad. Of the 146 eligible nations, 81 would eventually take part.[9]

It is widely assumed that the Soviets underestimated the intensity of Western response both to the Afghanistan operation and to the Olympic boycott proposal it brought back to life. But the Soviet response to the boycott campaign, despite certain hysterical overtones, was both coherent and multifaceted in its rhetorical strategy. Soviet counter-propaganda benefited from two factors. First, the idea of an anti-Moscow boycott was not new; and second, Soviet resentment of the boycott was widely echoed by Western voices.

The Soviet response can be separated into two strategies: on one level, a partisan but intelligible political analysis of "the anti-Olympic team"; on quite another level, a shrill and xenophobic campaign addressed to the Soviet public, warning of the "anti-Olympians from the CIA" and the scurrilous machinations they had prepared for the residents of Moscow.

"It was not today, or even yesterday," *Pravda* commented on March 18, 1980, "that Carter first called for a boycott of the 1980 Olympics. He set his sights on this target back in 1978. Suffice it to recall that during the trial of the American spy Shcharansky Washington threatened to 'wreck the Moscow Olympics'."[10] In fact, it had been Soviet dissidents and Western human rights groups—not the American President—who called for a boycott in the wake of the 1978 trials of dissidents such as Anatoly B. Shcharansky, Alexander Ginzburg, and others.

Even the obviously improvisatory character of the American boycott effort did not dissuade Soviet propagandists from emphasizing the idea of a longstanding conspiracy. "It is perfectly obvious," *Izvestia* stated on February 1, "that what we have here is a premeditated and coordinated act of hostility directed against mutual understanding and friendship among peoples and against peace and progress."[11] On January 13, *Sovietski Sport* had referred to the nascent boycott merely as a "reanimation" of previous anti-Soviet campaigns.[12] But on the same day, in *Pravda,* Leonid I. Brezhnev inadvertently acknowledged the spontaneous aspect of the whole idea. "President Carter," he said, "reacted like a spoiled child, emotionally."[13]

THE MOSCOW OLYMPIAD IN POLITICAL CONTEXT

A second Soviet argument interpreted the boycott as an unworthy attack on the Olympic movement in particular and international norms in general. "As the worldwide festival of young athletes draws closer, the foes of the Olympics are making fiercer attacks against the Olympic movement. It is indicative that the anti-Olympics team now includes politicians who don't like the spirit of Helsinki, spokesmen for racism in sports and anti-Sovieteers from various radios and television 'voices'—all sorts of double-dyed reactionaries."[14]

Western disunity regarding the boycott, and the long list of dissenters, presented Soviet publicists with an embarrassment of riches. Those objecting included Lord Killanin of the IOC; the French Minister of Youth, Sport and Leisure; the president of the Italian national Olympic committee; the head of the British Olympic Association; the president of the West German national Olympic committee and a leading opponent of the boycott, Willi Daume; the president of UNESCO's Intergovernmental Committee on Physical Education and Sport; a host of disappointed American athletes. To this list may be added the American businessmen who had been looking forward to Olympic profits and who were now, according to a Soviet official who met with them in April, "unbelievably depressed and disappointed."[15]

The Soviets also asserted that the boycott was a product of domestic political conditions in the United States. On January 21, the day after President Carter's ultimatum regarding the withdrawal of Soviet troops from Afghanistan, the official Soviet press agency, Tass, noted that this demand had been made just prior to the Iowa caucuses, the first step in the selection of convention delegates in an election year. The boycott, Tass said, "is clearly in the nature of an electoral campaign move designed to gain the support of the powers that be—those 'moneybags' who finance Presidential campaign candidates." President Carter, said Tass, was "trying to respond to the interests of those militarist and reactionary forces that in the past were regarded as the political base" of Senator Barry Goldwater, Republican of Arizona.[16] On February 6, *Izvestia* described the boycott campaign as "McCarthyism," and added, with a self-revealing irony: "Adventurism in US foreign policy is always accompanied by antidemocratic repression within the country."[17]

Finally, the boycott was occasionally represented as a sign of Western envy and a related fear that exposure to Soviet society might convince visiting athletes of its superiority. A Soviet party activists' manual described the boycott as a spoiler's action intended "to discredit the system of socialism itself, its potential, its achievements, Soviet democracy, our way of life."[18]

On July 20, the day after the opening ceremony of the Olympiad, *Sovietskaya Rossia* offered the following comment: "It's unlikely that those who stand at the helm of American policy feel sorry for the athletes, the majority of whom are Negroes. The logic here is simple: If today the Negroes perform in Moscow and become acquainted with the advantages of the Soviet way of life, then tomorrow, don't you see, they will give even more thought to their situation. So isn't it better to leave them home in 'free' America?"[19] The sheer implausibility of this idea—foreign athletes would have seen little if anything of "the Soviet way of life"—is not the point. For as one prominent Soviet intellectual was told when he objected to the crudeness of Soviet propaganda: "It's not meant for you. It's meant for others."[20]

The assumption that Soviet propagandists could count on the receptiveness of a xenophobic domestic audience appears to have been at least one basis for the numerous warnings issued in April 1980 concerning Western plans for subversion during the Games. These frantic bulletins offered a paranoid counterpoint to the official homilies about Muscovite hospitality which constituted the other side of the schizophrenic public campaign regarding the arrival of these foreign guests.

The ambivalence about visitors from abroad is evident in a *Pravda* article of March 3, titled "Spiritual Climate of the 1980 Olympics." On the other hand, "Muscovites hope to find out more about everyday life and customs in foreign countries and to get the foreigners' impressions of life in our country." On the other, "Muscovites realize that not all foreign guests will come to the Olympics with the sincere intention of becoming as well acquainted as possible with our reality or of 'rooting for' some particular athlete or team. They are ready to ideologically oppose those who hope somehow to poison the atmosphere of the sports festival."[21]

69

On April 16, the Moscow newspaper *Moskovskaya Pravda* reported that the Central Intelligence Agency was in the process of setting up an "anti-Soviet school" to train subversives who were to be infiltrated into the Soviet Union as Olympic "tourists." Under the direction of the American national security adviser, Zbigniew Brzezinski, the CIA was allegedly recruiting graduate students at Harvard University and at universities in the Philadelphia area who were fluent in Russian or other languages spoken in the Soviet Union. School children were warned that Westerners would be distributing poisoned chewing gum and exploding toys and that some would have concealed spray canisters up their sleeves which would cover them with deadly bacteria. The other task of these agents would be to "carry out hostile, subversive acts against sportsmen from the five continents who will gather in Moscow for the games."[22] The effects of such propaganda are impossible to assess. The adult Soviet citizen could assume, however, that its implausibility was a measure of its repressive intent.

2. The Dissidents and the Boycott

One of the accusations directed by *Moskovskaya Pravda* at the CIA is of special political interest. "The production of various shirts, jackets, bags, rain coats, umbrellas and other goods depicting all kinds of turncoats and traitors" was, it said, well under way. The images of these seditious characters would, in this manner, be circulated all over Moscow by athletes and Soviet naifs.[23]

The Soviet dissidents ("turncoats and traitors") had been at the very center of the boycott issue for two years prior to the Games themselves. The trials in 1978 of Anatoly Shcharansky, Yuri Orlov, and Alexander Ginzburg can be seen as the true beginning of the anti-Olympiad campaign in the West. These defendants had been associated with groups set up to monitor Soviet compliance with the human rights provisions of the 1975 Helsinki Agreement, and their prison and labor camp sentences shocked public opinion outside the Soviet Union.

"The British Foreign Secretary, David Owen, even went so far as to suggest in a television interview that, if the Soviet government 'continues to repress human rights', the Russians should not 'take it for granted' that the 1980 Olympics would be held in Moscow. Similar noises in the United States prompted NBC, the company which had negotiated exclusive American rights to televise the Moscow Games, to take out massive insurance on their huge investment. But within a month or two, the fuss died down."[24]

Significantly, the prehistory of the Moscow Olympiad (1974-1980) was characterized by relative political tranquillity prior to the invasion of Afghanistan. As more than one observer noted during the crisis of 1980, Western doubts about the propriety of holding the 1980 Olympic Games in Moscow should have been made explicit when the Soviet Union was granted the assignment in 1974. As we have seen in Chapter 2 (section 5), the IOC's refusal to site the 1976 Games in Moscow infuriated the Soviets and almost occasioned a serious crisis within the Olympic movement, for which the 1974 decision became quite literally a moment of truth.

One observer who realized the significance of this decision was the prominent physicist and dissident Andrei Sakharov, who would eventually receive the Nobel Peace Prize in 1975. On November 10, 1974, seventeen days after the IOC meeting in Vienna which had voted Moscow the Games, the Associated Press reported on a meeting between Sakharov and Senator James Buckley, Republican of New York. During their conversation, Sakharov had expressed the fear that Moscow would be "cleansed" of dissidents prior to the 1980 Olympiad.[25]

Eventually, Sakharov adopted an anti-boycott position (which he later abandoned). In an interview with the left-wing Paris Newspaper Le Matin published on September 14, 1978, he stated: "There is no point in boycotting the Games. The point is to assure that they come off the same way here as they would anywhere else, as in Tokyo or Montreal. The world must be able to see the conditions under which we live. The Games in Moscow, yes, but a political amnesty in Moscow, as well. We propose that every delegation coming to Moscow 'adopt' a political prisoner. In this way ten athletes can devote themselves to the liberation of one imprisoned member of the 'Helsinki Group'."[26]

But by the autumn of 1979, Sakharov's position had changed. At that time he called for a boycott, and on January 16, 1980, he repeated this appeal and expressed support for President Carter's position during an interview broadcast by the American television network ABC. "The Olympic committee has only two choices," he stated, "either to ignore the UN resolution or to take its consequences, even if this causes financial problems."[27] For Soviet officials who were already contemplating the prospect of Sakharov holding daily press conferences during the Games, this was the last straw.

On January 22, Sakharov was arrested and exiled to Gorky. On January 23, Izvestia announced that Sakharov had "recently embarked on a path of open appeals to reactionary circles in imperialist states to interfere in the USSR's internal affairs" and that he had been stripped of the title of Hero of Socialist Labor and his other prizes.[28] On January 24, an Izvestia article titled "A Just Decision" vilified Sakharov in that surreal idiom whose origins go back to the climate of terror surrounding the Purge trials of 1936-37. Sakharov, it said, "an extremely ambitious and conceited person," had "embarked on a path of outright betrayal," "heaped filth on the Soviet people and state," sunk to a level of "moral degradation," and had ended up a simple Judas: "A traitor is a traitor precisely because he sells himself."[29]

On January 22, a few hours before Sakharov's arrest, the "Moscow '80 Committee on Human Rights" held a meeting in Paris to appeal for an Olympic boycott. This conference brought together eight well-known Soviet dissidents, all of whom were veterans of the Gulag: Natalya Gorbanevskaya, Andrei Amalrik, Viktor Feinberg, Leonard Plyutsch, Vladimir Bukovsky, Eduard Kuznetsov, Alexander Ginzburg, and Vladimir Maximov.[30] Leonard Plyutsch had been a member of the "Collective for the Boycott of the Moscow Olympic Games"—including among others the author

Marguerite Duras and the philosopher-critic Roland Barthes—which had issued a manifesto in Paris on April 24, 1979.[31]

With one exception (see below), the Soviet dissidents supported the boycott campaign. The most publicized statements were those of Bukovsky, in Great Britain, and Ginzburg, in the United States. On January 20, 1980, Bukovsky published an article in the London *News of the World* describing the pre-Olympic repression which had been thinning the ranks of the dissident community; he also pointed out that among the members of the Soviet Olympic Organizing Committee were G.P. Goncharov, the head of the Communist Party propaganda apparatus, a senior KGB official, Alexander Gresko, who had been expelled from Britain in 1971 for spying, and Boris Onischenko, the fencer who had been disqualified at the Montreal Games for cheating.[32]

The dissident poet-journalist Alexander Ginzburg arrived in the United States in 1979 in the wake of his conviction the previous year for "anti-Soviet agitation." In early April 1980 he traveled to Colorado Springs to lobby for a boycott of the Moscow Olympiad while the House of Delegates of the U.S. Olympic Committee met to deliberate its fateful decision. Ginzburg's request to address the House of Delegates was denied. "The problem of the boycott has a long history," he said. "The opposition existed long before the invasion of Afghanistan." Outside as well as inside the USSR, however, his assertion that "there is a strong parallel between these Olympics and the 1936 Olympics in Germany"[33] attracted little interest.

The dissenter among the dissidents was Roy Medvedev, the reformist Marxist historian who had published (in the West) a famous critique of Stalinism, *Let History Judge* (1968), and the liberal manifesto *On Socialist Democracy* (1975). Medvedev's isolation on the boycott issue corresponded to his peculiar status within the dissident community itself. Having joined the Communist Party in 1961, he was expelled in 1969 for speaking out against plans to rehabilitate Stalin.[34]

Medvedev, according to an American journalist who knew him, is "the personification of the cool dissident. He is queasy at the combative mentality of rebels like the burly, bearded Pyotr Yakir who had been schooled in the Stalinist camps. Quite deliberately, he steers clear of the passionate moral indignation of either Solzhenitsyn or Sakharov. He has always maintained the sober, dispassionate stance of the thoughtful, armchair reformer."[35] Lacking the personal charisma and Slavophile passion of Solzhenitsyn, the gentle vulnerability and martyr's fate of Sakharov, and the clear-sighted, irrepressible defiance of Andrei Amalrik, Medvedev, despite his demonstrated capacity for courageous action, has been seen by other dissidents as an establishment liberal and even as an opportunist. In an interview with a Swedish correspondent published on January 25, 1980, Medvedev argued against the boycott on the grounds that the Olympiad "could change the political climate" in the USSR, in part by changing Soviet attitudes toward foreigners.

This statement is only one example of the "open society" thesis examined below. As we shall see, the Olympic crisis made visible to the world the strategies and the political-philosophical problems of the dissidents' project.

3. The Moscow Olympiad as Totalitarian Spectacle

The public celebration of political will is as old as the Soviet state. In his remarkable eyewitness account (1926) of the early Bolshevik years, René Fuelopp-Miller describes a revolutionary population caught up in a perpetual political festival: "Demonstration forms the framework of all Bolshevik mass festive performances. In Moscow and Leningrad, advantage is taken of the most trifling occasion to arrange a demonstration, and you can no longer conceive the streets of these towns except as filled with strolling masses of men. On such occasions, from all quarters and corners stream workers, soldiers, Soviet officials, whole organizations, unions, and schools, and soon even the most spacious squares are full of people. Motor-cars and all passing carriages are stopped and turned in a second into moving speaker's platforms, from which soldiers, workers, agitators, or students make flaming speeches to the people."[36]

This spontaneous ferment, however, disappeared from Soviet political life with the advent of Stalinism and the rigidified public ceremonial style which persists to this day. But political demonstrations of an impromptu character represent only one type of early Bolshevik political theater. Eminent culture figures, such as the director V. E. Meyerhold and the poet V. Mayakovsky, composed political propaganda plays to celebrate the purging violence of the Revolution and the dawning of a utopian age. But like so much of what he saw around him, this revolutionary dramaturgy left Fuelopp-Miller profoundly troubled.

> It would require a very considerable amount of preconceived enthusiasm to see in this and the other mass festival performances already described, anything but a completely naive symbolism, which keeps turning in a circle on the same spot, or to regard them as anything but the manifestation of an amateurish lack of taste, represented with a colossal supply of external resources. It would be an annihilating criticism of the possibilities of socialist art to say that the level of taste in these performances corresponds to the level of the proletariat, as the Bolsheviks maintain. These "compositions" are not, however, the work of proletarians; they originate entirely with the intelligentsia, and merely betray what a poor opinion Bolshevik leaders have of the level of this "mass man," to whom, in the same breath, they assign the sole right to artistic production.[37]

Fuelopp-Miller finds in the Soviet festivals of this period what is, in effect, a fundamental hypocrisy. On the one hand, there is the new "collective man" who "rejoices in play, in sunshine, in the untrammelled use of his throat and limbs,"[38] who "is seen, on the streets engaged in a demonstration, at festivals displaying a vociferous vitality,"[39] whose primitive energy would seem to guarantee his autonomy as he celebrates the coming of a new order. But there is also the fact of his manipulation by "Bolshevik aesthetes" and the larger implications of their cynicism.

The Moscow Olympiad of 1980 may be seen as the culmination of a tradition which, having been Stalinized during the 1930s,[40] has suppressed the spontaneity of public festivals. At the same time these festivals incorporate manipulative strategies—a fact that modern Soviet ritual specialists do not even bother to deny:

> They [Soviet ritual experts] suggest that even at the present stage of socialist development there are still people who cannot easily grasp abstract general ideas and norms and who, therefore, need to internalize them through the simplified form of ritual. They see no contradiction between this and the fact that Soviet society is trying to create a new, rational man as well as to eliminate the gap between social strata engaged in mental and physical labor. It is not iniquitous to them that one group of Soviet citizens applies its intellect to devise and disperse ideological notions, while another group is induced to dispense with rational judgment in favor

of an uncritical emotional approach. Nowhere is there a suggestion that the new ritual is a necessary evil which will be abandoned as soon as the gap between mental and physical labor has been eliminated. It is assumed that the new ritual will become a permanent element of Soviet society.[41]

From a Western standpoint, the idea of a Stalinist festival appears to be a contradiction in terms. How, one might ask, can emotional rigidity and emotional release be combined in one experience? Even before Stalin's ascendancy to power, Fuelopp-Miller had spoken of "the joyless joy of the Bolshevists.,"[42] and this is the tenor of much Western commentary on the Moscow Olympiad, which was described as "an unsatisfactory mock-festival, tightly disciplined and only fleetingly happy,"[43] "awesomely efficient yet somehow joyless and impassive,"[44] and as "among the sternest Olympics in the movement's history."[45] "Human walls of policemen and KGB men in identical light blue suits see to it that perfect order, perhaps too perfect, is maintained."[46]

The Soviets' "horror of anything spontaneous"[47] made spontaneity itself a topic for discussion. A week before the opening of the Games, Soviet officials were "guarded and defensive, quick to reject the merest suggestion that the Moscow Olympics will be in any way less joyous, spectacular and satisfying than previous ones."[48] It had evidently not occurred to Soviet planners that the banning of victory laps, on the grounds that they might "excite the public unnecessarily,"[49] could appear to foreigners as an example of repression.

The offical Soviet position on the spontaneity issue was provided in the course of a post-Olympic interview by the vice-chairman of the Soviet Olympic Organizing Committee, Vladimir Popov. When asked (by *Der Spiegel*) whether the "perfect organization" of the Olympic festival had not stifled "spontaneous emotions," Popov replied: "Perfect organization, that is a great compliment for which I thank you. Every organization, the more perfect it is, can come into contradiction with the emotions. I believe this is not exactly unknown to the Germans. That it is precisely super-organization for which you reproach us is good. But there is really no point in introducing outbreaks of feeling once the competition is over. It also violates the rules of the international committees. Personally, I cannot see any problem here, it is really a trivial matter."[50] At the root of this view is the Soviet idea that the societies of the West, and the emotional liberties they permit, are essentially anarchic and therefore impermissible.

The historical prototype for the Moscow Olympiad was the famous *Spartakiad* of 1928, "a tremendous show featuring a comprehensive sport program and launched with a gigantic sport parade of 30,000 banner-bearing athletes marching in colorful formation through Red Square—a forerunner of the heavily ornamented celebrations which were to characterize Stalinist Russia."[51] The 1928 festival was also the forerunner of a series which began with the First Spartakiad of the Peoples of the USSR, whose final competitions were held in Moscow in mid-August 1956. Since 1959 they have been held quadrennially in the year prior to the Olympic Games.[52]

Perhaps the most striking feature of the Soviet sports festival is the subordination of sport to pageantry. An important function of the *Spartakiads* is "to demonstrate patriotic feelings through festive parades and mass displays. A conscious attempt is made to simulate the sports ceremonies and rituals of the Ancient Greek Games that were held quadrennially at the foot of Mount Olympus between 776 B.C. and A.D. 395. Torchbearers run single-kilometer laps, starting in Moscow from the tomb of the unknown warrior in the Alexandrov Gardens alongside the Kremlin Wall, through the streets of the Lenin Stadium in the south-west of the city."[53]

Such a festival is also represented officially as a demonstration of multi-nationalism within the USSR: "The *Spartakiad* reflects a major component of our Leninist nationality policy—the convergence of cultural levels of all our peoples."[54] The sport competitions themselves, while considered pedagogically useful, do not employ pageantry and are therefore aesthetically anticlimactic in relation to the spectacles which open and close such festivals.

The opening ceremony of the Moscow Olympiad was widely regarded as the most spectacular pageant of its kind ever seen.[55] A British correspondent described it as follows:

> No one present, certainly none of the journalists alongside me, had ever seen anything like what unfolded before us over the next hour. In honor of the ancient Greek founders of the Games, the spectacle opened with a Ben Hur-like procession of Greek chariots, surrounded by hundreds of pink-clad Greek maidens. The arena then filled again and again with wave upon wave of performers (16,000 in all). There were dancers in the colorful costumes of the fifteen nations making up the Union of Soviet Socialist Republics—Estonians and Lithuanians, Georgians and Armenians, Ukrainians and Uzbeks. There were dancing gymnasts dressed as Misha Bears. There were jugglers, acrobats and other circus performers. To a succession of compositions, with titles like 'The Sun' and 'Dance Suite: People's Friendship', based on tunes by Borodin, or written by Soviet composers such as Rodion Shedrin, they formed and re-formed in a continuous kaleidoscope of colors and shapes— one moment making up the five Olympic rings, the next forming a succession of 'towers', each built up of several hundred performers standing on each other's shoulders, up to nine deep. It was an astonishing display of mass physical cohesion which with the music, the continuous cheering (even from the journalists), the exploding, swaying, expanding and contracting patterns of colour laid out below us, was quite mesmerizing.[56]

It should be clear that the appeal of such "an astonishing display" is not adequately expressed by references to "patriotic feelings" and "Leninist nationality policy." "Mass physical education displays," a Soviet author wrote in 1966, "must in every possible way further the strengthening of friendship, self-discipline, collectivism and the inculcation of the feeling of responsibility to one's collective."[57] The problem is that such euphemisms blur the distinction between pedagogy and domination. They are prime examples of that decerebrated vocabulary which invariably signifies authoritarian intent.

Mass gymnastics displays, which one observer has described as "a cross between sport, entertainment and ritual,"[58] offer a visual authoritarian idiom which Susan Sontag has analyzed in an essay on fascist aesthetics.

> The tastes for the monumental and for mass obeisance to the hero are common to both fascist and communist art, reflecting the view of all totalitarian regimes that art has the function of "immortalizing" its leaders and doctrines. The rendering of movement in grandiose and rigid patterns is another element in common, for such choreography rehearses the very unity of the polity. The masses are made to take form, be design. Hence mass athletic demonstrations, a choreographed display of bodies, are a valued activity in all totalitarian countries; and the art of the gymnast, so popular now in Eastern Europe, also evokes recurrent features of fascist aesthetics; the holding in or confining of force; military precision.[59]

As we shall see in the final section of this book, the massive non-verbalism of such choreography makes it an ideal Marxist-Leninist art form. We may even say that Marxism-Leninism is that ideology which places the language of the body and the languages of the arts on a common cultural level.

On February 11, 1980, the Count de Beaumont of France, a prominent member of the IOC, proposed a series of Olympic charter revisions "as the only way to denationalize the Olympic movement." These reforms included the elimination of all national anthems and flags, the abolition of all team competitions, and a parade of athletes by sports rather than by countries. "These changes are not for Moscow," he said. "But maybe for Los Angeles we can do it. We must do it for the future of the Olympic movement."[60] In March the IOC announced that it would study the possibility of allowing athletes to compete under the Olympic flag at the Moscow Olympiad in the event their countries participated in a boycott.[61] In April it was reported that the Soviets would "try to persuade the IOC in Lausanne to relax the Olympic rule forbidding individual athletes from competing on their own, without being sponsored by their national Olympic committees."[62] Given the Soviets' long-established commitment to Olympic nationalism, this campaign suggested desperation within the ranks of the Moscow organizing committee.

The crucial event before the denationalizing of the Moscow Games was the meeting on May 3 in Rome of officials representing eighteen West European national Olympic committees.[63] The purpose of this conference was to appeal for participation in the Moscow Games contingent upon the following conditions:

1. National delegations are to be represented in the opening parade by a name board followed by a flag bearer.

2. At all times the flag of the participating delegation will be the Olympic flag.

3. A shortened version of the Olympic hymn is to be used instead of national anthems.

4. At all ceremonies (the opening ceremony, the medal presentations, the closing ceremony), a shortened version of the Olympic hymn will be played and the Olympic flag will be raised.

5. Athletes' clothing will bear only the name of the appropriate national Olympic committee.

6. The IOC guarantees that no speeches of a political nature will be given during the opening ceremony.

7. Each delegation will confine its activities to the sporting events.

8. Delegations will not participate in the youth camp being planned to coincide with the Olympic Games.[64]

These points were ratified by Monique Berlioux, director of the IOC, who had attended the meeting.[65] The purpose of such conditions was to remove the custodianship of the Games—albeit symbolically and belatedly—from the Soviet hosts of the IOC. It is significant, moreover, that even this symbolic action by the IOC was attained, not through its own exertions, but upon the insistence of outside "political" forces.

The implementation of the West European demands was evident in the opening ceremony. The teams of Belgium, France, Italy, Luxembourg, the Netherlands, San Marino, and Switzerland were each represented by "a Russian girl in a red cape [who] carried the team's name-board, followed by a Russian man in red jacket and white trousers holding the Olympic flag. Britain, Ireland and Portugal were each represented by one of their own officials carrying the Olympic flag. Athletes from Andorra, Australia, Denmark and Puerto Rico followed the Olympic flag, and sportsmen from New Zealand and Spain marched behind the five-ringed flags of their national Olympic associations."[66] Soviet television went to great lengths to avoid presenting these signs of denationalization to its audience.

The widespread use of Olympic symbols in place of national ones was a bitter pill for Soviet organizers to swallow, even as they attempted to make the best of an embarrassing situation. When, for example, a Frenchwoman won a gold medal in women's fencing, deputy chairman Popov was asked (by a correspondent from the French communist newspaper L'Humanité) what he thought of the fact that "La Marseillaise" would not be played at the award ceremony. While conceding that the decision was a French matter, he affected a sympathetic concern: "personally, as an admirer of French culture and French history, I feel sorry for Pascale Trinquet, who was denied the opportunity of listening to her national anthem at the presentation ceremony."[67]

Soviet hostility to denationalization is ironic in that the USSR sees itself as the vanguard nation of an international movement. Lenin and his colleagues did not categorically reject nationalism, but rather distinguished between its progressive and retrogressive forms. Having invested enormous sums in the development of champions, modern Soviets have a real stake in perpetuating the notion that successful athletes demonstrate the vitality of the societies which produce them, and an atmosphere of national rivalry is the medium in which this popular notion thrives. In 1971 *Sovietski Sport* commented: "One can only hope that certain people, including, incidentally, certain circles in West Germany [the 1972 Olympic Games were held in Munich] will fail in their attempts to revise the Olympic ritual which vividly illustrates the Olympic oath obliging an athlete to fight on behalf of his country's honor."[68]

More curious, in a way, than the Soviets' uncritical promotion of nationalism is the IOC's longstanding resistance to the one-worldism the Olympic movement harbors and for which it would seem ideally suited. Coubertin's legacy plays a role here, but it must also be remembered that his influence on the movement had declined even before he died in 1937. We must assume that the absence of a genuine Olympic internationalism reflects a global consensus which the East bloc sport establishments, as the heaviest investors, are only too happy to support. The Olympic movement has successfully dressed national ambitions in an appropriately noble garb, making the reigning ideology a neo-Olympism. In 1981, for example, the *Soviet Military Review*, which offers a regular feature on "physical culture and sport," noted that "progressive organizers of sport" opposed "the discontinuation of the opening and closing ceremonies at the Games, because that would be contary to the Olympic ideals developed in antiquity and continued by Pierre de Coubertin. This would deprive sports of their humanistic value as one of the aspects of mankind's multinational culture."[69]

It has become clear that the IOC views denationalization as an exceptional, emergency procedure rather than as an ideal toward which the Olympic movement should strive. This is the lesson of the West European initiative of May 1980 and the essentially passive role played by the IOC in its implementation.

4. Could the Olympics Have Changed Soviet Society?

As a debate between two political worlds, the struggle over the Moscow Games was a conspicuous disappointment. With its belated misgivings and hastily improvised rhetoric, the West made a poor impression, while the Soviets offered little more than Stalinist philippics aimed at the imperialist defilers of world sport. In this sense, the boycott controversy was actually something of a non-event. Khrushchev had feared the perils of abstract expressionism more than the Politburo of 1980 feared Olympic orations from the West.

"Our enemies," Nikita Khrushchev told a Plenary Session of the Central Committee of the Communist Party in 1963, "have now concentrated their main efforts on ideological struggle against the socialist countries. The imperialist ideologists entertain the hope of undermining us from within with the aid of hostile ideology. Their thesis is that the more educated people there are in the Soviet Union, the more vulnerable Soviet society is with respect to ideology."[70]

It is clear, however, that the Politburo of 1980 did fear the cultural penetration possibly resulting from their Olympiad. "Foreigners," young Olympic guides were told, "may be secret agents, they carry unpleasant diseases, they will try to trap and use people. Do your job but don't be tempted to fraternize."[71] The difference between 1963 and 1980 was that Khrushchev turned his own cultural xenophobia into a one-man show which, even at the time, offered humorous moments. "I don't like jazz," he said. "When I hear jazz, it's as if I had gas on the stomach."[72] The public style of Brezhnev's Politburo was less burlesque.

Though overshadowed by the massive publicity given to the boycott, the latent issue of the Moscow Olympiad was the possibility that a significant influx of foreigners might initiate some sort of change within the Soviet Union. It should be noted, moreover, that this possibility greatly alarmed the Soviet leadership far more than it tempted those "ideological enemies" whose own boycott put a quick end to what was, in any case, an imagined threat. As we have seen, a xenophobic campaign intended for domestic Soviet consumption had to figure in Soviet planning, tempering the promise of the festival with warnings to confine the festivities within mandated limits.

The Communist festival raises the larger issue of what kind of cultural experience a Marxist-Leninist state can permit in the area of cultural exchange. Dialogical relationships of this kind are, of course, inhibited by ideological antagonisms. "The struggle of ideas," Izvestia stated in its major denunciation of Andrei Sakharov in January 1980, "is nothing new. It was not born yesterday, and it will not die tomorrow. While advocating peaceful coexistence and the deepening of the process of detente, Communists know very well that there never has been and cannot be any 'ideological coexistence' in relations between states with different social systems. Our adversaries are also well aware of this. But instead of waging a struggle of ideas, they are doing all they can to broaden the front of 'psychological warfare' by attempting to turn their mass information media into full-fledged tools of ideological sabotage, especially under cover of the artificially inflated furor in the West over so-called 'violations of human rights' in the socialist countries."[73] (A year earlier, Moscow Radio had accused Western broadcasters of carrying on "psychological warfare violating the spirit and the letter of the Helsinki accords."[74]) On March 3, 1980, Pravda called the idea that foreigners "will have no one [no average Soviet citizen] to talk to" at the Moscow Olympics "one more thesis of bourgeois propaganda." "The pushers of 'people-to-people contacts' (with specific ideological goals of course) obviously will not be pleased to find out that Muscovites intend to familiarize the Olympic guests first of all with the most noteworthy aspects of our life and Soviet reality."[75]

THE MOSCOW OLYMPIAD IN POLITICAL CONTEXT

Such quotations illustrate the predicament inherent in Soviet hospitality and the USSR's anxious dealings with the subject of competing ideologies. The policy of "peaceful coexistence" obligates Soviet ideologists to have at hand a term (the "struggle of ideas") which refers to the inescapable reality of doctrinal competition. But where does the "struggle of ideas" end and "psychological warfare" begin? This is a question Soviet commentators tend to avoid. The unspoken provision is that this struggle must not be imported into the USSR.

Could the Moscow Olympics have facilitated change inside the Soviet Union? Significantly, by early 1980 the only dissident who professed a belief in such a possibility was Roy Medvedev, who apparently welcomed any opportunity to liberalize the Soviet establishment. But even if the possibility of Olympic-powered change did not, by and large, interest the dissidents, it did appeal to some observers. "The Moscow Olympics," a former director of the American President's Commission on Olympic Sports wrote, "can still benefit the West. Consider this: When was the last time 8,000 journalists possessing freedom of movement under International Olympic Committee rules were in Moscow simultaneously?"[76] In a similar vein, Harrison E. Salisbury, a former Moscow correspondent of the New York Times, warned that a boycott would mean forfeiting a rare opportunity to inundate Moscow with more foreign visitors than the KGB could control. While it was true that many Russians would simply have tried to gather consumer items from the West, "not a few look forward to sampling more precious Western wares: literature, ideas, philosophy, a chance to talk with a foreigner beyond the scrutiny of Andropov's minions."[77]

It is significant that these predictions appeared many months before the Olympiad opened and before the world's journalists discovered the meaning of "freedom of movement under International Olympic Committee rules" in its Soviet context. One journalist who covered the Moscow Games told me that even three times as many visitors would not have made a difference to the security apparatus, that Moscow had been turned into "a city gutted of life and ordinary people."[78] As early as February 1980, Anthony Lewis of the New York Times appraised the inundation theory as follows: "Western scholars on Soviet affairs overwhelmingly believe that the Kremlin would find a boycott far harder to bear."[79]

Once upon a time, an international festival of youth was to be held in Moscow. This extravaganza would feature a great variety of athletic and artistic competitions, and even a special conference for stamp collectors. "No political, ideological or other tendencies will prevail," the Soviet hosts promised their guests. The theme of the festival was to be peaceful coexistence. Nevertheless, high government officials in Washington went to great lengths to discourage American participation. One group of outstanding young performers was pressured to drop its travel plans by a warning from the Secretary of State. The State Department, while claiming it would not deny a passport to anyone who wanted to go, proclaimed that this festival was "an instrument of Communist propaganda which serves the purposes of the Soviet Union and its orbit." "This show," said one official, "is costing the Soviets a tremendous amount of money, therefore it is obviously important to them that it succeed." Consequently, he added, "it is obviously not in our interest to help them succeed." Exiled dissidents warned that American participation would benefit only the Soviet regime, while supporters of American participation argued that an American delegation "could contribute to the ferment among Soviet youth."[80]

The festival described above did, in fact, take place; but it was not the Moscow

Olympiad of July 19-August 3, 1980. It was the Moscow World Youth Festival of July 28-August 11, 1957. The star performers who chose to stay home were not American athletes in awe of the mild-mannered Cyrus Vance, but American Rhodes Scholars intimidated by the blustering John Foster Dulles. The dissidents were not Soviet exiles protesting the seven-month-old occupation of Afghanistan, but Hungarians protesting the eight-month-old occupation of Hungary.

Today the Moscow Youth Festival is remembered by Soviet conservatives as an obscene invasion from abroad which brought sexual promiscuity, venereal disease, and Negroes to Mother Russia.[81] ("Jazz," said Khrushchev, "comes from the Negroes."[82]) For many Russians this was their first confrontation with black human beings, and there are agitated memories of wild Congolese playing bongos in the streets of Moscow. For the Stalinist xenophobes it was, in short, a nightmare.

For others it was a time "when, as Georgi Vladimov, the Russian writer remembers, young Russians and Americans and other Westerners strolled in groups and danced together in the streets and exchanged addresses and kissed each other good-bye with laughter and tears."[83] An American participant recalled: "A number of times when crowds I was talking to grew restless or too large, Russian police would approach. As soon as they were spied, the Russians listening would shout out a magic word which would cause the police to disappear. The word was 'Festival'. This word seemed, in effect, to be synonymous with 'freedom'—freedom to speak and listen and act as they wanted during the Festival."[84]

Nearly a quarter century later, the memory of the World Youth Festival convinced Harrison Salisbury that it could happen again:

> In 1957, the Russians with notable naivete sponsored a world youth congress in Moscow. Tens of thousands of young people, most of them supposedly ideologically screened, gathered. The mixing of these youths with Soviet young people had explosive results. Before the congress, the party and police had managed to hold the line against such intolerable symptoms of "bourgeois Western culture" as rock and roll and blue jeans. After it, Russian youth was never the same. In the end, the authorities simply gave up. Rock and roll and its stepchildren dominate Russian youth culture. So do jeans. What dynamite items the Olympics would introduce into Soviet culture probably never will be known if, as President Carter wishes, the boycott succeeds.[85]

There are two major objections to this argument. First, it underestimates the vigilance of the security organs, which were in fact able to seal off the entire Moscow area, clear its streets of residents, and regulate the movements of foreigners (including journalists) to a degree which is unimaginable to the citizens of democratic societies.[86] Second, the World Youth Festival coincided with the transformation of youth culture in the West, largely through popular music, an upheaval whose concluding phase is nowhere in sight. It is not surprising, therefore, that Salisbury does not attempt to answer his own rhetorical question: what else might we have brought them? New styles of rock and roll? Faded memories of 1968 (Berkeley, Paris, Berlin)? The full panoply of the West's culture of narcissism? Faced with Salisbury's rhetorical question we confront not the Russians, but ourselves.

IV. The Critique of Olympia

1. Introduction: Olympic Sport as a Modernism

The critique of the modern Olympic movement is as old as the movement itself. But it has intensified since 1894, the year of Coubertin's famous proclamation, when the *Spectator* called the idea of renewing the Games "a harmless whim."[1] A year later, this note of indifference recurs in the *Forum*, though now combined with an invidious comparison of the ancient and the modern. It is all very well that the world "loudly vociferates its approval of the gospel of physical culture, but the real leaders of life and thought can never again contemplate an athletic contest with the emotions of men who, like the poets, philosophers and statesmen of Greece, spent the best days of their youth in the gymnasium and often made it the centre of their social and intellectual life in later years."[2]

In 1896, the *Spectator* predicted once again that "Olympic games, ancient and modern, had and will have the effect of games merely, that is, of distractions, innocent or otherwise according to circumstances, from the work of the world."[3] As late as 1911, the French physical educationist George Hébert wrote Coubertin a public letter flatly stating that the Olympic Games' "influence on all that concerns education in the family, the schools, and in the army really amounts to nothing at all."[4]

The idea that the Olympic movement was simply irrelevant to modern life did not survive for long. On the contrary, the Olympic Games provoked extensive debate on several themes of cultural and political significance. The movement's internationalist character was resisted by the nationalistically minded; its commercialism was denounced by critics at both ends of the ideological spectrum; the significance of mass festival as cultural experience or political ceremony was debated; of competition and the pursuit of records challenged the ideals of communal solidarity and harmonious human development.

Specific criticisms of Olympic theory and practice have waxed and waned over the years. The idea that the Olympic festival represents a distasteful exercise in race-mixing is obviously out of favor if not quite extinct (see section 3). On the other hand, Coubertin's concerns about advertising[5] and the sporting press[6] (section 2) addressed a situation which has since hypertrophized beyond his wildest dreams.

The survey of the major critiques of Olympism presented in sections 3 and 4 requires the use of several categories. There is, for example, a rough division of these critiques into "pre-modern" and "modern" periods, separated by the Second World War. This dichotomy can be justified in several ways. First, 1945 marks the end of the age of fascism and the beginning of the United Nations and its multi-racial internationalism. From this point on, the very idea of a racially exclusive sport festival is an exercise in nostalgia. Second, 1952 marks the entry of the Soviet Union into the Olympic movement; at this point, both the politicization and scientization of high-performance sport take on novel dimensions. Finally, it is during the postwar period that the Olympic Games become a mass media and particularly a global television event with the attendant commercialization of its symbols and participants. For all of these reasons, the pre-modern critique of Olympia may incorporate premises that the historical process has changed or even destroyed.

These criticisms can also be shown to vary according to their orientation, whether nationalist or internationalist. What I have called a nationalist critique is specifically hostile to Olympic internationalism on the grounds of a national—racial—chauvinism; this is, of course, a right-wing position. The internationalist critique, on the other hand, regards the internationalism of the Olympic movement as flawed and offers a leftist substitute.

In 1929, for example, the socialist workers' sport leader Fritz Wildung compared the upcoming Workers' Olympiad in Vienna (1931) with the Olympism of the IOC. "Olympiads which have only a sportive significance," he states, "do not even deserve the name." Such a festival should also, according to Wildung, embody the ideals of international socialism.[7] Similarly, the Soviet *Spartakiad* of 1928, according to a Soviet *History of Physical Culture* (1956), was an alternative festival "which had international significance in that it featured many events in which Soviet sportsmen and foreign athletes participated."[8] The fact that "foreign athletes" represented fewer than fifteen percent of the participants was considered less important than the fact that these games were being held under progressive political auspices.

We may note in passing that, even with the disappearance of the European workers' sport movement and the integration of the Soviet Union into the Olympic establishment, an internationalist critique has in fact appeared during the postwar period (see section 4 below). In the meantime, the Soviets have been propounding a kind of internationalist critique from within the establishment itself, calling for the Olympic movement to develop along more "democratic" lines.

A third dichotomy distinguishes between reformist and extremist positions regarding the Olympic movement. The reformist can be defined as a critic who wants to improve upon the existing model. An extremist, on the other hand, calls for abstention from or abolition of the Olympic Games on the grounds that they represent a repugnant internationalism (e.g., the early Nazi position) or a tyrannical internationalism (e.g., the French ultra-left position). It should be noted, however, that the distinction between reformism and extremism is not always clear, since the Olympic model can accommodate a variety of forms, whether a *Spartakiad* or a "German Olympiad" celebrating Teutonic racial uniqueness. One might argue that the "Workers' Olympiads" were genuine examples of the internationalist reformist viewpoint, while the idea of a "German Olympiad" was actually an extremist position on account of its pseudo-internationalism. But if the criterion is pomp and ceremony, then this distinction is not at all clear, since stadium ceremony is beloved by all factions.

The Olympic Games are seldom criticized as an antiquarian aberration. This is due in part to the cultural prestige of their ancient model: Greek antiquity is rarely dismissed as retrograde in relation to modern standards. On the contrary, it is modernity which is conventionally held up for unfavorable comparison with the ancients.

"The Greeks," Friedrich Schiller wrote in his famous *Letter on the Aesthetic Education of Man* (1795), "put us to shame not only by their simplicity, which is alien to our age: they are at the same time our rivals, often indeed our models, in those very excellences with which we are wont to console ourselves for the unnaturalness of our manners. Combining fullness of form with fullness of content, at once philosophic and creative, at the same time tender and energetic, we see them uniting the youthfulness of fantasy with the manliness of reason in a splendid humanity." It is also "the peoples of Greece [who] in their athletic sports at Olympia, delighted in the bloodless combats of strength, of speed, of agility, and in the nobler combat of talents . . ."[9] This portrait of the Greeks and their noble athleticism is a perfect specimen of that Winckelmann-Hellenism which constitutes the charismatic core of the Olympic ideology. This tyranny of Greece over the moderns has contributed to making the neo-Olympic Games vulnerable to cultural critics who point to the "decline" of the Olympic ethos.

Almost all of the twentieth-century critiques of Olympia, with the prominent exception of the Marxist-Leninist version, are actually reactions against contemporary culture. As we have seen, conservative sport doctrinaires like Coubertin and Carl Diem could not avoid feeling a certain ambivalence about sport precisely because of its modern aspects: the relationship to technology, the problems associated with a mass culture of sport, the commercializing of sport, the distortions of human life introduced by specialized training, and so forth. In other words, their loyalty to modern sport had already run the gauntlet of conservative misgivings which were never finally extinguished. It is therefore not surprising that the Olympic critique of greatest cultural significance—promulgated by the Volkish ideologues in the German gymnastics movement around the turn of the century—is but one aspect of what the historian Fritz Stern, in his study of the Volkish movement, has called "the ideological attack on modernity."[10]

The critique of Olympia is predicated on a critique of modernity in general and a critique of modern sport in particular. It should be noted that studies of, and polemics against, the modern age have frequently employed sport as a symptom of cultural decline or, less frequently, as an instrumental mass culture at the disposal of the social engineer. (Although this instrumental use of sport is just what Coubertin had in mind, I have never seen any evidence that his theories about sport entered European social thought in any way.) The critique of Olympia is, then, subsumed by a larger critique of sport as a uniquely modern social phenomenon.

Sport as a type of modernism is the result of a development that dates from the middle of the nineteenth century and is British in origin. In his excellent study, *The Healthy Body and Victorian Culture* (1978), Bruce Haley states that the development of sport in England between 1850 and 1880 "can only be described as a national mania, perhaps the most widespread and long-lasting of any in the Victorian age."[11]

"This is not the era of sport," Thomas Carlyle wrote in 1831, "but of martyrdom and persecution. Will the new era never dawn? It requires a certain vigour of the imagination and of the social faculties before amusement, popular sports, can exist, which vigour is at this era all but total inanition."[12] If Carlyle associates the absence of sport with a kind of cultural energy deficit, twentieth-century cultural critics would later observe—often with dismay—that modern populations had all too much energy to expend at the stadium. However, this objection to modern sport, which really belongs to the critique of mass culture, is not a nineteenth-century theme. There must have been many Victorians who considered the newly popular sports a waste of time, but this is not the same thing as the later idea that sport is an opiate of the masses. For Carlyle the prospective "era of sport" promises, not manipulation, but vitality; and his association of sport with social vigor anticipates certain modern opinions. For example, in *The Revolt of the Masses* (1930), the Spanish cultural critic José Ortega y Gasset offers a similar vitalism: "It is a constant and well-known fact that in physical effort connected with sport, performances are 'put up' today which excel to an extraordinary degree those known in the past. It is not enough to wonder at each one in particular and to note that it beats the record, we must note the impression that their frequency leaves in the mind, convincing us that the human organism possesses in our days capacities superior to any it has previously had."[13]

Like Carlyle, Ortega associated sport with a general "increase of vital potentiality,"[14] thereby addressing sport's purported influence on society as a whole. But it will also be noted that, unlike Carlyle, Ortega believed this energizing effect was derived from the pursuit of the record performance. Whereas for Carlyle "a certain vigour of the imagination" was a prerequisite for sport, Ortega assumed that sport was a precondition for such vigor. The difference between these viewpoints illuminates the meaning of sportive modernity. For of all the European intellectuals who remarked on the social significance of sport during the interwar period (1920-1940), I cannot think of one who would have bothered to offer Carlyle's rather undramatic endorsement of "amusement" and "popular sport." The age of leisure, by this point, was being brought about by industrial civilization and was no longer, as it was for Carlyle, an unrealized golden age.

In general, modern sport has forced the cultural conservatives of our century to choose between the ideals of decorum and civility, on the one hand, and Ortega's sort of vitalism, on the other. Modern conservatives have often succumbed to the temptation to interpret sport as an index of cultural vitality. But this also means surrendering the civilities of amateur competition in favor of the deformations of body and spirit inherent in high-performance sport. This is the price of Ortega's "increase of vital potentiality," although there is nothing in his writings to suggest he was aware of it.

"Physical education," the founder of the Athletic Society of Great Britain stated in 1867, "is the great fact of the nineteenth century. The opposition to it has sunk from the general to the individual. . . . May the time soon come when weakly, misshapen men, and sickly, hysterical women will be the exception and not the rule among the inhabitants of our towns and cities."[15] Physical education, in other words, is functional hygiene; it is not a vitalistic doctrine of heroic performances. Its gentle meliorism requires neither specialized training nor the loss of civility inherent in modern competition.

The pre-modern ambiance of British sport during the latter half of the nineteenth century is evident in other statements contemporaneous with the citation above. An account of a hammer throw in the first Athletic Sports between Oxford and Cambridge (1864) includes the following anatomical observation: "The firm set muscles, at the top of each arm, were visible beneath his shirt."[16] The *Saturday Review* took note of "the grim struggle of a mile race," refusing to call such contests "games."[17] Such locutions take us back to the earliest moments of the new physical discipline, which would eventually lead to the development of muscle for its own sake and the removal of any limits on suffering in the cause of high performance.

The advent of chronometric sport pitted the human organism against abstract and insensate norms which could never be satisfied. In 1930, by which time the lessons of chronometrism had been learned, if not necessarily understood, Ortega y Gasset wrote: "It was a question of honor for man to triumph over cosmic space and time" by pursuing speed as a goal.[18] But there were other, competing notions of honor which were threatened, rather than inspired, by the cult of performance. As late as the Berlin Olympics of 1936, as Richard Mandell has pointed out: "Some British athletes and coaches commented that anyone who altered his existence so monstrously as to be fit to break the records then in existence thereby made a fool of himself."[19] In Germany, in particular, this kind of anti-modernism was rooted in a powerful cultural conservatism which put up stiff resistance both to modern sport and to Olympic internationalism. It is one of history's ironies that these anti-Olympic conservatives were eventually betrayed by the Nazi movement they had helped to make possible.

2. The Founder's Critique of Olympia

Coubertin's unflagging devotion to the Olympic movement did not overlook its vulnerabilities. His reservations are clearly spelled out in his published writings, though they are largely unknown and seldom discussed.

First of all, Coubertin saw in sport a profoundly ambivalent potential which "can set in motion the most noble passions or the most vile ones; it can develop disinterestedness and the sense of honor as well as the love of lucre; it can be chivalric or corrupt, virile or bestial; finally, it can be used to consolidate peace or prepare for war."[20]

Coubertin's purpose in this confession is to establish that sport is not a primary cause of human action. It can, rather, be tipped in the direction of good or evil by forces outside itself. This is perhaps the closest Coubertin ever came to acknowledging—however obliquely—the amoral core of the Olympic ideology described earlier, and it is significant that it takes the form of a caveat similar to that inherent in the sophistical notion that international sport is not an element of international politics. He exempts sport from moral judgment. Upon examination, then, this critique of sport is nothing less than an alibi formulated by Coubertin on behalf of sport's moral innocence.

As we have already seen, the very nature of modern sport forced both Coubertin and Diem to balance the modernism it implied against the cultural conservatism toward which both were inclined. This ambivalence is evident in Coubertin's treatment of the record performance, about which he published an essay in 1909 titled "La limite du record." Whereas Coubertin states elsewhere that there are instances where attempts to set records constitute a breach of his code,[21] most of his remarks on the record performance show approval and even fascination.

In this sense Coubertin represents the vitalist strain in the history of this idea, which sees sport and the challenges posed by record limits as a dynamic factor in the history of the human spirit. For while Coubertin's sport doctrine as a whole shows ambivalence toward equilibrium and excess, these themes are seen eventually to be associated with the social collectivity and the individual, respectively. Sport is intended to lower the socio-political temperature while raising the psychic temperature of the sportsman. "To seek to adapt athletics to a regime of obligatory moderation," Coubertin writes, "is to pursue a utopia. Its initiates require a 'freedom of excess'. That is why they have as their motto: "Citius, Altius, Fortius, always faster, higher, stronger, the motto of those who dare to make assaults on the records!"[22]

In "La limite du record," Coubertin endorses the record attempt while acknowledging the possible harmful effects of the specialization of training it involves. For the three sources of the record performance are "adaption to new types of equipment or movements, a general perfecting of the race, and specialization." Coubertin makes a point of distinguishing the "collective record" set by a group from the "record properly so called." For while the proponents of a "rational" physical education will favor the collective record, "the true sportman will always love to try to conquer himself or his neighbor by surpassing the previously attained result. And it is good that it should be so."[23]

Coubertin, while interested in specialization, was nevertheless cognizant of its dangers. He finds that the man who cultivates specialization acquires thereby "a new structure" which makes him "in a certain way, a different sort of animal from others of his species." In "La limite du record," Coubertin emphasizes the positive aspects of this difference: a "general amelioration" of the human race and "the truly wondrous results" which are achieved.[24] In "Le sport et la morale" (1910), he raises the spectre of an unhealthy type of specialization, a kind of "Nietzschean superman": "Adoring his own body like an idol, one would see him gradually subordinate everything to its development and the preservation of its perfection. One shudders to think of the reserves of refined ferocity and, consequently, the eventual barbarity which would affect human nature thus influenced." An indication of Coubertin's political orientation is found in the next sentence: "For it would require only a small number of such types surging out of the crowd to have a strong impact on those around them and to leave a terrible mark on the society of their time."[25]

Coubertin never conquered his ambivalence about the record performance. Nevertheless, the frequency of his references to its distorting effects suggests the persistence of his reservations. In the *Pédagogie sportive* (1922), Coubertin states that Sparta had actually withdrawn from the ancient Olympic Games on account of the "scientific tendency" that had come to prevail. In the same volume he disavows "the art of creating the human thoroughbred" and "scientific animalism."[26] In the *Mémoires olympiques* (1931), he notes that removing obstacles to record-setting is antithetical to the ancient Greek view that overcoming obstacles rendered a performance meritorious.[27]

It is interesting to note that Coubertin sees specialization in sport as only one aspect of a larger cultural syndrome. Criticizing (in 1931) the public's failure to demand the combined spectacle of outdoor sport and choral singing, he finds an explanation in "the deformation of taste and the habituation to virtuosity which have led in our time to a weakening of the harmonious eurhythmic sense and the development of a virtuosity which has accustomed us to the separation of our sensory impressions. Popular education in the arts must be revived in a new form."[28] The difficulty of virtuosity undermines both social solidarity and taste, which can be combined in a synaesthetic spectacle of eurhythmic bodies and voices. There can be no doubt that the idea of such a spectacle uniting an organic conception of culture with aesthetic standards had a profound appeal to the cultural conservative in Coubertin.

The *Mémoires olympiques* are Coubertin's *apologia pro vita sua,* and it is at the end of this volume that he draws up the balance sheet for the Olympic movement's first thirty-five years. Although "entirely satisfied with the evolution of neo-Olympism," Coubertin recognized its vulnerabilities. On September 13, 1930, he had issued a "Charter for Reforms in Sport," the text of which appears at the end of the *Mémoires.* This document begins by identifying the three major harmful effects attributed to sport: physical overexertion, anti-intellectualism, and the mercantile spirit.

But once again Coubertin pursues the theme of sport's essential innocence. "One cannot deny the existence of these maladies," he says, "but sportsmen are not responsible for them. The guilty parties are: the parents, the teachers, the public authorities and, secondarily the [sport] federation directors and the press."[29] Once again, sport is the innocent point around which noxious influences swirl.

The recommendations of the charter (the more technical points have been omitted) can be categorized as follows. First, Coubertin pursues an anti-mercantile line: "championships organized by casinos and hotels or on the occasion of expositions or public festivities" should be forbidden. As adjunct festivals to much larger expositions, the Paris (1900) and St. Louis (1904) Olympiads had been reduced to sideshows; earlier in the *Mémoires,* Coubertin recalls with distaste the "anthropological days" of the 1904 Games, which had featured competitions between the dark-skinned races: Negroes, Indians, Filipinos, Ainus, to whom, as Coubertin put it, "they dared to add Turks and Syrians."[30] Coubertin had already insisted that the Games must not take the form of a "chaotic and vulgar fair."[31]

Elsewhere in the *Mémoires,* Coubertin had referred to amateurism as an "admirable mummy which could be placed in the Boulak museum as a specimen of modern embalming! Half a century has passed without its seeming to have suffered from the incessant manipulations of which it has been the object. It seems intact. None of us were anticipating a career of such duration."[32] Coubertin's evident amusement at the improbably successful career of the amateur code derives from his claim that he had defended it with "a zeal lacking genuine conviction"; in fact, it had been no more than a strategem to gain the allegiance of sporting circles for whom amateur standards were a *sine qua non.*[33] Coubertin, however, concludes that the amateur doctrine amounts to little more than a "preoccupation with caste."[34] It is this impatience with class snobbery that accounts for the recommendation in his charter that each athlete sign a written oath listing his "various sources of potential profits."[35] It is clear that Coubertin's intention was to control the athlete's relationship to money rather than to abolish it.

"The only true Olympic hero, as I have always said, is the individual adult male. For that reason, no women and no teams. And yet, how can women, team sports, and all the other [undesirable] games be excluded from an Olympiad?"[36] This extract from Coubertin's alleged interview following the 1936 Berlin Games is consistent with one of the most conservative articles of his charter: the barring of women from "competitions in which men participate."[37] According to Diem, Coubertin's 1935 radio broadcast, "Pax Olympica," expresses unambiguous disapproval of public competitions featuring women.[38]

THE CRITIQUE OF OLYMPIA

Coubertin's hostility to specialization is also evident in his proposal that municipalities renounce "the construction of enormous stadiums designed for the sole purpose of staging sporting spectacles, substituting instead modernized versions of the ancient Greek gymnasium."[39]

Coubertin's sensitivity to the accusation that sport is an anti-intellectual influence is rarely noted. His oblique acknowledgment of this charge takes the form of two recommendations. First, he suggests that the Boy Scout movement be "intellectualized" by offering instruction in astronomy, history, and geography. Second, he proposes that the sporting press be "intellectualized" by means of articles devoted to "foreign policy and world events."[40] This is the voice of the cosmopolitan Coubertin who coexisted with the conservative one.

Finally, Coubertin was intent upon establishing the hegemony of the Olympic movement as an international institution. He therefore called for the abolition of "all World Games which duplicate the Olympic Games and are of an ethnic, political, or religious character."[41] The unification of world sport, or what Coubertin called *la jeunesse musculaire internationale*,[42] could not accommodate even that much pluralism.

3. The Fascist Critique of Olympia

a. The Historical Status of the Fascist Critique

The fascist critique of Olympia possesses a somewhat chimerical history. First, it has been promulgated only once by a fascist regime—which promptly betrayed its own anti-Olympic rhetoric. Second, its most eloquent formulations derive from (a) proto-fascist, rather than genuinely fascist, critiques of modern sport (the "premodern" phase), and (b) neo-fascist critics (of the "modern" phase) who are vestigial relics of a bygone fascist age. This analysis is confirmed by the three case studies (British, French, and German) which appear below.

The British example from 1908 shows that it is possible to propound an overtly racialistic Olympic doctrine (the only possible fascist Olympism) without professing an allegiance to fascism, since one need only invoke the authority of the ancient Greeks. The French material demonstrates, first, that Charles Maurras' critique of Olympia was formulated before he evolved into a fascist. Second, it shows that the neo-fascist critique of Olympia in France represents the vision of cultural critics who, having survived the extinction of fascist politics, find themselves political marginals. Finally, the German example shows that the Volkish critique of Olympia was one element of a proto-fascist cultural conservatism; however, Hitler's decision to jettison Volkish principles in favor of the propaganda advantages offered by the Berlin Olympiad was taken less than two months after his accession to power, thereby terminating the historical significance of the Volkish critique, which was absorbed into the highly ambivalent Nazi attitude toward the Olympic movement that evolved after Hitler's crucial decision of March 16, 1933. But despite its historical marginality, the fascist critique of Olympia represents an important current in the intellectual history of the Olympic movement. Its unifying characteristic is a preoccupation with race.

b. The Fascist Critique of Internationalism

Hostility to internationalism is implicit in fascist ideology which extols the cult of the nation, the glorification of war, and the doctrine of race. Fascist distaste for the fraternalism of the Olympic movement and the IOC's dream of mitigating political conflicts is rooted in a contempt for the liberal ideal of tolerance and diversity.

> Fascism, reduced to its essentials, is the ideology of permanent conflict. . . . One might object, but is not liberalism also an ideology of conflict? . . . However, the liberal does not seek to maximize conflict. He does not believe that the most extreme forms of conflict, organized violence and war, should be the paradigm. He seeks on the contrary to limit and regulate conflict and to establish rules of fairness which will be accepted by the contestants.[43]

It would be difficult to summarize Coubertin's internationalist vision more suc-
cinctly, and it is anathema to the fascist. As Mussolini put it in 1932: "as if history 89
were a hunting ground reserved to Liberalism and its professors, as if Liberalism were the definitive and no longer surpassable message of civilization."[44] In the same year, as though commenting on Olympism itself, Mussolini writes: "A doctrine, therefore, which begins with a prejudice in favor of peace is foreign to Fascism; as are foreign to the spirit of Fascism, even though acceptable by reason of the utility which they might have in given political situations, all internationalistic and socialistic systems which, as history proves, can be blown to the winds when emotional, idealistic and practical movements storm the hearts of peoples."[45] Mussolini contemplates with pleasure the fragility of internationalist schemes and their vulnerability to nationalistic passions.

During his Marxist phase (1902-1914), Mussolini had been a proletarian inter-
nationalist who savaged nationalistic sentiment with rhetorical ingenuity. "Socialism," he said in 1905, "knows no nationality." "The oppressed have no fatherland: they regard themselves as citizens of the universe."[46] He called the idea of patriotic loyalty "a lying and outdated fiction" and stated that "the national flag is for us a rag to plant on a dunghill."[47]

As a nationalist, Mussolini replaced the universality of Marxist internationalism with his notion of the universalized State; "for the fascist, everything is in the State, and nothing human or spiritual exists, much less has value, outside the State."[48] "The State, in fact, as the universal ethical will, is the creator of right."[49] "Fascism hencefor-
ward has in the world the universality of all those doctrines which, by fulfilling them-
selves, have significance in the history of the human spirit."[50]

It must be emphasized, however, that the fascist critique of internationalism signifies more than the glorification of the fascist state. Behind the fact that "fascism rejects universal concord"[51] lurk violent feelings about humanitarianism, rationalism, and pacifism which constitute the core of the fascist temperament. As Adrian Lyt-
tleton has commented, "one would be neglecting a valuable clue provided by the Fascists themselves if one did not pay attention to their definition of Fascism as more a 'style of life' than a philosophy."[52] The essence of this style is a hyper-virility which speaks a distinctly biological language.

Contempt for humanitarian feeling suffuses the political literature of Italian fas-
cism. In 1903 Enrico Corradini excoriates the Italian bourgeoisie for its "sentimen-
talism, doctrinairism, outmoded respect for transient human life, outmoded pity for the weak and humble . . ."[53] In his "Nationalist Program" of 1904, Giovanni Papini dismisses "that vague, confused and useless work Mankind" and comments: "Mourn-
ing over the dead, wasting one's time in sentimentality, humanitarian moaning, drawing back in the face of all the platitudes on the sacredness of human life, would be to deny the force of the life that is throbbing and growing and glowing all around

us."[54] In his novel *Lemmonio Boreo* (1912), Ardengo Soffici refers disparagingly to "those humanitarian phrase-mongers who go from place to place with their quack medicines and panaceas."[55] In a manifesto dating from 1918, Alfredo Rocco criticizes the "revival of disruptive individualism" that "at the international political level creates empty humanitarianism and universalism so that the national instinct of preservation and expansion vanishes into thin air, thereby abandoning its central function."[56]

At the crux of these quotes is the thesis that humanitarian concern is synonymous with physical and moral weakness. It is symptomatic, for example, that Corradini should see "pity for the weak and humble" as equivalent to "neglect of the higher potentialities of mankind, the ridiculing of heroism . . ." In a similar vein, Papini equates "humanitarian moaning" with a denial of "the force of life." In a very real sense, the Italian fascists' critique of internationalism is a critique of effeminacy, a theme that would eventually appear in Nazi ideology.

The cult of virility which characterized Italian fascism expressed itself in a taste for biological imagery. Papini calls the despised bourgeoisie "flabby and apathetic,"[57] whereas the elite, according to Vilfredo Pareto, requires "virile qualities."[58] Pareto also speaks of a "social physiology,"[59] while Papini extols "that mighty organism known as the nation."[60] "His force," Curzio Malaparte wrote of Mussolini, "is a specifically natural phenomenon, entirely physical, instinctive and human . . . His justice is of the body, not of the mind."[61] Indeed, there is much evidence that Mussolini made a public cult of his own virility.[62]

On the subject of the well-developed physique, both fascism and Olympism have a great deal to say. And both appreciate the sort of pageant that celebrates human physicality as a symbol of force. Given these important similarities, we must emphasize that fascism and Olympism compete for the sportive body as a political symbol, and the ideological variables that underlie this competition are the issues of rationalism and internationalism.

Despite the constant references to Coubertin and Diem[63] as "humanists," Olympism is a restricted kind of humanism, and it is not humanitarianism, which Coubertin calls a doctrine for the naive.[64] Like fascism, Olympism is a doctrine for the healthy and the strong. One genuine difference between them is rooted in Coubertin's horror of emotional excess, which is encouraged to expend its energies in the form of athletic passion. If excess can be confined to the sphere of sport, then the "internationalistic systems" held in such contempt by Mussolini will be able to survive.

In this sense, the difference between Olympism and fascism is the difference between rationalism and irrationalism. Coubertin, we recall, reacted to the spectre of Nietzsche's superman with instinctive disgust and alarm.[65] Mussolini, on the other hand, found that Nietzsche inspired in him a "spiritual eroticism." "In Nietzsche he found justification for his crusade against the Christian virtues of humility, resignation, charity, and goodness, and it was also in Nietzsche that he found some of his favourite phrases including 'live dangerously', and 'the will to power'. Here, too, was the splendid concept of the superman, the supreme egoist who defied both God and the masses, who despised egalitarianism and democracy, who believed in the weakest going to the wall and pushing them if they did not go fast enough."[66] (Mussolini probably skipped over Nietzsche's denunciation, in *The Will to Power*, of "bovine nationalism": "What value can there be now, when everything points to wider and more common interests, in encouraging this boorish self-conceit? And this in a state of affairs in which spiritual dependency and disnationalization meet the eye and in which the value and meaning of contemporary culture lie in mutual blending and fertilization!"[67] Nietzsche and Coubertin share this much modernism, if little else.)

As a social and political engineer attempting to build on an international scale, Coubertin feared precisely what a Mussolini exalted: those historical moments "when emotional, idealistic and practical movements storm the hearts of people." Coubertin's "notion of international harmony was fundamentally rationalistic; war and peace were matters of knowledge and ignorance. 'Wars break out because nations misunderstand each other. We shall not have peace until the prejudices which now separate the different races shall have been outlived. To attain this end, what better means than to bring the youth of all countries periodically together for amicable trials of muscular strength and agility?' "[68]

It is ironic that, in the *Mémoires olympiques* (1931), Coubertin salutes Mussolini for having "struggled courageously against a hostile destiny."[69] Given Mussolini's public disdain for internationalist schemes, this would seem to be an awkward compliment, illustrating what John J. MacAloon has aptly called Coubertin's "loose habits of mind."[70] On the other hand, it is entirely consistent with Coubertin's penchant for *dirigisme* within the Olympic movement. The political autonomy of Olympic internationalism could only be preserved, he believed, by retaining the authoritarian character of the IOC.[71]

Coubertin's internationalism is actually less an ideology than a scheme. For if we define an ideology, in its most general sense, as "a definite all-embracing system of ideas in one's social consciousness,"[72] then Olympism is an ideology only for that inner circle which administers the movement and for a relatively small number of Olympic devotees. One might even say that Coubertin's basic ideology was Third Republic liberalism, and that Olympism existed as a category within this world-view. The limitations of Olympic internationalism become particularly evident when compared with the Marxist variant, which offers, not an internationalism of play, but an internationalism of labor. Millions have died under the banner of Marxist internationalism, but no one has ever given his life for the Olympic rings.

c. British Imperialism, Racial Unity, and the Olympic Idea

In February 1894, Coubertin went to London to promote his International Congress for the revival of the Olympic Games, scheduled to meet in Paris on June 17 of that year. His dinner host at the London Sports Club was Sir John Astley, a peer and a member of the House of Lords,[73] who had published (under a pseudonym) two essays advocating what he variously called "an Anglo-Saxon Olympiad" or "the Pan-Britannic Gathering."[74] Despite his appointment by Coubertin to a nominal position in the upcoming Congress, Astley became both a defector and a critic of the Olympic movement in its infancy.

Astley is included in this discussion of fascist attitudes toward international sport because of his interest in "Race." His point of departure for the racial issues, like that of later neo-fascist commentators, was the racial purity of the Greek Olympics. Astley conceived the ancient Olympiad as a festival during which "all racial differences subsided for the time being, and every Greek was a brother and each contestant a hero."

This notion of racial difference is to put it mildly, a relative one, and Astley did not hesitate to apply it to the Anglo-Saxons: "We are, indeed, one of the most mixed

THE CRITIQUE OF OLYMPIA

races on the earth, but it is this mixed strain which has given us our nature of adaptability to circumstances, fitted us for a governing people." But how mixed a race can the Anglo-Saxons be? "Anglo-Saxon is a term which has been generically applied to us, but we are leavened throughout with the sympathetic, passionate Celtic elements."[75] Wrapped in the warm cocoon of his eugenic contentment, Astley's conception of miscegenation remained blissfully innocent of more exotic possibilities.

Race-mixing on the playing field, however, was quite another matter, although here Astley gives some contradictory signals. Having proposed (in 1908) a "cricket Olympiad," he comments: "Last year I was in some of our tropical African Colonies, and it was astonishing to see what the black man could do in the field, and with the bat and the ball."[76] In the same essay, however, he refers disparagingly to the race-mixing which characterizes Coubertin's neo-Olympia: "At the original Olympic games, only freeborn Greeks were allowed to compete, but in the present modern revival of them, the first of which was held in Athens in 1896, there is no racial, no language, no birth disability. It is purely a hybrid, babel, gathering."[77] It should be pointed out that Astley's published manifestos leave it unclear whether his principal objection is to racial heterogeneity *per se* or to the absence of *any* principle of homogeneity, be it racial, linguistic, or hereditary. In any case, it is a program with an inherent anti-pluralistic bias, and this is what distinguishes it from Coubertin's scheme while making it comparable to the fascist celebration of the racial community.

A periodic "National and Racial Festival," Astley suggests, "would keep the feeling of kinship among those who speak the same language and have inherited the same customs. . . . The principle of the scheme is based essentially on that of the family; it involves no artificial ties . . ."[78] Fifteen years later, Astley published a third commentary assessing what had and had not been accomplished. "Developments," he conceded in 1908, "have not been quite on the lines I framed, nor as one great organization," although he can point to "athletic contests, intellectual contests, and a universal anniversary day for the Empire, all of which have come to pass . . ." In the last of these essays the highest function of the Anglo-Saxon Olympiad is spelled out. The Greeks, Astley says, "included in their Olympic games other calisthenics in addition to the physical. They debated, considered, and thought out all things appertaining to the welfare of the race and State." What Astley has in mind is nothing less than a quadrennial sitting of the elders of the tribe, since the games themselves "are but the setting and the accompaniments of the jewel of the casket, which should be a periodical council of the wise and great of the nation and the race."[79]

Although Astley's project had been originally designed to comprise three sections—industrial, intellectual, and athletic—he saw special advantages to be derived from "the athletic portion." "By thus beginning on the sporting side, the arena of faction is left altogether, and large classes are reached in the colonies who would take an incredible interest in their champions."[80] Once "the arena of faction" has been left behind, opportunities for a ceremonial unity present themselves: "The dramatic symbolism of the gathering and the ceremony proposed ought to be a periodical object lesson as to what the Empire is, alike to Colonial and home-born." Why, he asks

> should not athletics provide a federating force round which all can gather, forgetful of the jarring interests of the Empire? I can see nothing in the conflicting political world, or the commercial world, which appeals more to the common instincts of the

race, and to its simpler and more sentimental side than such a gathering; and if we are to fall down and worship anything in unison for a time as a people, let us fall down and worship that which cannot be bought: health, pluck, physical vigor, self-denial and fair play . . . [81]

This passage contains two familiar themes: the idea that the appeal of sport transcends "the conflicting political world," and the idealizing of qualities "which cannot be bought." Like his successors in the Olympic movement, Astley insisted on the separation of sport and state: "any action even indirectly suggestive of patronage or control on the part of the State must be unhesitatingly discouraged,"[82] apparently because Astley associated the state with bureaucratic inefficiency. More interesting, and reminiscent of the Olympic circle's preoccupation with permanence, is Astley's concern that his Pan-Britannic Gathering develop "outside of existing political and commercial organisations which are sometimes of a disintegrating nature."[83]

Astley was also a partisan of amateur competitions, and in this regard he was representative of his class: "Let it be understood that the athletic contests, while open to the whole Democracy, are purely amateur; that is, they are to be for those who engage in such exercises for the pleasure they find in them and the benefits other than pecuniary that they derive from them."[84] He recommended that "no money prizes be given at all, but that instead some symbolic trophy be given to the victors in each event of the athletic contests: some gift from the race or nation to the man which would be treasured."[85] This is the gentleman's code which Coubertin claims (in the *Mémoires olympiques*) to have embraced for purely practical reasons.

d. Charles Maurras and the Neo-Fascist Critique of Olympia

Charles Maurras (1862-1952) was one of the remarkable political intellectuals of his era. On one level, Maurras could be labeled a Catholic royalist and a passionate French nationalist; on a deeper level, however, such general terms convey neither the facts nor the essence of his career.

Maurras was a Catholic whose political movement, the monarchist and anti-Semitic Action Française, was condemned by the Vatican in 1926. "Catholics by calculation, not by conviction," the Archbishop of Bordeau wrote to the youth of his diocese, "the men who lead the Action Française use the church, or hope at least to use it; but they do not serve it, since they reject the divine message which it is the church's mission to propagate."[86]

Maurras' royalism, like his Catholicism, derived from his attraction to the principle of authority and was explicitly repudiated by two royal pretenders. "Theoretically," wrote the Count of Paris, "his teaching leads to the monarchy based on reason; practically speaking, it leads to Caesarism and autocracy."[87] One disastrous result of Maurras' autocratic leanings was his uncritical support for the authoritarian "New Order" of the Vichy regime during the Second World War. In 1945 Maurras was tried and convicted of treason.

Maurras' "integral" nationalism, a pure form of antirevolutionary passion, was conditioned by the unrelenting fanaticism of his temperament. "A legitimate nationalism would be loyalty to the person of the King and the blood royal, an emotion essential to patriotism. To Maurras, however—and here he is quite Jacobinic—the King is the 'functionary' of the nation, and he regards heredity as a matter of political expediency. Maurras' nationalism is without precedent in history. He is the first to conceive of nationhood as a privilege, and to deny other peoples the right to nationality."[88] Maurras' hostility toward internationalism owes much to this pseudo-nationalist intolerance.

It is in the person of Charles Maurras that the Olympic movement visibly intersects the history of fascism. There are, in fact, two intersections, the first of which proved to be a false beginning. In 1887, commenting on proposed educational reforms, he refers approvingly to "the so very interesting observations reported from England by our colleague M. Pierre de Coubertin."[89] The irony is that Coubertin's application of these observations took the form of an internationalist movement whose ambitions Maurras could only despise.

In 1896 Maurras traveled to Athens to report on the newly revived Olympic Games for *La Gazette de France*.[90] In his fourth dispatch to the *Gazette,* Maurras admits that he had gone to this festival expecting the worst:

> When the idea was first published, I condemned it totally. The Internationalism of the games offended me. I feared the profaning of a beautiful name, that it would be turned into its contrary. And I saw an anachronism, as well. The Greek olympiads were made possible by the existence of a Greece. But since the Reformation, and particularly since the French Revolution, there is scarcely a Europe to speak of: what would be the meaning of an Olympiad open to the entire world? Finally, this *mélange* of races threatened to result, not in an intelligent and reasonable federation of modern peoples, but in the vague disorders of cosmopolitanism.[91]

Never, says Maurras, had there been such an opportunity "to try to distinguish precisely between cosmopolitanism, which is nothing but a confused *mélange* of diminished or destroyed nationalities, and that internationalism which predicates, first of all, the preservation of different national mentalities (*ésprits*)."[92]

Maurras' reaction to what he found at the Athens festival was ambivalent, and finally took the form of a perverse satisfaction. For while he did indeed find the distasteful *mélange* of nationalities he had expected, its effects proved to be a happy surprise. "As for cosmopolitanism," he says, "I did not see that there would be nothing to fear from this quarter for the simple reason that, in our age, when several distinct races are put together and constrained to mingle, they are repelled from each other and distance themselves at the very moment they think they are mixing." "So, far from suppressing national passions, all of this false cosmopolitanism of the Stadium just exacerbates them."[93]

Paradoxically, Maurras had discovered that internationalism was the best guarantor of nationalism itself. As Ernst Nolte has commented: "There in the Pan-Athenian stadium the competing nations stood revealed to Maurras as the fundamental reality of the age. This graphic experience was to remain with him for a long time as something much more powerful than his theoretical horror of revolution which, after all, he was never to see with his own eyes."[94] What is more, the athletic victories of Germans and Englishmen made him tremble for the future of a less virile France, which would never survive on what he later called "the artificial stimulants of democracy."[95]

"The outstanding facts of our time," Maurras wrote more than a half-century after the Athens Olympiad, "are national facts ... The nationalism of my friends and myself bears witness to a passion and a doctrine."[96] And it had all started at the Games.

Like Coubertin's Olympism, Maurras' anti-Olympism has been preserved essentially intact by his ideological inheritors. This doctrinal continuity has been made possible by Maurras' prestige on the French extreme right and by a pair of Maurrasian themes which continue to preoccupy neo-fascists: racial xenophobia and a vitriolic criticism of modern culture, its aesthetics, and its hostility to the fascist vision.

In an essay honoring such writers as Charles Péguy and Maurras, the prominent French neo-fascist Maurice Bardèche extols these pioneering spirits of the right: "These directors of consciousness, these guides, these exhorters, these men possessed by anger or by a sense of justice, these madmen who tear off their clothes in the plaza, all have chosen to be an incarnation of history, and they survive, in effect, in the memories of men, like heroes, petrified in a unique movement, symbols of an idea, the congealed lava of history, grandiose or frightening, fixed like owls on the great portals of time. It is their destiny which counts, not their words."[97] It is not fortuitous that Bardèche has also published a denunciation of the Olympic Games of comparable polemical violence. For one thing, postwar neo-fascists remember Maurras' dispatches from Athens and the portentous lessons he drew from the Olympic movement in its infancy. More important, the neo-fascist critics of Olympia, inhabitants of a different historical epoch and observers of a new Olympic culture, find Maurras' position analogous to their own. In this sense, Maurras is a living prophet.

Maurras' racial and cultural xenophobia originated in a virtually hysterical concern with the integrity and survival of France as a national culture. His suspicions about internationalist ideals were a consequence of this hyper-nationalism. Even the ultranationalist Gustave Hervé, Maurras wrote in 1926, "believes that, politically speaking, there are greater interests than national interests and that above the fatherland exists the human race. . . . We will swear, by God: fatherland and mankind. But if events say: fatherland or mankind, what is one to do in that case? Those who say . . . 'France first' are patriots, those who say: 'France, but . . . ,' are humanitarians."

"This dissociation of fatherland from mankind," Ernst Nolte comments, "is of the utmost significance. It is the guiding principle of fascist nationalism, which is always antihumanitarian and narcissistic."[98] Here Maurras lines up with Mussolini, whose public narcissim embodied nationalist vanity and the antihumanitarianism which always accompanies it.

Maurras' critique of internationalism was more, however, than a simple outgrowth of his nationalism. The revolutionary principle of fraternity, he wrote in 1922, "the essence of cosmopolitan brotherhood, imposed on the one hand a limitless indulgence towards all men, provided they lived far away from us, were unknown to us, spoke a different language, or, better still, had a skin of different color. On the other hand this splendid principle allowed us to regard anyone, be he even fellow citizen or brother, as a monster and a villain if he failed to share with us even our mildest attack of philanthropic fever."[99] The doctrine of universal fraternity had had the effect of setting Frenchmen at each other's throats.

The second and most important theme which links Maurras to the postwar ultra-right and its critique of Olympia is the idea that civilized standards were declining, succumbing to a global pestilence. Maurras' basic value was "discipline—mental, moral, aesthetic discipline—reason, law, order, taste in which was embodied all the civilizing influence of the classical spirit."[100] But for Maurras, the modern world had become a neoclassicist's nightmare. Like internationalism itself, to which it is thematically linked, his cultural pessimism is on a literally planetary scale. "An imperceptible degeneration has come to Florence, to Italy, to this whole planet, which day by day becomes colder, uglier, and more barbaric."[101] Or: "Should the liberal lie spread over the earth, should anarchism and universal democratism spread the 'panbeotie' announced by Renan, should the barbarians from the depths, as predicted by Macaulay, appear at the appropriate time, then man will disappear as a human being, just as he will have disappeared in the form of Frenchman, Greek, or Latin."[102]

Like the French right as a whole, Maurras sees himself in a desperate struggle against the French Revolution and the totality of its disastrous modern effects. What sets him apart is the ferocity of his conviction and the dimensions of the conspiracy theory which is its logical result. Maurras, as Ernst Nolte has said, "was the first man in Europe who as a thinker and a politician drove conservatism beyond the limits dividing it from incipient fascism."[103]

96

Of the extreme right-wing or fascist intellectuals to have survived, and then written against, the postwar antifascist purge in France, Maurice Bardèche is probably the most important by virtue of his intellectual and polemical skills,[104] the scandal over his polemic *Nuremberg or the Promised Land* (1948), which was confiscated and for which he served a year in prison,[105] the publication in 1960 of *What is Fascism?*, and his direction (since 1953) of the journal *Défense de l'Occident*.

Bardèche has evolved a neo-fascist ideology to cope with post-Nuremberg morality and its devastating assault on fascist values. Thus his dogma bears the mark of its desperately oppositional status, recalling the doctrine of Maurras. Bardèche's account of the transition from the fascist to the post-fascist period treats the purge as an invasive transformation of consciousness that also characterizes the modern age. His claim is that he represents thousands of his contemporaries of similar political temperament.[106] While this cannot be demonstrated in the ordinary political sense, a review of the literature emanating from the extreme right in France since 1945 makes it clear that Bardèche has articulated the fears and values of a political pariah caste. He also demonstrates the psychological consequences of prolonged ideological isolation and the defensive-aggressive reactions it engenders. If Maurras is the paradigmatic fascist, then Bardèche is the paradigmatic neo-fascist in France.[107]

Like Maurras, Bardèche perceives a continuing planetary catastrophe. "The real world," he writes in *Les temps modernes* (1956), "is disappearing before [our] very eyes, its complexity, its richness. Its natural contradictions are no longer apparent [to us]. [We] live [our] very mutilation, [we] live in a logical, coherent universe which dooms the real universe."[108] For Bardèche, as for Maurras, the Olympic phenomenon is but one symptom of this hostile and suffocating modern reality.

But why should we examine in such detail the critique of modernity formulated by so marginal a clique? This is a legitimate question which French historians have answered in two ways. First, these extremists are an intellectual resource. In his standard history of the French right, René Remond comments: "Overflowing with intellectual activity, speaking and writing, this Right furnishes ideas to other Rightist movements that are in short supply of significant thought. This fact permits the counter-revolutionary Right to extend its influence well beyond its own limits . . ."[109] One might add that the most disillusioned social critics are often the most penetrating ones, since they feel no obligation to the status quo. If their dangerous fantasies are, in some way, our own, then we should confront them.

This possibility calls into question the marginality of certain neo-fascist ideas. The problems expressed by the extreme right, René Chiroux wrote in 1974, "are, at bottom, identical to those of the moderate Right and even, often enough, to the concerns of a large segment of public opinion which, disturbed by too rapid a development of the modern world, has difficulty getting its bearings in a France in total flux." The extreme right, Chiroux suggests, confronts the disorientation others may repress or fail to recognize. What distinguishes the extremists, then, is their style: "the manner in which the problems are presented, the tone which is employed, the polemical vigor, the provocative aspect, the personalization of attacks."[110] This is the style of Maurras and Bardèche.

The neo-fascist resistance to Olympia comprises five major themes: a nostalgia for the ancient Games, a nostalgia for the Berlin Olympiad of 1936, a xenophobic scorn for internationalist ideals, a contempt for sport as a modern spectacle, and a racist disgust at the sight of the foreigner (métèque). The unifying themes are race and a contempt for the modern world.

1. Philhellenism is hardly limited to the extreme right, but it is the right that gives the "racial purity" of the ancient Greek athletes inordinate emphasis. As Bardèche claims, "In ancient times, the 'Barbarians'—the non-Greeks—were excluded, and the Games signified the unity of a civilization which, for a time, constituted itself across divisions of politics and wealth. But modern, 'globalized' Olympism is anyone at all and, preferably, the exotic: the 'Barbarians'—or non-occidentals—reign here uncontested." "The Olympic Games," Bardèche wrote in 1972, "as they have developed in the form of a democratic travesty, have lost all meaning. The Greeks' admiration for their athletes was not based on the cult of muscle and gaping astonishment at performances. The Olympic Games of antiquity rendered homage to virile qualities, to the discipline which the athlete imposed upon himself, to the courage he put to the test, to the energy he expended in his effort."[111]

2. The only modern Olympiad of any value was the Berlin Olympiad of 1936, toward which the neo-fascists feel a kind of religious awe. Never, says one writer, had the Games "reached such heights, such a point of exaltation."[112] These were the "Wagnerian Games of 1936," and Coubertin himself had blessed the grandeur of their emotional violence.[113] The right sings praises to Leni Riefenstahl's film masterpiece on the Berlin Games, "Olympia," whose special powers reside "in a kind of return to the sacred, in a quasi-musical mythology which finds its nourishment in acts of muscular precision, isolated details, magnified and slowed down by a factor of a thousand." This film, says Paul Werrie, is elevated by a "mystical element."[114]

> That this mystical element was inspired by Hitler changes nothing. The fact is that it ruled over the stadium, as perceptible and as palpable as a fog. Leni Riefenstahl had only to capture it in order to give it an orchestral arrangement. At first it was a frightening magnetism, a magic. A suspect magic, of course, and a dangerous one. Like all magic and all grandeur, or the dream of grandeur. This is the mysticism with which Wagner fills himself. Erotic passion, as destructive as it can be, is still vital to the nurture of masterpieces. Every time the medium appeared in the stadium—this is the truth—the tiers became a sea of outstretched hands, like the heads of lances. From this enormous rheostat radiated emanations which electrified the defenders of the German colors who, suddenly, transcended themselves.[115]

"The stadium at Nuremberg," says Bardèche, "was not built to offer applause to 'mighty arms', but to salute force, health, and the plenitude of the 'hero' whom the new civilization of energy presents as its human ideal."[116]

3. In its hostility to internationalism, neo-fascism perceives modern sport as "one of the transcendental lies of the epoch."[117] This "universal panacea"[118] is false, and

the merchants, capitalizing on the Olympic obsession, offer the "fraternity of the peoples" as part of their "ideological Camelot."[119]

> A motley and amorphous mass, a great mixing together of the nations, infatuated by a vague and insipid ideal of fraternalism, relativism, and a sanctimonious pacifism. Greek Olympism had a unifying sense; modern Olympism reunites in order to disunite a bit more, or to achieve unification on the animal level.[120]

4. The neo-fascist critique of modern sport incorporates many of the standard cultural conservative themes: a perception that sport has degenerated into a spectacle analogous to the circus or the cinema;[121] the claim that the play element has been lost and *homo ludens* has been transformed into *homo faber*;[122] hostility to professionalism ("the great denaturation"[123]) and advertising ("*parade publicitaire*"[124]); a denunciation of the tragedy of mass culture,[125] the idea of the State athlete (a "monster"[126]), and the passivity of the spectators;[127] condemnation of the creation of artificial conditions to promote records[128] and the creation of artificial human beings to set them. "The champions who are admired [today]," says Bardèche, "represent a variation on the human cannonball. They are products of the forcing technique, like calves stuffed with hormones or chickens with pills embedded in their necks."[129]

Paul Werrie echoes Coubertin's fear of the overdeveloped "monster" and derives from it a racist logic: "Where, I ask you, is the natural element in these professionals, these monster-types who are often drugged, in these Olympic supermen, this hyperproduction of cells, muscles and nerves which is what a record-holder amounts to nowadays; in this governance by hypophysis and thyroids, these glandular treatments, this invasion by endocrinology, [or] the racist, cattle-breeding [*cheptelien*] eugenic delirium which pervaded the stadium last year in Rome [at the 1960 Olympic Games] at the appearance of the black male [Ray] Norton and the black female [Wilma] Rudolph, fiancés who are to be mated in order to bring into the world a race of athletic supermen?"[130]

For Werrie, the cult of the record performance requires a perilous and sickening venture into the distortion of human nature. But one must also note that Bardèche, who shares Werrie's disgust at such biological manipulations of the human organism, believes that society has a stake in the setting of records, arguing that "les recordmen"[131] are among those whose exploits demonstrate that virility has not disappeared from the face of the earth.

None of these criticisms of modern sport originates with the neo-fascists. They are, rather, elements of an anti-modernism which first developed within the sport cultures of nineteenth-century England and Germany. What is new, as René Chiroux points out, is the tone: the visceral anger, the elaborate formulations of disgust, the *total* character of the cultural emergency. If there is any thematic originality which can be credited to the neo-fascists, it is their racial critique of the Olympic movement.

5. The neo-fascist critique of sport is inseparable from a compulsive racial xenophobia which exhibits a particular fixation on the threatening and distasteful figure of the Negro athlete. "Athleticism and aesthetics," says one colleague of Bardèche, "are one and the same thing: Greek thought's invention of the Beautiful begins with the cult of the naked athlete."[132] More specifically, athleticism requires the discipline of a racial aesthetics.

The racial critique of Olympia begins with a racist anthropology. Africa and Asia offer civilizations that "are nothing more than enormous growths of vegetation," while "our own" is of Greek origin.[133] Consequently, the Olympic stadium has become an arena in which "white order" struggles against "black disorder," in which "the sub-human (*l'homme peu humain*) can exploit his animality: they go into ecstasies over the beauty of the athletes of the black race. They practice a— virtuous—racism, calling them 'thoroughbreds'."[134]

The race-mixing spectacle of the Olympic Games demonstrates the need for a "fascist Peace," representing "the just violence of Culture." "The Occident has the mission of imposing Peace on the savage, that is to say, of colonizing him." The most profound perversion is, in this view, not to leave the savage to his savagery, but to adopt the "ethnological barbarity" bequeathed to us by two (conveniently Jewish) anthropologists, Lévy-Bruhl and Lévi-Strauss, according to whom it is "the savage who colonizes culture, or rather culture which, decadent and suicidal, consents to be colonized by savagery (Olympism enthrones in the West the negritude of Akii-Bua and Matthews, just as Lévi-Strauss enthrones the art of life as practiced by the Bororos)."[135] In a word, the very idea of the black champion is culturally subversive and should be suppressed.

If the principal threat is black, it is also possible to discern a yellow peril. In his *Notes on Public Education* (1901), Coubertin had maintained that "the sporting instinct" was not a part of the heritage of the Orient.[136] One neo-fascist author, overlooking the fact that Coubertin wanted to integrate the Asians, not exclude them, turns him into a prophet of racial struggle. Coubertin, he says, "grasps clearly the conflict of tomorrow, this ineluctable struggle of the white man and the yellow, separated by a fundamental irreducibility. Coubertin knows where the heart of the problem lies and he defends 'this principle of individual autonomy so contrary to the pantheistic and communistic intellect of ancient Asia'. Here is a completely disregarded aspect of Coubertin which proclaims, however, the advent of the modern age."[137]

Whereas Maurras greeted the intercultural confrontations in the stadium at Athens with a certain malicious satisfaction, his neo-fascist inheritors denounce interracial contests as forums for "racist passion." They believe such "racial fanaticisms" are a political instrument of "the colored peoples" and their propaganda.[138] This ideology of resentment is seen as a mania which endangers global stability while it claims innocent victims such as the sportsmen of the Republic of South Africa.

The most conspicuous aesthetic issue for the neo-fascists is what might be called Olympic deportment. Here Maurrassian discipline—mental, moral, and aesthetic— has broken down, and again it is the black victor who is singled out for special attention. "After his 400 meter victory, Akii-Bua goes into obscene contortions and, standing on the podium, kisses his gold medal frenetically."[139] Self-control, that cardinal sportsman's virtue, has, in this view, been replaced by jungle rhythms and the latent insanity of the savage.

The aesthetic disaster that follows upon the total collapse of Olympic deportment is dramatically rendered in Paul Werrie's appalled meditation on the finale of the 1964 Tokyo Games. The 5,541 athletes,

> instead of leaving the stadium in a dignified manner, the way they had entered and *as the Japanese were doing,* broke from their moorings, upending all the barriers, invaded the infield, mingled together, ran around yelling, danced to the sounds of the orchestras that were stirring and churning them up, women hoisted onto the

shoulders of the men. And there were the buffooneries: Western athletes kneeling in parodic fashion and pretending to pray before the Emperor who has ceased to be God, but has become an oceanographer. And there were the bronze-skinned beings, their hair done up as at a mascarade [sic], jutting out their chests, flashing their white teeth, brandishing sticks and keeping time, then finally, hilariously, taking the lead to conduct this ecumenical carnival toward God knows what conquest.[140]

Here, indeed, are the preoccupations of Maurras: the fear of tumult and disorder, the loathsome alien, dignity's ghastly fate in a world of vandals, the vision of cultural ruin on a planetary scale.

100

At the same time, there are hazards Maurras either did not imagine or did not take the trouble to record: the deforming of the body to achieve high performance, the commercialization of sport (meaning the death of values), the disappearance from sport of the play element (the competitions witnessed by Maurras in 1896 were a carefree romp by modern standards), prestigious victories by racial aliens, or the subtle infiltrations of technology which have transformed sport itself.

Despite its hysteria, its racism, its pseudoclassicism, and its Hitler nostalgia, the neo-fascist critique of Olympia is not entirely without value. Its contribution is the emphasis on the social value of style, or what might be called the aesthetics of the public sphere. Unmoved by the functionalism of the democratic welfare states, the neo-fascists argue that a world in which aesthetics is debased is a demoralized one.

In this respect they are not alone. For many observers, and not just those on the extreme right, the "imperceptible degeneration" Maurras saw afflicting the whole planet has become all too perceptible. In the sphere of nature we find ecological devastation; in the sphere of culture we find disastrous architectural developments, the rise of advertising as a new public consciousness, providing a surrogate aesthetic for entire populations—these are social phenomena which have concerned many social critics. As we shall see below, the neo-fascist critique of Olympia can be viewed as a radical anti-modernism which transcends ideological boundaries.

e. The Volkish Critique of Olympia
(1) The Pre-Nazi Phase

The Volkish critique of Olympia, unlike the French neo-fascist critique, is rooted in the value system of an established physical culture, namely German gymnastics (*Turnen*), which dates from the first decades of the nineteenth century. During the period from 1880 to 1914, the German gymnastics movement confronted the two cultural forces which would eventually replace it as Germany's predominant sport culture—modern sport and the Olympic movement.[141] Sensing the possibility of its own extinction as a subculture, the *Turner* mounted an aggressive propaganda campaign against the double evil of modern athleticism and the foreign influences it represented.

The Volkish mentality, as described earlier, is a specifically German cultural conservatism. Its major themes—mystical racism, xenophobic nationalism, anti-Semitism, anti-industrialism, anti-intellectualism, anti-modernism—virtually require an anti-internationalist outlook. As George Mosse has pointed out, all of these themes play a role in Volkish hostility to the city:

> The image of the city always conjured up the dread of the rootless elements, their incompatibility with the Volk, and an antagonism to foreign persons or cultures.

Volkish thinkers saw the specter of internationalism in the rapid expansion of the cities. [Wilhelm] Riehl, who was credited with this apocalyptic vision, criticized big cities for wanting to become international urban centers, to achieve equality with all the large cities in the world and form a community of interest. Within such a union, Riehl feared, the 'world bourgeoisie' and 'world proletariat' would recognize their mutual compatibility and exercise a suzerainty over a world in which all that was natural had been destroyed, especially the estates.[142]

Riehl's fears were justified: after the First World War, Weimar Germany did indeed become far more international and urban than Volkish, and a conspicuous symptom of this modernization was the meteoric rise of modern sport. As Wolfgang Rothe points out, "even inherently non-contact sedentary activities such as chess, riddle-solving, and card-playing now become the competitive sports of chess, mental quiz, and skat-matches. Hunting is transmuted into a sport, and after Hitler's assumption of power, martial arts become a concept as flexible as it is unambiguous. And each of these sports has its associations and clubs, and hence its sports officials. Everything is regulated and organized to the nth degree—truly a new world."[143] On one level, the Nazis' destruction of the Weimar Republic represented the revenge of the Volkish spirit. But in the case of sport, as we shall see, the Nazis' initial hostility to sport proved to be a false regression which eventually could not conceal a modern essence.

Volkish resistance to internationalism in the area of physical culture goes back to Friedrich Ludwig Jahn, the founder of the racialist-nationalist gymnastics movement in Germany and perhaps the foremost Volkish culture hero. After his death in 1852, Jahn's legacy found its most important vehicle in the German Gymnastics League (DT), established in 1868. In 1877, the same year an international gymnastics competition was held in Italy, the Germans refused to make the German Gymnastics Festival in Breslau an international event. A year later, the newspaper of the DT declared that the internationalist sympathies of social democrats made them unfit for membership in what was, in effect, a Volkish organization. Volkish influence even extended into the ranks of German sportsmen, some of whom apparently managed to combine nationalist isolationism with their adoption of a foreign physical culture.[144]

It is also interesting to note the appearance of a pseudo-internationalism among the Volkish gymnasts not far removed from Astley's idea of a Pan-Britannic Gathering. During the 1860s, German gymnastics clubs (*Turnvereine*) were formed in cities as dispersed as Paris, London, Manchester, Budapest, Bucharest, Verona, Stockholm, Moscow, Constantinople, Rio de Janeiro, and Melbourne; some of these were represented at a *Turnfest* in Frankfurt.[145] The appearance of Coubertin's festival inspired in Volkish gymnasts the same racist objections expressed by Astley and Maurras: "The real Olympic Games were national to the core, and that was their glory; the international Olympics are rotten to the core. Don't talk to us about the brotherhood of man and those false notions about humanity. The brotherhood of man can be achieved only on the basis of economic agreements. Nationalities cannot be talked out of existence, and they cannot be mixed together" (1910).[146] As early as 1896, the year of the Athens Games, the DT had declared that any German who promoted or attended Coubertin's Olympiad would be excluded from the *Volk*.[147] Globalism, it seems, was fine on the condition that it expressed racial unity.

The Volkish critique of sport addresses both the inferiority of sport as a physical culture and the undesirability of associated cultural phenomena which are peripheral to sport but of significance for the aesthetics of the public sphere.

The first category includes objections to the performance principle, the introduction of technical improvements, "record mania," undue emphasis on the quantitative measurement of performance, and "unaesthetic" contortions.[148] Men, the DT organ stated in 1884, should not be trained like racehorses or "to the point of insanity." There are objections to specialization (the "refined onesidedness of sport"), to "the onesidedness and uniformity of the movements sport requires," to treating the body as a machine, and even to "the hypnotic effect of competition" (1914). As late as 1930 one author refers to "the record epidemic," "medicalization," and "pedagogicalization" as the three major threats to physical culture.[149]

Of more general historical interest are the contemporary interpretations of sport as a cultural malady affecting the public sphere as a whole. There is Volkish disdain for the sportsmen's outfits: brightly colored or striped tight pants, striped jerseys and shorts,[150] which some considered "dishonorable" and all too reminiscent of "circus clowns." (The possibility of the degeneration of sport into a form of circus or carnival is a standard, culturally conservative theme which recurs in Coubertin,[151] the French neo-fascists,[152] and Avery Brundage.) Sport brings in its wake flashy placards, overblown press coverage, tumultuous ovations, and costly prizes.[153] Aesthetic tradition is discarded,[154] an invidious individualism is promoted at the expense of the community,[155] publicity and advertising assume a role which calls into question the integrity of what they are promoting.[156] And there is the Volkish criticism of the notion, embraced by certain journalists, that athletic performance is an index of national character.[157]

It should be emphasized that this cultural opposition came from both sides of the political spectrum, as Henning Eichberg has pointed out in an important essay titled "Thing-, Fest- und Weihespiele in Nationalsozialismus, Arbeiterkultur und Olympismus." As Eichberg has shown, Volkish influence extended into the ranks of the social democratic Workers' Gymnastics League (ATB), founded in 1893. Here, too, there is principled opposition to sheer performance, to the egotism inherent in record mania and the cult of the star, to unaesthetic dress and movements, to the loss of the communal solidarity implicit in the idea of Turnen, to novel medical dangers.[158]

This is not to say, however, that the conservatives of the DT and the social democrats of the ATB were ideologically indistinguishable. On the contrary, Volkish hostility toward the urban proletariat, the persecution of the socialist movement by the Prussian authorities, and radically different attitudes toward internationalism made political unanimity impossible. What is more, the Volkish doctrine of the DT and the socialist physical culture of the ATB would, by the 1920s, eventually develop into antagonistic ideologies: Nazi sport doctrine and workers' sport doctrine, respectively. It is all the more interesting, therefore, to note virtually identical antimodernistic attitudes in both camps. As we shall see in the next section, this coincidence of ideological opposites points to a radical anti-modernism which seems to lack ideological specificity.

(2) The Nazi Phase

The Nazi critique of sport represents a more political, more racial, and more militarized version of the Volkish program. In addition, it takes Volkish doubts about the value of reason and turns them into a coarse (and anti-Semitic) anti-intellectualism which glorifies the body over "cold intellect." A physically healthy person, Hitler says in *Mein Kampf*, is always to be preferred to a brainy weakling.[159]

Like the Volkish doctrinaires, the Nazis consider modern sport subversive to the community and its authority. The Nazis prefer "the political education of the body" to the abstract individualism of the performance principle and "the political life of the community" to the "limited tasks" of the sportsman. To the record-setter they oppose the soldier who defends the community, and to the shot-putter they oppose the grenade-thrower. The "bourgeois" ideal of "unpolitical sport" is dismissed as an illusion.[160]

Like the Italian fascists, the Nazis equate internationalist sentiments with weakness and effeminacy, and the special enemy in this regard is the Jew. The Jews' ambition, says the sport propagandist Bruno Malitz, is to feminize the German male by turning him toward pacifism and internationalism, substituting the innocuous contests of athletes for the struggles of warriors.[161]

The Nazi critique of Olympia comprises two doctrinal stages whose transitional phase is not particularly well defined. On March 16, 1933, Hitler met with Theodor Lewald, the chairman of the German Olympic Organizing Committee, and with Joseph Goebbels, who recognized a propaganda opportunity when he saw one.[162] Hitler had in 1932 already given an unofficial indication of his interest in the 1936 Olympiad (awarded to the Weimar government in 1930); in the 1933 meeting he confirmed that interest.[163] (As Arnd Krüger has pointed out, so long as the Nazis were an opposition party, it was hardly advantageous to promote an Olympiad that would surely add to the prestige of their democratic opponents.)[164] After this meeting, during which Lewald applied his powers of persuasion to an already receptive *Führer*, the 1936 Olympiad took on the character of a national mission.[165]

It must be emphasized, however, that while Hitler's decision did initiate a new policy, this was not a clear transition between the two phases of Nazi Olympic doctrine, the first being hostility to the "Olympic idea," and the second a qualified (and hypocritical) endorsement. The boundary between these two phases is blurred simply because even Hitler's endorsement of the Games could not stifle Volkish resentment directed against them.

Hostility to internationalism in the sphere of physical culture goes back to the earliest days of the National Socialist movement. In 1923, Alfred Rosenberg, then editor of the Nazi party organ *Völkischer Beobachter*, demanded of the *Turner* the "total rejection of the internationalist idea."[166] In 1928, Rosenberg called the Olympic Games a crime because of their international character.[167]

In 1929, the *Völkischer Beobachter* declared that, due to her "pride," Germany would stay away from international sporting competitions until she regained her rightful place in the world.[168] This rhetorical strategem appears again in a text published by Bruno Malitz in 1933. His point is that, despite liberal rhetoric that sport served the "reconciliation of the peoples of the world," Germany was still subject to the "paragraphs of shame" contained in the Versailles Treaty; the international victories of German athletes had not managed to suspend these scandalous provisions.[169]

During the winter semester of 1932/33, a group of German students warned of the "noisy Olympic preparations of clever business circles," proposing instead "genuinely national tasks."[170] In January 1933, only two months before Hitler's decisive conference with Lewald, university personnel associated with the Physical Culture Office (AfL) passed an "Anti-Olympia Resolution." And a radical student association, responding to a call for a Volkish conception of sport, formed a "struggle group" against the Games.[171]

Like the French neo-fascists, the Nazis were deeply offended by sporting contacts with "primitive" races, and particularly by contact with Negro athletes. In 1932, the *Völkischer Beobachter* published the following commentary: "Negroes have no place at an Olympiad . . . unfortunately, one finds today that the free man must often compete against unfree blacks, against Negroes, for the victory wreath. This is an unparalleled disgrace and degradation, and the ancient Greeks would turn in their graves if they knew what modern men have made out of their holy National Games . . . The next Olympic Games will take place in 1936 in Berlin. Hopefully, the men who are responsible in this regard will know what their duty is. The blacks must be excluded. We expect nothing less."[172]

Such an exclusion was, of course, out of the question, since it would have violated Hitler's agreement with the IOC, which had extracted certain promises of good behavior. And there was certainly no support for the idea in modern Olympic tradition. In a 1912 essay, Coubertin had noted that some European colonialists feared the consequences of a victory by "the dominated race" over the "dominating race" on the grounds that it might engender rebellious notions in black heads. On the contrary, says Coubertin, such contacts—as British practice in India had demonstrated—were in fact "a vigorous instrument of discipline" and should be encouraged.[173] Diem, too, took an unalarmed view. Writing in 1941, he noted that among those who oppose the global character of the Games, "there are many who, consciously or unconsciously, believe that their race should avoid engaging in physical competition with more primitive races." On the contrary, says Diem, the "masterful position of the superior race" will last only as long as Europe is willing to compete against the best bodies the world has to offer.[174]

Hitler, of course, took a less liberal view of the matter, as his much publicized pique at the successes of Jesse Owens in 1936 indicated. According to Albert Speer, this annoyance was quite real. But in a conversation with Speer during the Games, Hitler also showed he was capable of taking the long view on the racial issue: "People whose antecedents came from the jungle were primitive," Hitler said with a shrug; "their physiques were stronger than those of civilized whites. They represented unfair competition and hence must be excluded from future games."[175]

The decision of March 16, 1933, was, of course, a betrayal of the Volkish position on international sport contacts. On the other hand, an Olympiad represented a unique propaganda opportunity, as well as a chance for Hitler to indulge his architectural fantasies on a monumental scale.[176] As a result, certain ideological adjustments become evident in Volkish pronouncements. In May 1933, for example, "Turnführer" Leistritz concedes the possibility of Olympic Games on a "national basis," although not without adding a grudging motto: "A proud and withdrawn Germany will be obligated to watch the Olympic Games of 1936."[177]

A more upbeat rationale for participation appears in the first set of guidelines for Olympic propaganda issued in October 1934: "One of the fundamental principles of National Socialism is that the new German carries out the schooling of the body, the soul, and the spirit in the same manner. In this sense the Olympic idea is a cultural requirement of National Socialism which concerns the entire German people."[178] The same attempt to combine the Olympic idea and Volkish norms appears as late as 1936: "The present form of the Olympic Games is only conditionally acceptable to

National Socialist pedagogy, for it is shaped and propagated by a spirit which derives from the world conquered by the revolutionary breakthrough of National Socialism."[179]

· These were attempts to adapt the Volkish line to political necessity, but not all Volkish opinion chose to adapt. In 1934, the only Nazi sport philosopher of note, the Nietzsche specialist Prof. Alfred Baeumler, complained that: "To the practical internationalism of the Olympic Games there corresponds an inner internationalism: here as elsewhere, neutrality is just the word for a concealed political position on the path of least resistance . . . "

In 1937, a year after the Berlin Olympiad, Baeumler called the "Olympic idea" the "crowning development of the abstract idea of performance"—an unambiguous insult, since "from the abstract performance principle and its individualism there is a line that runs straight to internationalism."[180] One is as bad as the other. A year later, at a meeting of the Office of Physical Training, there was resistance to "sporting competitions held in accordance with international rules and norms."[181] The Volkish norms had refused to give up the struggle.

But the Volkish doctrine could not win, either, and to understand why takes us to the core of Nazism itself. Volkish ideology had been the cultural soil in which Nazi doctrine was cultivated. But at a crucial point, the Nazis' commitment to the building of an industrialized, technological, militarized state required them to sever certain ideological ties to the Volkish cultural conservatives. For example, as George Mosse points out,

> the rejection of modernity was characteristic of Volkish thought. However, recent research has begun to emphasize the connection between Volkish ideas and technology. The Nazis made use of the most up-to-date technology in all fields, from transport to propaganda. Here we must distinguish between natural sciences and technology. National Socialists rejected the latest developments in physics as "Jewish," but their program "Beauty of Labor" modernized the work place. Preindustrial forms were often applied to the industrial process as successful modernization: Volkish art, clear and simple architectural design, fresh air, lawns, and trees were to transform working conditions. . . .[182]

Such examples illustrate the problematic status of technology and the struggle between modernism (the Nazis) and anti-modernism (the conservative Volkish types). In the compromise that resulted, efficiency and anti-Semitism coexisted as equals, and a common enemy (the Jewish mind) was suppressed.

The Olympic issue, however, offered no comparable solution, since it was a contradiction to try to nationalize an international festival. The Volkish rhetoric we have heard argues, in effect, for a re-hellenizing of the Olympic idea under Nazi auspices, with racial purity emerging intact.

Sport lent itself much better to compromise because the internationalist issue could be excluded. Modern sport offered a visible dynamism of movement and force that expressed well the narcissistic and aggressive elements of the Nazi ethos. One example of sport's irresistible appeal in this regard is provided by Edmund Neuendorff, a longtime official of the DT who, in 1933, as its *Führer*, presided over the integration of the DT into the Nazi order.

In 1932, in the course of a meditation on his own world-view (composed in the third person), Neuendorff spoke of "the hardness of our age, which is everywhere pressing for high performance (*Leistung*)."[183] An unvolkish thought from a Volkish head, but hardly inconsistent with Hitler's values. As Hajo Bernett points out, the performance principle could be incorporated into National Socialist ideology by evoking "the warrior-like training of the will."[184]

A second example of the split between Hitler and the Volkish conservatives concerned boxing, which happened to be Hitler's favorite sport. (As early as 1921, Hitler had planned a "Boxing and Storm Troop" to terrify his political opponents.[185]) Whereas the Volkish types spurned boxing as both foreign and unaesthetic, Hitler embraced its symbolic message of sheer domination and could not fathom the squeamish objections of "educated types."[186] In this sense, as Henning Eichberg notes, boxing is an excellent example of a specifically modern sport form.

106 Even before Hitler's Olympic decision, boxing (and, therefore, modernity) had already achieved an important breakthrough within the National Socialist establishment. Ludwig Haymann, a former German heavyweight champion, had been hired by the paramilitary SA in 1921 to create a street commando spearheaded by boxers. In 1932 Haymann was named sports editor of the *Völkischer Beobachter,* and from this point on sport was no longer an officially "*unvölkisch*" physical culture.[187] When Hitler noted (in 1938) that National Socialism had built "sport arenas" rather than "cultic groves,"[188] he was dissociating the Nazi movement from its cultically inclined Volkish forebears and promoting a specifically modern cult of the body. Sport, like technology, was the wave of the future.

4. The Neo-Marxist Critique of Olympia

a. Pre-Modern Marxist Anti-Olympism

The fascist critique of Olympia is unified by its racist core. Hitler's apparent about-face was simply a tactical maneuver; as he eventually revealed to Albert Speer, the Olympic Games of the future would reintroduce the principle of racial exclusivity.

We cannot speak of a Marxist critique of comparable unity. For one thing, the Marxist-Leninist (i.e., Soviet bloc) position regarding the Olympic movement underwent a genuine reversal in 1951, when Stalin elected to apply for Soviet membership. Soviet successes at the 1952 Helsinki Games strengthened a resolve which has seldom wavered. The pre-modern Soviet position, however, had been one of strict disapproval, arguing that the Olympic Games aimed "to deflect the workers from the class struggle while training them for new imperialist wars."[189] "Over a considerable period of time," two Soviet authors wrote in 1981, "the Olympic movement developed in the context of capitalist society. Therefore, it bore the imprint of class contradictions, class and racial oppression and social inequality. The leaders who determined IOC policy indulged in talk about their independence and actually isolated the Committee from the world of sport."[190]

Soviet participation in the 1952 Games, itself a harbinger of the policy of "peaceful coexistence,"[191] brought to the Olympic movement "an absolutely new character."[192] "The idea behind the Olympic Games," *Sovietski Sport* stated on April 16, 1955, "is a wonderful one. It cannot but help attract youth with its purity, striving for peace, friendship and cooperation among peoples."[193]

A second obstacle to a unified Marxist position was the bitter feud between the Red Sport International (RSI) and the social democratic Socialist Workers' Sport International (SWSI), until 1927 the Lucerne Sport International (LSI).[194] Between 1921 and 1927, the LSI was continually resisting the RSI's attempts to absorb it, and by 1928 relations between the left's two alternatives to "bourgeois" sport and *its* International, the Olympic movement, had completely broken down. An RSI delegation was not permitted to take part in the first workers' Olympiad, held in Frankfurt in 1925 by the LSI; nor did the leadership of the RSI allow LSI clubs, which had in fact received invitations, to participate in the Moscow Spartakiad of 1928.[195] The "bourgeois International" of Coubertin and his successors was thereby handed an important victory by default.

It is clear that neither the socialist (LSI) nor the communist (RSI) faction objected to sports festivals per se. In fact, they were trying to outbid each other on the same territory. In 1924, the RSI threatened that it "would, if it did not receive an invitation to Frankfurt, plan a world olympiad of all 'proletarian physical culture organizations' for 1926."[196]

The workers' sport activists of the LSI attempted to create a distinctly socialist sport culture and Workers' Olympiads to celebrate it; this necessitated a critique of the "bourgeois" Games. For example, the LSI "planned to avoid the quest for records and the idolization of individual athletes that pervaded the bourgeois Olympics."[197] Fritz Wildung, the leader of the German Central Commission for Workers' Sport and Physical Culture and a member of the International Bureau of the LSI,[198] faulted Coubertin's Olympiads as unworthy of their ancient model. "As was once the case at Olympia, this event must express a great cultural idea with solemn splendor." In the modern world, this idea "can only be that of international socialism."[199] (It is interesting that neither the LSI's Frankfurt Olympiad of 1925 nor the Moscow Spartakiad of 1928 had met Wildung's standards; his hopes in 1929 rested with the Vienna Workers' Olympiad of 1931.) In his *Sport and Workers' Sport* (1931), Helmut Wagner distinguishes the workers' Olympiads from their "bourgeois counterparts" by noting that the former, unlike the latter, "are based on genuine international solidarity, not on national pride . . ."[200]

The LSI attempt to bring forth an ideologically distinct (and purified) sport culture is an interesting study in the relationship between political ideology and culture. As an example let us take the Frankfurt Olympiad of 1925.

> Through opening ceremonies overflowing with red flags, mass free exercises in which hundreds of participants engaged in simultaneous coordinated movements, the mass pyramids with which the festival ended and the Weihespiel 'Kampf um die Erde' (Struggle for the World), a powerful dramatic presentation using large speaking and acting choruses that portrayed sport as the source of strength for the creation of a new world, the olympiad demonstrated proletarian solidarity and brotherhood.[201]

As formal exercises, these ceremonies would appear to be similar to their "bourgeois" counterparts. But the official publication of the Frankfurt *Arbeiterolympiade* insists upon a crucial distinction: "Not festival games [*Festspiel*], but devotional games [*Weihespiel*]! For they break with the dreary bourgeois festivalizing [*Festspielmacherei*] which works with pathetic rhymes and byzantine phrases. With that sort of thing our Olympic Games have nothing in common. They are the first deliberate attempt at modern games which speak to the masses in the enormity of open space."[202] Such subtleties leave ceremonial virtue very much in the eye of the beholder, who may or may not detect the proper spirit behind the festivities.

As the sport historian Henning Eichberg has pointed out, the workers' Olympiads made an important contribution to "the cultic exaltation of sport: an opening ceremony as the nations marched in, the lighting of the flame, the oath of the athletes standing behind their red flags, the solemn vow of one speaker in the name of all the athletes to serve workers' sport and the socialist workers' movement as a whole, followed by an entire series of devotional actions."[203] Eichberg notes that the ceremonial style of the Frankfurt (1925) and Vienna (1931) workers' Olympiads actually pointed the way toward the Nazi Olympiad of 1936.

When the "bourgeois" Olympic Games came to Paris in 1924, L'Humanité, the newspaper of the French Communist Party (PCF), devoted considerable space to a hostile, and sometimes waspish, critique. Like the German socialists active in the workers' sport movement, the PCF could point to an alternative, and allegedly superior, sport culture of its own, in this case the Labor Sport Federation (FST), whose convocations constituted a "dual festival of Muscle and revolutionary Thought."[204]

For the PCF, bourgeois sport was tainted at its source. "There can be no such thing as honest sport under a capitalist regime,"[205] because the "inherent genius" of capitalism is "to exploit in the most sordid fashion every innocent human activity."[206] The communists maintained that a "loyal and unselfish sporting spirit"[207] is violated by a bourgeois Olympiad. Commercialism, chauvinism, and political opportunism all play noxious roles. "At Colombes," said one headline, referring to the Olympic stadium, "the boutiques are growing like mushrooms,"[208] and profiteers were supposedly everywhere.

In addition, the IOC (of which Coubertin was still president) had excluded Germany from participation in the 1924 Games, thereby expressing a narrow-minded revanchism to which the PCF contrasted its own "intransigent internationalism."[209] "The profiteers who organized the great Olympic festival at Colombes have deliberately turned away from their stadium both the Germans and the Russians. . . .[210] We communists, 'without a country and poor Frenchmen to boot', do not have the same scruples."[211]

What sport-conscious French communists cherished was a "splendid dream of the future: Olympic Games in a proletarian universe, the global festival of virile health and nobility, the athletes' fraternal struggles, the stadium situated between fields and factories, the immense stadium from which hirelings, clients, and profiteers will be banished."[212] Such a festival would never subject socialist athletes to the sort of "odious Olympic cross country race" that in 1924 reduced the runners—with the exception of Paavo Nurmi—to "human rags."[213]

The PCF eventually changed its position on the Olympic movement in order to follow the Soviet line. While continuing to denounce "mercantilism" and "chauvinism," it now called the Olympic Games a "living demonstration of the possibilities of peaceful coexistence in our era and of the rejection of racial discrimination."[214]

More striking, however, is the similarity of the PCF critique of 1924 to that of the French neo-fascists. Both are scathingly anti-capitalist and both take aim at the aesthetic consequences of commercialism. L'Humanité uses terms like fiasco, bluff, and farce[215] to describe the overall effect of the Games, and goes so far as to criticize the unsightliness of the stadium roofs, which had been erected over stands "which will seat the rich, who pay well because they are afraid of the sun and the rain" ("what ignoble laws is the capitalist regime not willing to impose upon architecture!").[216]

The pre-modern communist and postwar neo-fascist critiques are not, of course, identical. The PCF would never permit its organ to compare a stadium crowd to "guano birds perched on the ledges of their island."[217] Nevertheless, the PCF's sarcastic observations about failed Olympic aesthetics point to the transideological critique of the Olympic Games discussed at the end of this section.

b. The Neo-Marxist Critique of Olympia

The unity of the Marxist critique of Olympia has been precluded, as we have seen, by the Soviet reversal of 1951 and by the political feuding between European socialist and communist sportsmen during the 1920s. To these obstacles one could add the profound differences which separated Stalinist sport, which remains essentially intact in the USSR, from its Maoist counterpart. The latter has undergone considerable decay since Mao's death in 1976 and has now yielded to the highly competitive ethos it once spurned.

Today Marxist sport doctrine is divided between the Marxist-Leninist camp, i.e., the Soviet bloc, and the neo-Marxist sport critics who emerged at the end of the 1960s in conjunction with the student revolts in France and West Germany. Despite differences of tone and emphasis rooted in their distinct intellectual traditions, the French and German sport radicals subscribe to a single, unified theory of sport.[218]

The neo-Marxists attack the global culture of high-performance sport, regarded correctly as a uniform athleticism that has triumphed over non-competitive and unmeasurable forms of physical culture. The Olympic Games, in turn, are the principal showcase for this sport culture, which properly belongs, not to the East or to the West, but to the rationalized world of technology. The technophobia of the neo-Marxist doctrine indicates that it represents only the latest development of a traditional anti-modern critique of sport.

"Only sport," a West German sport radical wrote in 1972, "moves the masses in a really massive way. In whose interest does it move them?"[219] One answer, proposed the same year by a French colleague, was that sport had become "State sport,"[220] regardless of official ideology. The neo-Marxists attack both the "bourgeois" sport of the West and the "neo-Stalinist" or "cybernetic" sport of the East, which celebrates the ethos of competition and measured effort at the Olympic Games. Their critique of Olympic sport can be briefly, and inadequately, summarized as five theses:

1. Sport has ceased to be a genuine alternative to work and has become instead its structural analogue or even, as in intensive training, its equivalent. "The principle of specialization is an integral part of modern sports and is symptomatic of the problem. Specialization has gone so far that the top-level athlete now needs vacations—from sports."[221] A corollary of this thesis is that sport is the modern—and degenerate—form of the primal play-impulse; or, as Ulrike Prokop puts it, "that form of play which has been deformed by capitalism."[222]

2. Like the labor regime it has come to approximate, sport adheres to a performance principle that combines competition and performance quotas, which must be met over and over again. Sport is "the systematic perversion of the agonal [striving] play-instinct by competition";[223] sportive performances are turned into commodities.[224]

3. Sport is an effective instrument of social control, an "ideological apparatus" whose bureaucracy (and leading personalities) are at the disposal of the state.[225] It is "the poetry of hierarchy,"[226] "order" itself.[227] On the one hand, it is (repressively) depoliticizing;[228] on the other, it is directly politicizing in that it inculcates "bourgeois

values (individualism, aggressiveness, virility, the myth of the superman, phallocracy, the cult of the strong man, the myth of continuous progress, the promotion of competition, of industrial efficiency, sado-masochism, etc.) . . ."[229]

4. Participation in high-performance sport requires a high degree of emotional repression and, therefore, self-alienation. Typical of this syndrome are asceticism,[230] the censoring of imagination and spontaneity,[231] and masochism.[232] The neo-Marxists also identify sport with anti-intellectual tendencies.[233]

5. The "star syndrome," which makes idols out of champion sportsmen, is comparable to the relationship between a dictator and the masses.[234] This phenomenon is exploited both by "bourgeois" and by Marxist-Leninist doctrinaires. "Champions," a PCF publication stated in 1969, "are the pilots of the human species."[235]

The neo-Marxist critique of the Olympic movement is aimed at the high-performance athlete as a human type and at the Olympic festival itself, which is denounced as a counterfeit celebration of global reconciliation. "The Olympic ideology is universally accepted as the common property of humanity. 'Sport is democratic and international by nature and by vocation.' Coubertin's Olympic idea has thus become the transcendental ideal of all sporting peoples."[236] Conservative opposition to Olympic internationalism was overcome after the turn of the century, according to this view, by expansionist ambitions that ultimately took the form of imperialism.[237]

The first, and still the most detailed, neo-Marxist analysis is Ulrike Prokop's *Sociology of the Olympic Games: Sport and Capitalism* (1971), praised by a French sympathizer as a work which demonstrates "the positivist (Comtean) origins of the baron Pierre de Coubertin's philosophy of social imperialism."[238] For reasons which are not immediately evident from Coubertin's intellectual biography, Prokop puts him in the debt of August Comte (1798-1857), the utopian sociologist whose ideas Marx had once referred to as "this Positivist muck."[239] Both Coubertin and Comte were defenders of social stability and the principle of hierarchy.[240] Such general similarities, however, do not conceal the rather arbitrary choice of Comte as Coubertin's ideological mentor. As we have seen, Coubertin's exemplary career as a Third Republic bourgeois establishmentarian does not require a Comtean lineage. In addition, it should be noted that whereas Comte tended to be a dreamer and a fanatic, Coubertin's utopianism was far more pragmatic and could benefit from diplomatic skills Comte never possessed. Nor does Coubertin deserve to be identified with Comte's indiscriminate authoritarianism. More sensitively attuned to the requirements of social equilibrium in the modern world, Coubertin was more discriminating about political leadership than was Comte.[241]

Prokop annexes Comte and Coubertin as forerunners of totalitarian social engineering. Her basic thesis is that Olympic sport, in its theatricality, "offers a graphic symbolic system suggesting that the System is capable of resolving existing problems in a technically effective way."[242]

There is indeed much evidence to suggest a compatibility between modern sport and certain totalitarian goals. The problem is that Prokop interprets Coubertin's actions and motives too retrospectively, as though he were a modern rather than the pre-modern he actually was. As a result, Coubertin's establishmentarianism and moderation are presented as if they had issued from a conspiracy rather than from the process of history. These retrospective strictures express the indignation of the Marxist observer who is continually discovering that it is the bourgeois who control their own domain.

c. The Radical Critique of Olympia

The evidence presented above suggests that the most hostile critiques of the Olympic phenomenon are rooted in a radicalism which transcends ideology. For Olympic visionaries, these festivals represent a form of radical therapy. But for the fiercer critics, the Games are a radical hoax, not merely because they offer a counterfeit peace, but because they exalt a technological human type. The radical critic, whether of the left or of the right, interprets the Olympic movement as the conspiracy of a global center and its monopolizing of world sport. Politically, this center represents an unholy alliance of the liberal democracies of the West with the police states of the East; aesthetically, it represents the mediocrity of mass culture masquerading as style.

It is interesting to note that the French Communist Party has found the transideological dimension of the neo-Marxist critique both obvious and scandalous. In 1972 the French ultra-leftist sport critics were delighted to reprint the following PCF attack (among others) on their own doctrine: "One finds again the old reactionary idea of a culture of the body, of free, spontaneous, natural enjoyment, a sort of cult of the *élan vital* and of that instinct already glorified by Bergson which finds apparent scientific justification through appeals to Freud and the fashionable thinker Marcuse . . ."[243] In fact, the PCF is correct when it asserts that an interest in the body has usually been found on the political right. But its disapproval of "free, spontaneous, natural enjoyment" helps to explain why the French radicals of the May-June 1968 uprising spurned the PCF as one more Establishment interest group. Marxist-Leninist asceticism had no authority among the New Leftists.

Most observers have failed to note the similarities between the cultural conservative critique, in its pre-modern (Volkish) and modern (neo-fascist) variants, and the modern (neo-Marxist) analysis. To these variants may be added the PCF critique of 1924 which, even prior to the Stalinization of the Party, sounds more like the postwar neo-fascist critique than that of the neo-Marxists.[244]

The common attitude that runs through the Volkish, early PCF, neo-fascist, and neo-Marxist critique, is anti-modernism. This anti-modernism comprises four major areas of concern: aesthetics, authenticity, technology, and the human image.

1. For the Volkish critics of sport, aesthetic value was seen in their own (gymnastic) tradition rather than in the new doctrine of utility and measured performance, new sartorial standards, and unseemly forms of publicity such as placards and sensational journalism.[245] In 1924 *L'Humanité* comments derisively on an "absence of aesthetic sensibility" and notes with amazement that the bourgeois organizers of the Games had assumed they could bring to life the ambiance of the ancient Olympic festival "amidst smoking factory chimneys and metal structures."[246] As we have seen, the French neo-fascists took up the same theme, claiming that only the Nazis could approach the Greeks. They, too, speak of an "absence of style," of "trivialization," of the failure of ceremonial aesthetics.[247]

The anti-urban aesthetics of the Volkish thinkers appear as late as 1933 in the following prophecy: "Gradually, then, the symbols of our asphalt culture which have penetrated physical culture will disappear: the cement stadium, the cinder track, the measuring tape, the stopwatch, well-tended lawns, and running shoes which have served to intensify the pursuit of 'sheer performance'. In their place will be the simple meadow, untrammeled nature."[248] It would be difficult to formulate a less accurate vision of sport's destiny in the modern world. Nevertheless, this happy daydream registers an important aesthetic discontent with the evolution of modern sport. The aesthetic critique addresses both the practice of sport and the Olympic stage on which it is presented.

2. Related to aesthetic norms is the charge of phoniness or inauthenticity. In 1886 a Volkish commentator called sport "a fashionable distortion of true gymnastics,"[249] the implication being that it lacks substance and integrity. More often this kind of disapproval has been directed against the Olympic Games. "Ceremony without grandeur, purely theatrical, at times even ridiculous," L'Humanité commented in 1924.[250]

For the neo-fascists, modern sport itself is "spectacle, false theater, circus, or any other name you want to give it."[251] The Tokyo Olympiad of 1964 had concluded in chaos, punctuated by revolting "buffooneries";[252] the Munich Games of 1972 had amounted to no more than "titanic disorder."[253] L'Humanité took pleasure in reporting the derisive whistling and cries of "fake!" which had greeted the phony Chinese (in reality, a Caucasian) who had been hired to carry the Chinese flag during the opening procession of the 1924 Games; it scorned the use of Negro bootblacks, rounded up at the Gare Saint-Lazare, who had been pressed into service as "Haitians" and "Philippinos."[254] In a similar vein, Maurice Bardèche takes an even fiercer joy in denouncing Olympic athletes who are in fact "phony students, phony sailors, phony peasants who are disguised, travestied, like the phony schoolgirls and phony little ingenues one used to meet at Chabanais."[255]

The resentment of fraud is by no means a monopoly of the political extremes. "It is because of the lack of efficient leadership," the politically moderate Karl Jaspers wrote in his well-known polemic, Man in the Modern Age (1931), "that disintegration, window-dressing, and jiggery-pokery of all kinds are rife; that unsavory bargaining, procrastination, compromise, ill-considered decisions, and humbug are so common."[256] But it is the ideologically motivated critics who are most willing, and sometimes best able, to expose the foundations of cultural institutions. The neo-Marxists are correct to call attention to the *global* character of modern sport and indicate the possibility that the Olympic ideology represents "the hypocritical image of genuine human fraternity."[257] They are correct to point out that sport "is supposed to be an entity transcending history and the class struggle."[258] For them the fraud is not the failure of Olympic ceremony but the claims which are made in the name of "the universal circle of sport."[259]

3. Hostility to the technology of modern sport is a standard part of the radical critique. Volkish opinion condemned the new reign of numbers and its relentless measurement of performance, or the idea that the body was a perfectible machine.[260] Volkish objections (in 1887) to "the onesidedness and uniformity of the movements required by sport"[261] reappear almost a century later as neo-Marxist criticism of specific movements which are "practiced to the point of somnambulistic, habitualized mastery."[262] Eventually, this line of criticism addressed "the programmatic technicity of useful gestures" and the "abstract, mathematical spatio-temporality" in which the athlete's body is enveloped. "The sport robot is being born"[263] in the "sport factory" of East Germany, "this immense *laboratory of sport.*"[264]

4. Many serious observers have interpreted modern sport as a flight *from* the machine or as assimilation *to* the machine. Both possibilities concern what can be called the human image of the athlete. Volkish conservatives found it distasteful (in 1884) that an athlete should be trained "like a racehorse."[265] Both Volkish[266] and

neo-Marxist[267] critics point to the egocentricity of the athlete in search of technical perfection. Both neo-fascist[268] and neo-Marxist[269] observers deplore the physical transformation of athletes into "monsters."

The radical critique of Olympia integrates these four categories into a coherent anti-modern doctrine within which each category contains the others. Aesthetic failure can mean inauthenticity, or artificiality, or the deformation of the human body. Inauthenticity may appear as the consequence of "scientific" expedients which improve performance. The technologizing of sport may offend taste or force athletes to adapt their movements to the impersonal demands of new devices. The athlete's human image may be subverted by his loss of autonomy within a world of equipment and the tyranny of numbers. The trans-ideological nature of the radical critique reflects the revolt against the center (symbolized by the IOC) in which these anti-establishmentarians are engaged. Neo-fascist[270] and neo-Marxist[271] join hands to hail the PLO terror at Munich (1972) as a radical act of exposure, a demythologizing of the counterfeit Olympic peace. This is the paroxysmal moment of the radical critique. Prior to this point, it is essentially an up-to-date cultural conservatism. Here, however, we glimpse a nihilistic core. Is this criticism, or is it the revenge of the excluded?

5. Olympism, Communism, Art and Technology

The Soviet bloc's ardent embrace of the Olympic movement represents more than a shared taste for open-air ritual and the choreography of muscled grace. For behind this shared fascination with the aesthetics of the sportive body there is a basic compatibility between the doctrine implicit in high-performance Olympic sport and Marxist-Leninist ideas about culture and its political function. Olympism and Marxism-Leninism in fact share a conception of culture that truncates and simplifies the life of the mind.

The doctrine of high-performance sport, which is the feature attraction of any Olympiad, and communist doctrine agree on two important points. First, both adhere to a conception of culture which incorporates mass convocations, ceremonial aesthetics, a doctrine of optimism, and a "humanism" which offers the prospect of global harmony. Both find in sport an ideal culture which is accorded the status of art. Second, high-performance Olympic sport and communism are ideologies of sheer performance, of technique in the comprehensive sense suggested by the French social philosopher Jacques Ellul.[272] Both ideologies find the fulfillment of human existence in the attaining of technical norms and in the adaptation of human beings to technology.

a. The Sport-Art Synthesis

Sport is the one form of culture that is wholly compatible with the ideological requirements of those Marxist-Leninist bureaucrats whose task it is to preserve cultural orthodoxy within the Soviet bloc. One of the basic features of Marxism-Leninism is an interest in reducing all culture to the level of sport culture, which is devoid of irony, intolerant of ambiguity, easy to judge, and as transparently pedagogical as one wishes to make it. As a form of culture, the sportive performance exhibits the simple and truncated ambitions of Socialist Realism, the official aesthetic of Marxist-Leninist societies.

Addressing a world congress of sport scholars held in Moscow in 1974, the East German Olympic champion Margitta Gummel offered the following excursus on Marxist aesthetics:

> Today, and to an ever increasing degree, sport is related to the concept of beauty. Here I am interpreting the category of the beautiful in its Marxist sense, that is, in the unity of aesthetics, purpose, meaning, and social significance. That is where I stand, and in the course of my career in sport I have become ever more convinced that the person who strives for a meaningful goal is also, in her exertions, beautiful. For example, ideas about female beauty, which were long based upon the ideal of the Venus de Milo, have changed under current conditions and will continue to change. A woman's beauty is revealed in the totality of her personality.[273]

We can disregard the fact that this statement represents a veiled word on behalf of the virilized female champions of the East. The more important point is that its merging of sport and aesthetics is substantiated by official ideologists. In 1959 the daily newspaper of the East German Socialist Unity Party proclaimed the appearance of "a new type of art, in which sport, gymnastics and acrobatics, dance, movement, music, chorus, color, and the plastic and performing arts combine. This new 'total art work' contains great creative possibilities."[274] Writing in 1964 in the most important philosophical journal of the German Democratic Republic, one author states: "In sportive movement the boundaries of art have been reached and surpassed." Marxist aesthetics, he says, must extend the aesthetic appreciation of human movement from the realm of dance into that of sport.[275] In 1980 the authoritative physical culture journal of the GDR reported that, since the early 1970s, sport colleges in the Soviet Union had been waging a campaign to suffuse the world of sport with "aesthetic principles."[276] "Under the conditions offered by genuine socialism, sport and art are permanently conjoined," since both "are areas of human activity and social phenomena in which man expresses himself as a social being, and both have a class character." Artists with reservations about high-performance sport should make an effort to lose their prejudices by acquiring some first-hand knowledge of the subject.[277]

The fusion of sport and art is also endorsed by Andrzej Wohl, a Polish sport sociologist who is the East bloc sport doctrinaire best known to Western readers in the field. In his *Social-Historical Foundations of Bourgeois Sport* (1973), Wohl ascribes to sport "cultural functions such as emotion and entertainment." Movement replaces language, and the result is an appeal that "by virtue of its immediacy and simplicity captivates people regardless of their intellectual, educational, or cultural level." At the same time, Wohl is aware of possible objections. "The simplicity of the sportive performance is not, however, synonymous with poverty of expression, emotion, or content." Indeed, he says, sport is comparable to theater, and Polish drama critics might well envy the expertise with which teenaged soccer fans analyze the styles of their favorite players.[278]

The Soviet sport philosopher Nikolai Ponomaryov observes, but does not condemn, the simplicity of sport. "Sport spectacles," he writes, "are distinguished by the visual and obvious nature of what is happening: everything is being decided before the eyes of the spectators . . . Of course, the ease and unforced nature of movement which the spectators admire is obtained only by great efforts, sometimes even in conditions of conflict."[279]

Unlike Wohl, Ponomaryov does not flirt with the idea that sport is comparable to art. "In our opinion," he states, "there are no good reasons for identifying sport and art . . . Sport lacks an artistic image, since sports phenomena consist of life itself." But he does not disavow what he calls "the so-called psycho-hygienic function of art":

> Nowadays, as a result of scientific and technological progress and its associated urbanization and the increasing flow of diverse information, the human psyche is experiencing enormous nervous overloading. There arises the need to remove some of the pressures. Art transfers people into a special world of relationships and experiences, it distracts them, concentrates attention on new objects, switches psychic activity, creates an outlet and removes pressures. Thus, aesthetic development is also related to spiritual as well as physical health. Undoubtedly, such a phenomenon is typical of sport as well as a spectacle.[280]

115

Ponomaryov distances himself from the sport-art synthesis by keeping the sport-art analogy as vague as possible. Apparently, ideological constraints require a presentation of the sport-art relationship, even if it is not an entirely favorable one.

As shown in the final section of Chapter 1, there are Olympic officials, too, who adhere to the view "that Sport itself is indeed one of the Fine Arts." Within the Olympic fraternity, this idea goes back to the founder himself. Coubertin's interest in artistic competitions that would complement the athletic contests is well known, and was based on the ancient Greek model and its assumption that the pursuit of excellence is undifferentiated at its source.[281] As John J. MacAloon points out, Coubertin "would make a career drawing fanciful 'ballplayers in the Colosseum' off museum walls, out of art, and into action. Performing anew, they would play new games in new coliseums, to be put up in the center of modern public life. Along the way, they would make of the 'manly arts' an art form, and claim it to be *the* democratic art form."[282]

Coubertin was also concerned about the ambiance that should envelop Olympic sport. Art should transfer to sport a measure of its cultural dignity. After all, amid the "ceremonies and solemnities" of the ancient Greek Games, religion and art had "reigned in perpetuity."[283] A visit to Bayreuth and immersion in its "passionate Wagnerian tones" permitted Coubertin "to contemplate in peace the Olympic horizon." "Music and sport," he adds, "have always been for me the most perfect 'insulators', the most fertile instruments of reflection and vision, powerful stimulants to perseverance and the 'massaging of the will'."[284] For Coubertin, sport and art are twin intoxications whose value resides in their power to transport the willing imagination.

Like his mentor, Diem speculated enthusiastically about the sport-art synthesis, although here, too, his penchant for cautious ambiguity is evident. Coubertin, he notes, had warned against exaggerated hopes in this area.[285] And there is a cautionary touch to Diem's observation that "formal movements are a kind of preliminary exercise like the 'études' of piano instruction."[286]

Diem's rhetorical strategy is to pile up a critical mass of analogies which will take on the appearance of an identity. The flowing movement of a runner, he says, dissolves tensions which, in others, are released by listening to music.[287] Sport and art both belong to "the great domain of human 'play';" both can be pursued to the point of perfection; both possess a "transcendental significance;" both express a "creative will." "The point is to give rise to a genuine art which has somehow been ignited by sportive performance."[238]

This is not to say that Olympic enthusiasts embrace Socialist Realism. There is,

THE CRITIQUE OF OLYMPIA

after all a great difference between making sport spiritually instrumental ("one of the Fine Arts," Coubertin's "most perfect 'insulator' ") and making it politically instrumental in the manner of the Soviets and the East Germans. But the sport culture promoted by the Olympic movement, and its reluctance to tolerate criticism or scepticism, are easily appropriated by the cultural commissars of the East.

Socialist Realism, as one commentator notes, is a prescription for "the total politicalization of art."[289] "Our literature," A.A. Zhdanov wrote in 1934, "is impregnated with enthusiasm and heroism."[290] Socialist Realism is a functional aesthetic which sees art as an inspirational technique. "As the fundamental hero of our books," wrote Maxim Gorky, "we must choose labor, that is, man organized by the labor-process, which is armed here with the full power of technology, man in his turn making labor easier, more productive, raising it to the level of art."[291] The Stalinist concept of labor is entirely compatible with the Stalinist cult of sport. In fact, the point of sport is to serve as an idealized image of labor. They are merely different expressions of a performance principle. From the Soviet point of view, Olympic sport is a hymn to productivity and the willpower which makes it possible. It is no accident that the ideal of the record-breaking Soviet sportsman appeared during the mid-1930s, at the same time as the Stakhanovite super-worker who broke records on the production line.

b. The Sport-Technology Synthesis

In "our time," Nikita Khrushchev said in 1963, "the time of the atom, electronics, cybernetics, automation, and production lines, it is all the more necessary to have harmony, ideal coordination, and organization in all the links of the social system, both in the field of material production and in the sphere of spiritual life."[292] In a world shaped by technology, conformity is taken for granted.

Soviet bloc sport theory is based upon a belief that sport plays an evolutionary role in the development of human motor skills. The basic relationship here joins man and the machine, and Soviet ideology is pointedly optimistic about the combination. Andrzej Wohl's central thesis regarding modern sport holds that its most important function is to facilitate the adaptation of the human organism to the requirements of modern technology. Wohl dreams of "a transformation of the human body, to adapt it to the human world we have created." "We have embarked upon the era of cosmic flight, which has clearly shown how important it is to improve the motor ability of human beings. In this situation improvement of the motor skill of people can no longer remain the private affair of individuals."[293]

It is the cosmonaut who embodies the fusion of athleticism and technology. This idealized figure combines the ethos of sport, the cult of the military, technological optimism, and submission to political authority. During the 1930s, this role was filled by record-setting aviators and arctic explorers whose heroic dimensions were carefully limited by the public homage they paid to Stalin.[294] During the space age, the aviator and the explorer have been combined in the figure of the cosmonaut who flies for the Politburo.

The cosmonaut and the high-performance athlete exemplify "adaptation of the human organism" to novel conditions of stress and the latest "technical achievements."[295] Both experience potentially life-threatening conditions. According to Major E. Ozolin, Merited Master of Sport, during high-level bicycle and ski races "the biochemical indicators of the sportsman's blood reach magnitudes lethal to a man in normal conditions;"[296] and the cosmonaut, too, faces physiological terrors.

Both cosmonaut and athlete rely on medical support teams. The research laboratory of the Central Army Sports Club, according to Major Ozolin, "has formed complex scientific groups of physiologists, biochemists, psychologists and pedagogues."[297] The cosmonaut is usually a military pilot who, like the athlete, possesses a "hardened organism."[298] The athlete, in turn, is probably a member of the Red Army or the KGB.[299] The cosmonaut, like the athlete, sets "world records." The athlete and the military pilot perform for the State. The cosmonaut visits the Lenin mausoleum before and after every flight into space.[300]

The cosmonaut and the "scientific" athlete represent what Soviet ideologists claim is an emerging human type. "The whole life of any man," says Pilot-Cosmonaut A.A. Leonov, is "nothing but psychological training."[301] With this final triumph of functionalism, human life becomes a pure mobilization which makes sense only within a technological and authoritarian order.

"Scientific" sport is not, however, a purely technological enterprise, even if its quantitative improvements are due in part to training machines, computer-assisted kinesthetic studies, applied physiology, the use of videotape, and pharmacological aids. It would be more accurate to say that modern high-performance sport partakes of the spirit of technology.

"Scientific" sport can be understood in terms of Jacques Ellul's concept of technique (Fr. *technique*) as it is elaborated in *The Technological Society*. Technique, says Ellul, is "the *totality of methods rationally arrived at and having absolute efficiency* (for a given stage of development) in *every* field of human activity."[302] Technique is efficient procedure per se, an irresistible and homogenizing force that "has taken over all of man's activities." It "is efficient and brings efficiency to everything," striving for "the mechanization of everything it encounters." "Technique has become autonomous; it has fashioned an omnivorous world which obeys its own laws and which has renounced all tradition." Its "refusal to tolerate moral judgments" is due to the fact that it "has only one principle: efficient ordering."[303] Technique, in short, is a ubiquitous *modus operandi* which has seduced modern civilization.

"In every conceivable way," says Ellul, "sport is an extension of the technical spirit. Its mechanisms reach into the individual's innermost life, working a transformation of his body and its motions as a function of technique and not as a function of some traditional end foreign to technique, as, for example, harmony, joy, or the realization of spiritual good. In sport, as elsewhere, nothing gratuitous is allowed to exist; everything must be useful and must come up to technical expectations."[304]

Ellul's critique of sport in the age of industry and technology is essentially correct; high-performance sport does require the cultivation of method in order to achieve its goal of efficient effort. At times the aping of the industrial process, as in the case of American football, can take on a ludicrous aspect with coaches prowling the sidelines in massive earphones, endless poring over game films, specialization that makes players, in effect, technicians, pseudo-technical chatter about game plans, and so on. But Ellul confuses this infusion of technical trappings with the entirety of sport. Technique, he says, "tends to bring mechanics to bear on all that is spontaneous or irrational."[305] But modern sport, even conceding the scope of its surrender to technique, preserves a sphere in which spontaneity does survive. Still, as Ellul would point out, it is the triumph of technique, not the remnants of spontaneity, that is truly representative of sport's destiny in the technological era.

6. Conclusion: The Defense of Olympia

The defense of the Olympic movement is ultimately the defense of its reconciling possibilities, of the idea that sport is, as Jean Giraudoux put it, "the Esperanto of the races."[306] "To ask the peoples of the world to love one another," Coubertin wrote in 1929, "is merely a form of childishness. To ask them to respect one another is not in the least utopian, but in order to respect one another it is first necessary to know one another."[307]

Avery Brundage's defense of Olympia was less temperate. The Olympic movement, he stated in 1965, is "perhaps the greatest social force in the world." Three years later, and speaking only five days after the Tlatelolco massacre of which he was, in fact, aware, he insisted that "despite the opposition presented by the ambitions of an overwhelmingly materialistic world, the essence of the Olympic ideal maintains its purity as an oasis where correct human relations and concepts of moral order still prevail."[308] Coubertin, too, had worried about the purity of the Games as a unique kind of collective experience. But Brundage's defense of the movement, couched in a rhetoric that borders on hysteria, gives the "oasis" theme a new and almost desperate importance.

To the traditionalists' defense of Olympia must be added its Soviet bloc counterpart, which aims at rescuing the movement from the "bourgeois" establishment which gave it birth. As the *GDR Review* put it in 1976:

> When imperialism's cultural pessimism steadily expands to the field of sports—where it is expressed in prophecies about the end of the Games, an increasing measure of anti-communism as an obbligato to the press reports, and also in direct provocations—this shows clearly that the Olympic idea is not excluded from the influence of the general crisis of capitalism. It is from this fact that the obligation of the socialist countries and all humanist forces in all parts of the world arises to do everything in their power to protect the great ideas of the Olympic Movement from the shortcomings of imperialism.[309]

Such criticism serves ideological requirements without seriously impeding the administration of the Olympic movement as an international institution.

"Coubertin's vision of a world community," John J. MacAloon has pointed out, "was based upon a philosophical anthropology." Its practical principle, " 'true internationalism', understands cultural differences as an enduring and marvelous feature of the human landscape and argues that world peace depends upon a celebration of human diversity and not the eradication of it." Coubertin defines "true internationalism" as "the state of mind of those who love their country above all, who seek to draw to it the friendship of foreigners by professing for the countries of those foreigners an intelligent and enlightened sympathy."[310]

It is a striking fact that Coubertin, who contributed to a journal titled *Cosmopolis*,[311] never refers to the eighteenth-century Enlightenment cosmopolitans, such as Voltaire, who would seem to be his natural precursors. As MacAloon notes, Coubertin's "notion of international harmony was fundamentally rationalistic; war and peace were matters of knowledge and ignorance."[312] But Coubertin's conservatism did not permit an alliance with the Enlightenment rationalists whose internationalistic schemes very closely resemble his own.

There are some striking similarities between eighteenth-century cosmopolitanism and that of the IOC. As Thomas J. Schlereth has shown, "a necessary credential of the eighteenth-century philosophe was that he be a loyal citizen of an *idea* world that knew no inhibiting national boundaries and, hence, also an *ideal* world that knew no inconvenient practical realities." But, like Coubertin and his followers, "these self-acclaimed 'citizens of the world' did not translate their world view into a radical political cosmopolitanism that might have abolished all nation-states as viable political entities." Benjamin Franklin's call for a gathering of "the good and virtuous men of all nations into a regular body," directing what Schlereth terms "a vast laic church," sounds very much like the IOC itself. Furthermore, an internationalist culture should enjoy immunity from the disruptions of war. The spirit of Olympism is certainly alive in two edicts issued by the American Philosophical Society of Philadelphia in 1778: "It shall and may be lawful for the said Society, by their proper officers, at all times, whether in peace or war, to correspond with learned societies, as well as learned men of any nation, or country upon matters merely belonging to the business of the said society." For: "Nations truly civilized (however unhappily at variance on other accounts) will never wage war with the Arts and Sciences and the common Interests of Humanity."[313] The principled hostility of the IOC to boycotts of any kind could not be expressed more succinctly. Whether sport is actually equivalent to "the Arts and Sciences" is a separate question.

The two arguments on behalf of the Olympic movement which can lay claim to intellectual respectability may be termed the *macrophenomenal* and the *microphenomenal* interpretations of the Games. The first approach offers necessarily speculative hypotheses about the capacities of an Olympiad (1) to divert aggressive impulses from the international political arena into nonwarlike forms of sportive competition or (2) to promote mutual tolerance among people who at first confront each other as cultural aliens. Macrophenomenal analysis regards the Olympic movement and its festivals as an enormous (if largely unknown) process which can be thought about in terms of large-scale psycho-social processes. The microphenomenal approach looks in a more detailed and specific way at the cultural exchange that an Olympiad makes possible. It is an adjunct to the macrophenomenal analysis it presupposes.

A well-known example of the macrophenomenal approach appears in the "Avowal of Optimism" with which Konrad Lorenz concludes his famous book *On Aggression* (1963).

> The most important function of sport lies in furnishing a healthy safety valve for that most indispensable and, at the same time, most dangerous form of aggression that I have described as collective militant enthusiasm in the preceding chapter. The Olympic Games are virtually the only occasion when the anthem of one nation can be played without arousing any hostility against another. This is so because the sportsman's dedication to the international social norms of his sport, to the ideals of chivalry and fair play, is equal to any national enthusiasm. The team spirit inherent in all international sport gives scope to a number of truly valuable patterns of social behavior which are essentially motivated by aggression and which, in all probability, evolved under the selection pressure of tribal warfare at the very dawn of culture.[314]

The problem with this sort of theorizing is that it raises more questions than it answers. For example, is there evidence that political leaders have cathartic experiences after watching their athlete-compatriots in international competition? Do the athletes who have cosmopolitan experiences at Olympiads ever assume policy-making roles in their native societies? Might the sight of international competition stimulate more aggressive ambition than it discharges? The critique of these "festivals of humanity" must question the nature, the depth, and the duration of their effects on those who watch or participate in them. If an Olympiad is, as it is sometimes claimed, a kind of pedagogical theater, then what is being taught?

Lorenz did not do the microphenomenal research that might have provided empirical support for his assumptions about the value of sport. "Sporting contests between nations are beneficial not only because they provide an outlet for the collective militant enthusiasm of nations, but also because they have two other effects that counter the danger of war: they promote personal acquaintance between people of different nations or parties and they unite, in enthusiasm for a common cause, people who otherwise would have little in common."[315] A true son of the Enlightenment, Lorenz takes its cosmopolitan premises as self-evident truths which obviate the need for more specific inquiries into the complexities of festivals and the symbolic dramas they offer. Like an eighteenth-century philosophe, Lorenz is looking for the world language on whose behalf Condorcet planned a World Institute of Learning.[316] His strategy is to add sport to the "three great human enterprises, collective in the truest sense of the word, whose ultimate and unconditional value no normal human being can doubt: Art, the pursuit of beauty; Science, the pursuit of truth; and, as an independent third which is neither art nor science, though it makes use of both, Medicine, the attempt to mitigate human suffering." Lorenz assumes that "the sanctity of the Red Cross"[317] has its Olympic analogue.

The West German sociologist Helmut Schelsky shares Lorenz's view that the Red Cross and international associations of scientists, artists, and scholars are proper models for a hypothetical world order. And Schelsky, too, endorses Olympic cosmopolitanism without reservation. But Schelsky's *Peace in Time: The Future of the Olympic Games* (1973), while sharing Lorenz's Enlightenment premises, offers a much more detailed analysis of the Olympic phenomenon. Schelsky does not examine the premises of Lorenz's macrophenomenal theory of the Games' cosmopolitanizing effects. Instead he offers a set of practical suggestions for maximizing the exemplary effects of an Olympiad while minimizing the possibilities for disrupting it. The most remarkable feature of Schelsky's book—remarkable at any rate for an academic—is the degree of personal animus directed against his anti-sportive fellow intellectuals, whose "defamation" of the Olympic movement he regards as both harmful and ignorant.

Schelsky believes that there is an "international psychological equilibrium" which benefits from national sport.[318] But it is not served by utopian notions of world peace. Schelsky steers clear of impractical idealism by distinguishing between a total or integral conception of peace and a limited type of peace which can exist in an isolated setting such as an Olympic festival.

Schelsky proposes a thorough depoliticizing of the Games except in one respect. Denationalization, the removal of national flags and anthems, is not part of his program. Nations cannot be reconciled at an Olympiad if they are not present as meaningful national entities. Cathartic international competition requires self-consciously national contestants.

Schelsky's fundamental principle is a wholly nonpartisan procedure which aims at universalism. Writing just after the 1972 Munich Olympiad, he expresses the hope that the Games will be held in Moscow in 1980. The real winners of the Munich

Games, he says, were the Israelis, whose athletes were murdered, and the Rhodesians who had been excluded; the losers were the Arabs, who took satisfaction in the Israeli casualties, and the black Africans who took satisfaction in excluding the Rhodesians. "Civilized humanity" is absolutely tolerant on the issue of Olympic participation with only two exceptions to the rule: nations at war should be excluded, and national teams which present irresistible targets for terrorists should have the grace to withdraw for the good of the festival. Olympic sites should not be turned into armed camps. (One need only think of the Montreal or Moscow Games to appreciate this point.) The only athletes who should be excluded from the Games are those who are not prepared to abide by their peaceful standards. Schelsky expects of Olympic athletes a kind of apolitical solidarity which should have made a point of censuring, for example, the American athletes whose Black Power demonstrations were the political sensation of the 1968 Games in Mexico City.[319]

Schelsky adheres to Avery Brundage's conception of the Games as an "oasis." This rather idyllic idea of the Olympic festival requires, in turn, a considerable degree of self-restraint on the part of the journalists who cover the Games. Schelsky expects these reporters to avoid polemical or defamatory commentary about other national groups or their athletic representatives. His Olympic program calls, in short, for a kind of gentrification of the public sphere.[320]

As noted earlier, Schelsky saves his harshest commentary for those West European intellectuals whose disapproval of high-performance sport and those who practice it he regards as both ignorant and perverse. The intellectuals, he says, are too insular to appreciate a type of human being who does not conform to the norms of their own non-aggressive, intellectually oriented ideal type. (Schelsky's claim that East-bloc intellectuals, unlike their Western counterparts, appreciate the value of Olympic sport is naive. There is, of course, a group of scholars and journalists in, for example, East Germany who enthusiastically endorse high-performance sport. But it would be a mistake to assume that their views are representative of all East-bloc intellectuals. When the official party newspaper in East Germany calls on artists to emulate athletes, it is not preaching to the already converted.)[321]

Schelsky openly scorns the sort of (neo-Marxist) *Sportkritik* which first appeared in West Germany in 1969[322] and took on a certain modish popularity. This sport criticism is strongly anti-competitive, and Schelsky disapproves of the way it portrays athletes as "inhuman figures" who are taken as symbols of aggressive nationalism or the ruthless ethos of competitive capitalism. The discipline of the athlete, he notes, has its counterpart in the discipline of the artist. And Schelsky offers some invidious comparisons, as well. The showier kinds of public debate in which intellectuals revel are a form of sublimated aggression which is actually less disciplined and rule-bound than sportive competition. Intellectuals, he says, would be in a better position to criticize if their performance could show the sort of progress achieved by the athletic community. It is time, he concludes, that intellectuals stop projecting their own existential problems onto athletes and stop projecting conflicts from the world of ideas into Olympic festivals where they do not belong.[323]

The strengths of Schelsky's analysis lie in its consistency and its iconoclasm. His "oasis" concept is hardly original; Avery Brundage promoted this ideal for many years. But Schelsky's consistency leads him to say things many IOC members probably think in private but dare not say in public. Perhaps the most important example of Schelsky's candor is his proposal that South Africa be re-admitted into the Olympic family, apartheid notwithstanding. His suggestion that certain national contingents will at times present overwhelming security problems, and that this should prompt their withdrawal, would be very controversial if the IOC were to suggest it. But the IOC is not the target of his iconoclasm. Indeed, Schelsky may be thought of as the IOC's idea of its own conscience.[324]

Curiously enough, Schelsky's critique of the intellectuals' disdain for sport and the Olympic ideals may be the most important part of his book. On the one hand, he may be congratulated for pointing out a visceral hostility to sport on the part of many intellectuals that is not defensible on rational grounds. At the same time, however, he seriously underestimates the value of the neo-Marxist critique of sport. He seems to be unaware that the sociology of sport exists as an academic discipline (especially in West Germany), and he overlooks the fact that the modern critique of sport expresses misgivings about modernity itself which date, as we have seen, from before the turn of the century.

Schelsky's pragmatic Olympism is almost identical to the amoral universalism of the IOC, and that is its principal defect. Schelsky assumes that an Olympiad produces mass behavioral effects of a positive character; but he does not choose to examine the possible moral costs of this strategy. It is interesting, for example, that Schelsky's thoughts on a Moscow Olympiad[325] prompt him to imagine, somewhat uncomfortably, a situation which actually came to pass in 1980, namely the forced removal of dissidents (including Andrei Sakharov) from Moscow for the duration of the Games. But he never draws a moral line beyond which his pragmatism is negated by larger events.

In July 1983 the French writer Maurice Druon published a very sceptical commentary on a proposed universal exposition to commemorate the passing of the twentieth century. "The universal exposition," he says, "is an idea which belongs to the last century. It corresponds to the first dazzling stages of the industrial age, to the first achievements of technology, and to the dawn of the era of rapid communications. A universal exposition is based on curiosity, surprise, and wonder."

Druon argues that this type of cosmopolitan spectacle is outdated for two reasons. First, modern technology has surpassed the wildest dreams of Jules Verne and has lost its power to fascinate the masses as it once did. And second, the need for a localized format in which the public can encounter alien and exotic cultures has disappeared. "Today what does leaving one's native habitat really mean? Where is exoticism when vacationing has become synonymous with traveling, and when limits on the right to leave national territory are the most resented of all?" In an age when images of and information about the most remote peoples are available at the touch of a button, the cosmopolitan festival is superfluous.[326]

This view is challenged in the work of John J. MacAloon, an American cultural anthropologist who has produced both macrophenomenal and microphenomenal analyses of considerable originality. MacAloon views the Olympiad as a virtually unique macrophenomenon, "an institution without parallel in nature and scope in the twentieth century. Insofar as there exists, in the Hegelian-Marxian phrase, a 'world-historical process', the Olympics have emerged as its privileged expression and celebration." The "idea of 'world community' is no longer simply a humanistic pipe dream, but increasingly a set of facts and challenges."[327] The Olympic Games are, in other words, a microcosmic version of a macrophenomenal process. For this reason they can be used to study this larger process and perhaps even to affect it, even if these effects must be regarded at this point as hypothetical.

The most important theoretical innovation to be found in MacAloon's work is the idea that the Olympic Games represent what he calls "a ramified performance type" consisting of four genres—spectacle, festival, ritual, game—that are "distinctive forms of symbolic action." "The genres are intimately and complexly interconnected on all levels: historically, ideologically, structurally, and performatively. Thus we are forced to recognize that the Olympic Games represent a special kind of cultural performance, a ramified performance type, and we are forced to seek for new models and methods of analysis that will allow us to understand the relationships between the various forms of symbolic action without losing sight of their distinctive properties."[328]

MacAloon proposes that a key genre for understanding the Olympic Games as "cultural performance" is the spectacle because of its refusal to demand participation by those who watch it.

> Why did festival not suffice as a metagenre promoting the (re-)joining of ritual and game in Olympic history? So far, the following answers have been offered. By requiring joyfulness, the festival frame cannot incorporate the very unjoyous, saddening, alienating, sometimes tragic events that have come to be part of Olympic experience. Spectacle can do so for it specifies no further affect than diffuse wonder or awe. Festival demands engaged participation, leaving little room for dispassionate behavior. Spectacle, on the other hand, licenses such behavior in the mode of distanced observation—spectatorship. By prescribing only watching, leaving the rest to the dialogue between the observer and the "sights," spectacle accommodates the optionality and individual choice, which are widespread modern values.[329]

Like other macrophenomenal theorists such as Lorenz and Schelsky, MacAloon believes that an Olympiad has a positive, i.e., reconciling, effect on its international audience. (Spectacle, unlike festival, lends itself to being televised.) The difference between MacAloon's claims and those of his predecessors is that his are more modest and more carefully formulated. "Perhaps the growth of the spectacle genre in the modern world is to be understood as a public form of thinking out, of telling stories about certain growing ambiguities and ambivalences in our shared existence." The "reimagining and reencountering of structure, of the ordinary, goes on continuously at and in and through the Olympic Games. Are capitalists predatory sharks out solely for themselves and the almighty dollar? Are communists all robots under mind control? Are black people physically superior to whites? Do athletes have underdeveloped personalities? . . . Is there such a thing as humankind? Or are there only humans? As much as they are an antistructure, the Olympic Games create a sort of hyperstructure in which categories and stereotypes are condensed, exaggerated, and dramatized, rescued from the 'taken for granted' and made the objects of explicit and lively awareness for a brief period every four years."[330] MacAloon is more interested in analyzing the appeal of the spectacle than in advertising its therapeutic effects.

Trained as a cultural anthropologist, MacAloon conducted "field work" at the 1976 Montreal Games. "The volume of symbolic exchange—interpersonal, national, and cross-cultural—defies quantitative description, but it is even more prodigious and remarkable." MacAloon describes the "mass street festival" in which the actual competitions are embedded and describes individuals' reactions to this cosmopolitan experience.[331]

Another example of microphenomenal analysis is the author's observation of "competitors who were so restricted by their physical and psychological training regimens at the Games that they too were mostly unaware of the vast festival surrounding the athletic competition."[332] This is the sort of observation which puts the lie to Lorenz's happy reveries of "chivalry and fair play." Neither he nor Schelsky seem to know anything about the personalities of high-performance athletes, their monomania or their egotism. Schelsky, in particular, would have been pleased to discover how many athletes are as politically indiscriminate as he wants them to be, but he did not bother to investigate their attitudes toward sport or politics.

MacAloon, however, is well aware of how many problems afflict every modern Olympiad. The world expects an Olympic festival to lift its spirits. "But these days a strong foreboding remains about the fate of the Games in general and about the likelihood of joyfulness persisting from one day to the next within each Olympics. The immediate causes vary from one Games to the next, but the overall shift is steady and unremitting. The emotional unpredictability of the spectacle has challenged, and perhaps now supersedes, the more reliable affective structure of the festival." MacAloon's list of factors which threaten "the festival frame" of an Olympiad is long and sobering: "professionalization of sports and the transformation of athletes into celebrities, the growing number-fetishism and specialization in athletics, the increased role of technology and of hyperextended training periods in sports success, the growth of athletic bureaucracies," and so on.[333] The spectacle is an advantageous "megagenre" for the modern age precisely because it can accommodate so much that is so different. But this supercapacity of the spectacle can also degrade the "cultural performance" it contains.

The "tragic consciousness that haunts an Olympic Games," as MacAloon puts it, could be eliminated by a largely pacified Olympic festival which, having exchanged competitive sports for cooperative ones, would also forfeit certain crucial dramatic experiences. Such "soft Games" are the dream of the West German futurologist Robert Jungk, whose plan for complete denationalization of the Games calls for the "formation of nationally mixed teams in which participants from different countries and races would learn to cooperate." Winners would share their "superior knowledge and ability" with the losers, and training secrets would be prohibited.

Jungk's vision transcends the familiar anti-competitive model by aiming at a multidimensional reformation of the athletic identity. He recommends, for example, the aestheticizing of athletic performance in the manner of ice skating competitions, which include a choreographic component. "The 'how' involved in jumping, throwing, running, swimming, or handling a ball" should be judged along with sheer quantifiable performance. This aestheticizing serves a larger anthropological project. "The diminished sensory capacities of all workers in the high technology societies would be restored by means of a consciously intensified sensory training of the body, including seeing, touching, hearing, and smelling as they are still known among the primitive peoples now facing extinction."[334]

Jungk's call for more aesthetically advanced athletic costumes is somewhat ironic from a historical standpoint. As we have seen, Volkish conservatives in Germany at the turn of the century objected to aesthetically innovative costumes which appeared along with the competitive ethos—not as a response to its asceticism. In fact, Jungk's relationship to pre-modern (e.g., Volkish) norms is ambiguous. As a sartorial radical and denationalizer, he is a modernist. As an aesthetically oriented dequantifier, he is a pre-modernist.

In one respect, at least, Jungk's utopia has already come to Bulgaria where, according to Ponomaryov, "they hold a competition 'for the model sporting public'. According to the conditions of the competition, fans can by their exemplary behavior bring a certain number of points to their team; if they act in an unworthy manner, however, points are deducted correspondingly. Furthermore, information on disciplined and undisciplined fans is published in the press."[335] There is no evidence, however, that this sort of refinement, which recalls the highly developed *politesse* of Maoist sport culture, has tempered the cult of performance which characterizes East bloc sport at its higher levels.

There remains the possibility that it is precisely the most spectacular and moving manifestations of the "festival of humanity"—including "the sight of heretofore stoic and 'Olympian' athletes weeping under the immense symbolic weight of the victory rite"[336]—which constitute the certain proof of its impotence vis-à-vis the historical violence which mocks the Olympic "oasis." This is the bleak judgment Theodor W. Adorno pronounced on another form of international culture:

> At music festivals and similar events official gentlemen continue to make encomiastic speeches on the international character of music, on its bridge-building between peoples. Even in the Hitler era, when the Nazi music politicians tried to replace the International Society for Contemporary Music with a backward-directed organization, there was no shortage of such professions of faith. They have something pleasurable about them, as when countries engaged in cold warfare against one another participate in joint earthquake relief operations, or when a European doctor demonstratively cures natives on a distant continent. Such outbreaks of brotherhood testify that nothing is too bad to allow something universally human to flower, though the humane holidays do not even slightly inhibit what goes on socially and politically, day in, day out.[337]

Even a cautious optimist like MacAloon is haunted by the terrible implications of Adorno's stoic cynicism.

> If the images of shared humanity generated by the Games simply ignore the structural realities that separate men from one another; if they encourage actors and spectators to take "life as but a game"; if our romance with a Romanian gymnast, awe at a Cuban sprinter, and admiration of a Canadian high jumper lead to thoughts of state socialism and capitalist democracy as "all the same"; if our delight as white Americans, English, or French in the victories of black countrymen is taken uncritically as evidence for racial progress at home—then the spectacle has made us victims of the most dangerous illusions. If so, then the language of Olympism is a lexicon of deceit, and the Games are a theater of self-delusion.[338]

What redeems the Games is their profoundly ambiguous nature. "This sort of thing happens all the time in and through the Olympic Games. Simultaneously, however, the Games generate completely contrary experiences. Spectacle, at least Olympic spectacle, *is* full of events that make us notice and heed moral and social boundaries that have become blurred and banal in daily life. Our daily existence is fraught with illusions."[339] The value of the Games, in other words, resides in their power to offer an enormous public a massive lesson in the epistemology of everyday life.

So can the massive quadrennial investment in the Olympic movement be justified? Are the Games worth the candle? If, as I believe, almost any international institution is preferable to none at all, then the answer is yes. The crucial caveat is that

Olympism must learn to recognize and abjure the amoral tendencies which lead only to disgrace and the loss of authority which inevitably follows.

For in the modern world internationalism is not an option; it is an obligation for the most urgent practical reasons. But in addition to promoting human survival, internationalism is an inherently dignified ideal. It is easy to fault international organizations for their failure to bring about the harmonious global order which is their inherent promise. It is the ongoing effort, untainted by appeasement, that counts. "For the dream of an integrated world order has been one of the oldest rational visions of civilized man, perhaps a dream against the grain of his egotism, but an epic quest nonetheless."[340]

126

Epilogue: The Olympic Crisis of 1984

On May 8, 1984, the Soviet Olympic Committee announced that Soviet athletes would not participate in the Los Angeles Olympic Games. The Committee cited "rude violations by the organizers of the Games of the rules of the Olympic Charter and the anti-Soviet campaign launched by reactionary circles in the United States with the connivance of the official authorities." This decision, which took most observers by surprise, followed a month of public controversy during which the Soviet Olympic Committee had complained about entry requirements and security arrangements for its athletes, the commercialization of the Games, and an alleged attempt on the part of the U.S. administration "to use the Olympic Games on the eve of the elections for its selfish political aims."[1]

Even before the statement of May 8, Soviet spokesmen had repeatedly declared that Soviet non-participation would not be equivalent to a "boycott." On April 6, Marat V. Gramov, head of the Soviet National Olympic Committee and chairman of the State Committee for Physical Culture and Sport, stated: "We never use the word boycott and we will never use it. We have no intention of boycotting. We make a difference [sic] between boycotting and not attending."[2] On April 21, Sergei Romanov, a Soviet cultural attaché, stated: "We are against a boycott. A boycott would be an incorrect approach. The Games are designed to be an international festival of friendship and peace."[3]

As Soviet authorities pressed this point of semantics, their boycott strategy, which was deeply resented in East European capitals, became clear. By June 26, thirteen nations allied with the Soviet Union had withdrawn from the Games: Bulgaria, East Germany, Vietnam, Mongolia, Laos, Czechoslovakia, Afghanistan, Hungary, Poland, Cuba, South Yemen, Ethiopia, North Korea, and Angola.

The Soviet campaign against the Los Angeles Games provoked criticism across a broad ideological spectrum. The Reagan administration called the Soviet charges "a classic case of complete distortion and twisting of facts to fit a particular Soviet line."[4] On May 15 Amadou Lamine Ba, secretary general of the Supreme Council for Sport in Africa, said that he believed "Africa plans to participate" and called the Soviet action "a sovereign act which is not for us to approve or disapprove." He added that withdrawals by African nations "on the request or influence of the Soviet Union . . . is not envisioned for the moment;" the Council's executive committee is scheduled to meet in Upper Volta June 16-17 "to analyze objectively the situation and decide the position to take."[5]

In West Germany, both Helmut Kohl, the Christian Democratic Chancellor, and Willy Brandt, chairman of the opposition Social Democratic Party, protested the Soviet move in a familiar, and clichéd, idiom. Kohl averred that "anyone who says 'yes' to dialogue must also say 'yes' to the athletic games of the youth of the world," while Brandt spoke of "a heavy blow for the peaceful ideal" of the Olympic Games and denigrated the boycott strategy per se. Georges Marchais, the head of the French Communist Party, "deplored" the Soviet action; *L'Unita*, the newspaper of the Italian Communist Party, called the Soviet decision "improper and not acceptable."[6] The head of Yugoslavia's major sports organization stated: "We deplore the decision of the Soviet Union as it brings into question the universality of an event which greatly transcends the sport framework."[7]

Why did Moscow choose to forfeit its exemplary status within the Olympic movement by initiating a boycott? On May 14 Marat V. Gramov asserted that the Soviet decision was a response to three stages of provocation. First, there had been a meeting in March 1983 between President Reagan and American Olympic officials at which "the position came out clearly that 'we need victory at any cost'." Second, there had been the formation of the "Ban the Soviets Coalition" after the shooting-down of the South Korean airliner in September 1983. The third factor was a plan to subject Soviet athletes to "psychological pressures" which would subvert their performances, including "methods devised for the abduction of Soviet people, for compelling them not to return to their motherland, and for treating them with special drugs, including psychotropic preparations that destroy the nervous system."[8]

This is not a convincing account of Soviet motives; it rather provides pieces of a much larger mosaic. First, the Soviet withdrawal is a response to the deterioration of Soviet-American relations which dates from the Soviet occupation of Afghanistan in December 1979. It is a dramatic gesture which defies President Reagan's repeated assurances that superpower relations, though strained, are not in a state of crisis. In a widely noted article which appeared in the February 16, 1984 issue of the *New York Review of Books*, Seweryn Bialer pointed to "the far from normal hostility of the two powers, which persists notwithstanding the recent gestures of the Reagan administration." Bialer associates the intensification of "neo-Stalinism" with the American leader's predilection for insulting language: "President Reagan's rhetoric has badly shaken the self-esteem and patriotic pride of the Soviet political elites. . . . No one who seeks to understand the political culture of Soviet Russia, not to speak of its historical tradition, should underestimate the potency of words. Among the Soviet elites, who have spent much of their lives manipulating the nuances of ideology, words are taken very seriously."[9] State Department officials who were dumbfounded by the Olympic withdrawal had underestimated the effects of verbal aggression.

Second, the Soviet boycott was a response to the American-led boycott of the 1980 Moscow Games, which should be seen as one precipitating factor among others. The evidence to date suggests that the Soviet decision to boycott was reached early in 1984, and that the "revenge" motive could have been neutralized by better diplomatic relations.

Finally, the Soviets feared the global televising of anti-Soviet demonstrations, defections by star athletes, and even subpar performances.[10] It is especially difficult for Kremlin leaders to believe that a "Ban the Soviets Coalition" is not an organ of the state. They can scarcely conceive of an officially sanctioned festival permitting vocal political dissidence on its very periphery which is not a direct instrument of White House policy. Despite Soviet suspicions, plans by the Immigration and Naturalization Service to process defectors,[11] and a State Department human rights officer's address (on March 17) to the Baltic American Freedom League,[12] do not amount to a concerted campaign. As we have seen, the more significant anti-Soviet campaign has been carried on at a higher level.

According to Richard Pound, a Canadian member of the IOC, the Soviet campaign against the Los Angeles Games began in 1978. Then as now, the complaints concerned security, IOC charter violations, smog, and commercialism.[13] It is worth noting that 1978 also marked the beginning of a drive against Soviet dissidents in anticipation of the Moscow Olympiad. In fact, the paranoid tone of the campaign against the Los Angeles festival recalls, even in its details, the xenophobic hysteria of the 1980 campaign on behalf of the Moscow Games. The "anti-Olympic basis" ascribed to "reactionary political, emigré and religious groupings" recalls the CIA "anti-Olympic teams" of 1980. In early April, *Izvestia* warned that pornographers were planning to exploit the Los Angeles Games.[14] The Soviet youth newspaper, *Komsomolskaya Pravda*, published an article by a former Olympic champion claiming that anti-Soviet groups were plotting to kill Soviet athletes.[15] Tass, the official Soviet news agency, described the granting of press credentials to Radio Free Europe and Radio Liberty as an attempt "to bring the spirit of psychological war and ideological subversion to the world Olympic movement."[16] Soviet charges about the prospective use of mind-altering drugs occur in both 1980 and 1984.

This xenophobic rhetoric expresses what the journalist Kevin Klose has called the "broader phenomenon of Soviet retreat from the community of nations in recent years." The Olympic boycott is only the latest in a series of isolationist measures which date from 1980: the resumption of jamming operations against foreign broadcasts, a reduction in the number of exit visas issued to Jews, a new law aimed at passing information to foreigners, and the disconnecting of the country's direct-dial international telephone system which had been installed for the 1980 Olympics.[17]

The cumulative impact of successive superpower-led boycotts has produced unprecedented signs of change within the Olympic hierarchy. The current president of the IOC, Juan Antonio Samaranch, has already spoken of compulsory participation in Olympic Games and the expulsion of non-attenders from the movement.[18] Still it is well to remember that Olympism is by definition a conservatism. It will be the more recent, rather than the more established, members of the Olympic movement who will promote change.

As of this writing (June 1984), the most interesting commentary from the inner circle has come from Willi Daume, a prominent West German member of the IOC and a bitter opponent of the 1980 boycott. Daume's interview with *Der Spiegel* combines a candor born of ideological exhaustion with the indefatigable determination characteristic of IOC stalwarts. "From the beginning," he states, "excessive moral demands have been made on the Olympic Games, as though they had to take place on some Island of the Blessed." He concedes that the movement has been guilty of moral opportunism and that, "in the last analysis, the IOC will always be vulnerable to blackmail (*erpressbar*)." The Olympic Charter, he continues, "is in a continuous state of development," and the IOC itself cannot be expected to demonstrate "all that much political breadth of vision." This is candid stuff from a pillar of the movement.

But Daume is also certain that the movement will survive, thanks in large measure to enormous television revenues and a growing number of applicants interested in staging future Olympiads (see below). As he points out, the movement has heard many premature obituaries.[19]

Within the United States Olympic Committee (USOC), the winds of reform have been blowing more briskly. "We must open our hearts and our minds and forget past prejudices, and commence the dialogue that will result in the creation of a new Olympic movement that recognizes the world as it is today. It should be obvious to all that the Olympic movement will emerge from this second disruption as a different entity." So spoke William E. Simon, president of the USOC, who went on to endorse the selection of permanent Olympic sites on five continents.[20] Five days earlier, on May 13, Peter V. Ueberroth, president of the Los Angeles Olympic Organizing Committee (LAOOC), had stated: "If you want a solution, maybe you have to have [the Games] in the Third World, developing nations or small nations."[21] (Just after the announcement of the Soviet boycott, the Greek President Constantine Caramanlis reiterated his proposal of 1980 that the Games be held permanently at Ancient Olympia.)

Ueberroth also made a more radical proposal bearing on the Olympic eligibility of athletes who are citizens of boycotting nations. On May 25 he said he would seek permission for such athletes to compete at the Los Angeles Games as individuals under the Olympic flag; he maintained that such an arrangement can be endorsed by an athlete's home sports federation.[22] Ueberroth has stated that the LAOOC has received between ten and twenty requests to compete without the approval of their national Olympic committees. But this proposal was rejected by Monique Berlioux, director of the IOC, at a press conference in Lausanne on May 29. "It is impossible for the IOC to accept these entries," she said. "It would be a violation of Olympic rules. No athlete can compete unless he is sponsored by his national Olympic committee."[23] The IOC, in effect, reiterated the position it had taken in 1976 in the James Gilkes case (see Chapter 2).

A second, and potentially more controversial, issue concerning Olympic eligibility is the status of Zola Budd, a 17-year-old runner from South Africa who, on January 5, 1984, set an unofficial world record for the 5000-meter run. On March 23 she flew to London and, on the basis of having a British-born grandfather, applied for British citizenship. On April 6 she was granted British citizenship so that she could be considered eligible for Olympic competition. South Africa last participated in an Olympiad in 1960 (Rome) and was expelled from the Olympic movement in 1970 because of its racial policy of apartheid.

An application for British citizenship usually takes from six to nine months to clear; Zola Budd was granted citizenship after a waiting period of only two weeks. In addition, passage to England for her and her parents had been arranged by the *Daily Mail*, a London tabloid which has retained exclusive interview rights in exchange, reportedly, for a "Zola Budd trust fund," a car, and a house.[24]

Aside from the dubious role of yellow journalism in this episode, the Zola Budd affair raises practical and theoretical issues which are related. First, the inclusion of this crypto-South African athlete (or any one of seven others who aspire to compete under other national flags[25]) is a potential boycott issue, even though the Supreme

Council for Sport in Africa announced in early June that Zola Budd's participation in the Los Angeles Games would not trigger a boycott by the nations it represents.

Second, this case raises "the larger issue of whether South African athletes should be allowed to circumvent an international boycott by switching nationalities."[26] A bylaw to Rule 8 of the Olympic Charter states that "a nationalized competitor . . . may not participate in the Olympic Games to represent his new country until three years after his nationalization." But the bylaw goes on to say: "The period following naturalization may be reduced or even canceled with the agreement of the National Olympic Committee and International Federations concerned and the final approval of the IOC executive board."[27] It is a measure of the IOC's political dexterity (or timidity) that, equipped with this infinitely flexible regulation, it has apparently chosen to deflect responsibility for this decision onto the national level. As Monique Berlioux put it after the IOC eligibility panel met on April 27: "Zola Budd is a British problem, not an IOC problem."[28]

131

The ideal which haunts this case and others like it is the possibility of world citizenship for world-class athletes and the transformation of Olympic territory into a supranational domain. Such a development would, of course, require an improbable surrender of power by the Olympic bureaucracy. But let us set aside this formidable obstacle and attempt to judge this ideal on its merits.

The ideal of Olympic citizenship exercises the appeal associated with any dramatic inversion of the status quo. The utopian overtones which accompany the promise of radical change have a siren-like quality on a tense and deadlocked globe. But merely denationalizing the world-class athlete is not a panacea. Olympic citizenship is not— *pace* Olympic ideology—an inherently humane identity in a world which has established publicity as its basic cultural currency. The Nazis demonstrated this as early as 1936 by combining Olympic participation with the celebration of racial doctrine.

The generic global athlete of tomorrow may have no values whatsoever beyond the pursuit of high performance; or he may turn out to have values which are simply scandalous. It is worth noting that the Hell's Angels motorcycle club, long associated with a variety of criminal activities, has purchased the right to carry the Olympic torch for a kilometer of its journey across the United States.[29] There is no reason to assume that sportive variations of this type, emboldened by talent, wealth, and notoriety, could not appear on the Olympic stage to amaze, and horrify, a public primed for more wholesome fare. At the same time, the global audience which devours the "action" films of Clint Eastwood and Bruce Lee might find the "outlaw athlete" a very appealing figure.

While the denationalized hoodlum-athlete remains a possibility for the future, the Zola Budd controversy is already upon us. What it shows is that de facto denationalization does not necessarily mean the decline of nationalism ("I'll run my heart out for Britain"). Its immediate effect is rather to challenge the internationalism represented by anti-racialistic norms. Such cases show why Olympic citizenship requires an ethos which could be prescribed—and enforced. Such an ethos is the Olympic festival's guarantee against the sort of degeneration which robs a festival of all but spectacular value.

Proposals for permanent Olympic sites and athletes who compete under the Olympic flag represent what may be called an internationalist, and therefore de-nationalizing, trend within the USOC. But U.S.-Soviet conflict within the Olympic movement has also produced a nationalist countertrend within the USOC which threatens the international authority of the IOC itself. This dispute arose during a bitterly contested debate over press accreditation for Radio Free Europe (RFE) and Radio Liberty (RL) at the 1984 Winter Olympics in Sarajevo, Yugoslavia. The Soviet Union, which deeply resents (and jams) their broadcasts to its Eastern bloc satellites, opposed the IOC's granting of credentials to these United States government-funded stations. The IOC, in turn, responded to Soviet pressure by working out a compromise with F. Don Miller, the executive director of the USOC, which accredited fewer station employees than had been requested.

Among the IOC members voting for the compromise formula was Julian K. Roosevelt, one of two Americans on the IOC and a member of its Executive Committee. When RFE-RL officials rejected the compromise, Roosevelt and his IOC colleagues voted to allow the stations no credentials at all.

The USOC leadership was indignant at Roosevelt's votes against what they perceived as the national interest. The President of the USOC complained that Roosevelt had "repeatedly voted in the IOC counter to the USOC stance, and that's absolutely wrong," and Roosevelt was officially censured by the USOC.[30]

This episode illustrates the clash of two important principles: unlimited media access to a public event versus the political autonomy of IOC members. Following the IOC's exclusion of RFE-RL, its president, James L. Buckley, commented: "the present course is a dangerous one: dangerous to the true spirit of the Olympic movement and dangerous to the basic principles guaranteeing free flow of information."[31] This interpretation is in accordance with Rule 49 of the Olympic Charter ("to ensure the widest possible audience for the Olympic Games").

But Rule 12 of the Charter guarantees IOC members a kind of Olympic citizenship: "Members of the International Olympic Committee are representatives of the IOC in their countries and not their delegates to the IOC. They may not accept from governments, or from any organization or individual, instructions which will in any way bind them or interfere with the independence of their vote."[32] Rule 12 says, in short, that a member of the IOC is entitled to vote his Olympic conscience.

It should be noted that this particular conflict of principles was not inevitable. An American IOC member's vote against an American interest group is a function, not simply of IOC membership, but of an individual temperament in which the IOC ethos and national bias play indeterminate roles. So when the USOC's president, William E. Simon, dismissed Roosevelt's position as too idealistic,[33] he was attacking the very core of Olympic internationalism.

The Olympic crisis of 1984 has already had the effect of injecting some political realism into the thinking of the IOC. But it is unlikely that policy changes will be initiated by the IOC's inner circle. When confronted with political conditions beyond its control, the IOC elite reacts instinctively as the conservator of the Olympic status quo, not as a vanguard of change.

This conservatism was evident when, on May 20, 1984, F. Don Miller of the USOC announced that the national Olympic committees of the United States and the Soviet Union, at an emergency meeting of the IOC in Lausanne, had reached an agreement in principle to "join together in support of the Olympic movement and work together to preserve the Olympic movement." This was the meeting at which the American delegation proposed that Summer Olympic Games be rotated through five permanent sites, an idea to which the president of the IOC offered no immediate response.[34] Ironically, the intellectual leadership of the Olympic movement is being assumed by the national Olympic committees which have carried out—albeit without enthusiasm—the most damaging boycotts ever mounted against it. The pronunciamentos are coming, not from Juan Antonio Samaranch, but from Americans and Russians who are nominally his subordinates (see Rule 23 of the Olympic Charter). Even prior to the announcement of the Soviet-American Olympic compact, Marat V. Gramov had emphasized the peripheral role of the IOC. "The International Olympic Committee," he stated, "is not competent to discuss Soviet nonparticipation."[35]

The Olympic movement is likely to survive into the foreseeable future for several reasons. First, the superpowers' Olympic detente demonstrates the importance of high-performance sport—and its principal forum—to both societies. Second, the IOC and its many sympathizers around the world will struggle tenaciously to preserve the movement. The idea that it remains, in the recent words of William E. Simon, "a positive force for peace,"[36] is widespread. Third, the staging of an Olympiad is still widely regarded as an important instrument of economic or political policy. The regime in Seoul, for example, expects the 1988 Games to promote both economic growth and, by securing the participation of the Chinese, their foreign policy.[37] Bids to put on the 1992 Summer Games have already been received from Paris, New Delhi, Barcelona, Stockholm, Brisbane, and Amsterdam or Rotterdam; six other bids have been submitted for the 1992 Winter Games. And, according to a Japanese news bureau, China has asked Japan to assist in staging a Peking Olympiad for the year 2000.[38] It is clear that the Olympic Games are still considered an effective vehicle for national "image-building."

Finally, it appears that early rumors of a "Red Olympics" or "Counter-Olympics" were exaggerated. These alternative competitions will be scheduled after, rather than against, the Olympic Games so as not to violate implicit provisions of the Olympic Charter. Unless East-West relations decline even more dramatically than they have in recent years, there will be no return to Stalinist rejectionism vis-à-vis the Olympic movement.

. "Most of Key British Athletes Favor Moscow Games," *New York Times*, March 4, 1980.

. Aloys Behler, "Die Schlacht im falschen Saal," *Die Zeit*, January 25, 1980, p. 21

. "Bentsen hits Mexico, Iran Olympic stance," *Dallas Times Herald*, January 31, 1980.

. Henry Morton, *Soviet Sport* (New York: Collier Books, 1963), p. 92.

. Kenny Moore, "Crowned on Coronation Drive," *Sports Illustrated*, October 18, 1982, p. 64.

. "India opens Asian Games," *Boston Globe*, November 20, 1982, p. 7.

. "Korea's Chun: absolute control," *Boston Globe*, April 25, 1983, p. 2.

. "Soviet Psychiatrists, Faced With Censure, Leave World Group," *New York Times*, February 11, 1983, p. A8.

. "Czechs Quit World Psychiatric Association," *New York Times*, June 11, 1983, p. 24.

New York Times Magazine, January 30, 1983, p. 50.

"Czechs Quit World Psychiatric Association," p. 24.

See, for example, "H.H. Paul VI: the educational factor of sport," *Olympic Review*, Nos. 125-26 (March-April 1978), pp. 170-72; "Religion and sport," *Olympic Review*, Nos. 132-33 (Oct.-Nov. 1978), pp. 587-93, 611.

ort and the Moral Order

Peter J. Beck, "Politics and the Olympics: The Lesson of 1924," *History Today*, Vol. 30 (July 1980), pp. 7-9.

Christian Graf von Krockow, quoted in *Fussball und Folter: Argentinien '78* (Reinbek bei Hamburg: Rowohlt, 1978), p. 42.

3. Peter McIntosh, *Fair Play: Ethics in Sport and Education* (London: Heinemann, 1979), p. 11.

4. Charles Cheney Hyde, "The Boycott as a Sanction of International Law," *Political Science Quarterly*, Vol. 48 (1933), p. 211.

5. See, for example, Samuel Untermyer, "The Boycott is Our Only Weapon Against Nazi Germany" (New York: American League for the Defense of Jewish Rights, 1933).

6. "The Boycott as a Sanction of International Law," p. 213.

7. "Tossing the Olympics Javelin," *New York Times*, January 17, 1980, p. A22.

8. "Soviet Opens Big Push to Get Olympics," *New York Times*, October 13, 1974, Section 5, p. 5; see also "Sozialistischer Gang," *Der Spiegel*, August 27, 1973, p. 2.

9. B. Bazunov, "Olympic Horizons," *Sport in the USSR* (1974: 12), p. 12.

10. "Olympia dient der Erhaltung des Friedens," *Neues Deutschland* (East Berlin), January 25, 1979, p. 5.

11. "Olympic Horizons," p. 12.

12. "Olympics: To Go or Not to Go," *Time*, January 28, 1980, p. 15.

13. "100,000 Cheers Greet Mobutu 'Gift', a Rebuilt Stadium," *New York Times*, September 23, 1974.

14. See *Keesing's Contemporary Archives* (London), September 1-7, 1975, p. 27307.

15. *From Helsinki to Belgrade: The Soviet Union and the Implementation of the Final Act of the European Conference* (Moscow: Progress Publishers, 1977), pp. 11, 226.

16. S. Popov, *Socialism and Humanism* (Moscow: Progress Publishers, 1977), p. 11.

17. Ibid., p. 226.

18. David E. Powell, *Antireligious Propaganda in the Soviet Union* (Cambridge, Mass.: The MIT Press, 1978), pp. 9, 43.

19. See *Antireligious Propaganda*, p. 53; Jean Meynaud, *Sport et politique* (Paris: Payot, 1966), p. 312.

20. "Requiem for a Friend," *Sports Illustrated*, October 20, 1958, p. 27.

21. "Olympics Aides Consult Vance, Resist a Boycott," *New York Times*, January 19, 1980, p. 8: Letter to the editor, *New York Times*, January 31, 1980.

22. "Bei uns ist immer Olympia," *Der Spiegel*, August 7, 1972, p. 90.

23. "Wohln wir wollen," *Der Spiegel*, October 15, 1979.

24. "Walker Sees Runaway By Soviet Bloc in Games," *New York Times*, February 6, 1979.

25. Sigmund Freud, *Totem and Taboo* (New York: Vintage Books, n.d.), pp. 181-82.

26. Pierre de Coubertin, *Notes sur l'éducation publique* (Paris: Hachette, 1901), p. 214.

27. Jean-Pierre Clerc, "Argentina in a state of shock," *Manchester Guardian Weekly*, June 18, 1978, p. 13.

28. "Ein Appell der argentinischen Regierung: Arbeit soll ein Ausdruck der Freude sein," *Frankfurter Allgemeine Zeitung*, June 26, 1978, p. 15; "Herr Präsident, wir wollen heute nicht arbeiten," *Die Welt*, June 28, 1978.

29. Leopold Unger, "Soviet Tourniquet Tightens," *International Herald Tribune*, July 5, 1978.

30. "Väst bör tona ned bojkotthotet," *Dagens Nyheter* (Stockholm), January 25, 1980.

31. "Soviet Tourniquet Tightens."

32. "Prague Said to Plan Trial of 10 Leading Dissidents on Subversion Charge," *New York Times*, July 15, 1979, p. 3.

33. "Sacharov släpps när OS är över," *Dagens Nyheter*, January 24, 1980.

34. See "How I spent my Summer Vacation," *Sports Illustrated*, November 12, 1979, p. 34; Harrison E. Salisbury, "A Boon for· the K.G.B.," *New York Times*, January 31, 1980.

35. Pierre de Coubertin, *Mémoires olympiques* (Lausanne: Bureau International de Péda-

gogie Sportive, 1931), pp. 49-50.

36. "A Boon for the K.G.B."

37. "For Russia, Olympics Aren't Fun an Games," *New York Times*, January 27, 1980

38. Octavio Paz, *The Other Mexico: Critique the Pyramid* (New York: Grove Press, 1972 pp. 16-17.

39. Ibid, pp. 12-13.

40. "The Games Nations Play," *New York Time* January 8, 1980.

41. It is even more astonishing that in the 198 edition of *The Politics of the Olympic Game* (Berkeley: University of California Pres 1979), Richard Espy never mentions th Tlatelolco massacre, referring instead to Mex can students who "rioted just before th Games" (p. 104) and to "the demonstratior of the Mexican students which had threatene to cancel the Games" (p. 120). For anothe account of the Tlatelolco massacre, see M chael C. Meyer and William L. Sherman, *Th Course of Mexican History* (New York: O) ford University Press, 1983), pp. 669-671.

42. K.S. Karol, *Guerillas in Power* (New Yor Hill and Wang, 1970), pp. 502-3.

43. "Aber wir haben den Krieg gewonnen," *D Spiegel*, June 23, 1974, pp. 94f.

44. "Aber wir haben den Krieg gewonnen," *D Spiegel*, May 20, 1974, p. 108.

45. Ibid., pp. 116, 119.

46. Ibid., p. 108.

47. "Aber wir haben den Krieg gewonnen," *D Spiegel*, May 27, 1974, p. 105.

48. Ibid., p. 106.

49. Ibid., p. 106, 110.

50. Ibid., p. 106.

51. "Olympics Racing Against Time," *New Yor Times*, January 30, 1980.

52. *Fussball und Folter: Argentinien '78*, op. cit pp. 37-38.

53. Ibid., p. 64.

54. "A U.S. Boycott of Moscow Olympics," *Ne York Times*, January 26, 1980.

55. "Nazi accused of murder 'did what he wa ordered'," *Dallas Times Herald*, February 1980.

56. "Cuba Pulls Baseball Team Out of Nicaragu Series," *New York Times*, November 9, 197

57. *Guerillas in Power*, p. 503.

58. Robert F. Wheeler, "Organized Sport and Organized Labour: The Workers' Sports Movement," *Journal of Contemporary History,* Vol. 13 (1978), p. 200.

59. Jürgen Fischer, "Die Olympiade der Sozialistischen Arbeitersportinternationale in Frankfurt 1925," in Hans-Jürgen Schulke, ed. *Die Zukunft der Olympischen Spiele* (Köln: Pahl-Rugenstein, 1976), p. 101.

60. "Organized Sport and Organized Labour," p. 201.

61. See, for example, Gerhard A. Ritter, "Workers' Culture in Imperial Germany," *Journal of Contemporary History,* Vol. 13 (1978), pp. 165-89. For a longer treatment see Wilfried van der Will and Rob Burns, *Arbeiterkulturbewegung in der Weimarer Republik* (Frankfurt/M: Ullstein, 1982), 2 vols.

62. The best known manifestos are Julius Deutsch, *Sport und Politik* (Berlin, 1928); Fritz Wildung, *Arbeitersport* (Berlin, 1929); Paul Franken, *Vom Werden einer neuen Kultur* (Berlin, 1930); Helmut Wagner, *Sport und Arbeitersport* (Berlin, 1931). For a history of the workers' sport movement see Heinz Timmermann, *Geschichte und Struktur der Arbeitersportbewegung 1893-1933* (Ahrensburg bei Hamburg: Verlag Ingrid Czwalina, 1973).

63. Robert Creamer, "Of Greeks—and Russians," *Sports Illustrated,* February 6, 1956, p. 32.

64. For a brief—and apologetic—survey of von Halt's political and Olympic career, see Karl Adolf Scherer, *Der Männerorden: Die Geschichte des Internationalen Olympischen Komitees* (Frankfurt/M: Limpert, 1974), pp. 74-77. For a more detailed and reliable account of von Halt's contributions to the Nazi sport apparatus see Arnd Krüger, *Die Olympischen Spiele 1936 und die Weltmeinung* (Berlin, München, Frankfurt/M: Verlag Bartels & Wernitz KG, 1972). While Scherer (p. 76) dispels a false rumor that von Halt had belonged to the SS, Krüger (p. 128) confirms that he had been a member of the SA and the NSDAP.

65. "Bei uns ist immer Olympia," *Der Spiegel,* August 7, 1972, p. 78.

66. See Richard Edward Lapchick, *The Politics of Race and International Sport: The Case of South Africa* (Westport, Conn.: The Greenwood Press, 1975), pp. 4, 31, 75, 115-17, 119, 124, 125, 141, 186.

67. Ibid., p. 116.

68. Idem.

69. "Das Todesstadion," *Der Spiegel,* November 12, 1973, p. 172.

70. "No Soviet Soccer in Stadium," *Chile Newsletter,* Vol. I, No. 2 (December 1, 1973), p. 3.

71. "Aber wir haben den Krieg gewonnen," *Der Spiegel,* May 20, 1974, p. 105.

72. "Das Todesstadion," p. 172.

73. Ibid., p. 174.

74. Willi Knecht, "Moskaus ultimative Kandidatur," *Deutschland Arkiv,* Vol. 7, No. 5 (May 1974), p. 465.

75. Quoted in "For Russia, Olympics Aren't Fun and Games," op. cit.

76. "Aber wir haben den Krieg gewonnen," *Der Spiegel,* May 20, 1974, p. 105.

77. "Das Todesstadion," p. 174.

78. "Ich weiss, Ihr werdet mich nicht vergessen," *Neues Deutschland,* October 24, 1979, p. 4.

79. "Argentina Expects World Soccer to Test Its Image," *New York Times,* April 30, 1978.

80. "Pourquoi Videla a perdu le Mundial," *Le Nouvel Observateur,* July 17, 1978, p. 36.

81. "Idrotten får avgöra själv," *Dagens Nyheter,* November 1, 1977.

82. Fussballweltmeisterschaft findet im Winter statt," *Neues Deutschland,* March 21, 1978, p. 5.

83. *Fussball und Folter: Argentinien '78,* op. cit., p. 36.

84. "Idrotten får avgöra själv."

85. "A Marxist Soccer Star is Newest Hero of West Germany's New Left," *New York Times,* July 20, 1972, p. 12.

86. "Wie zehn Arbeiter," *Der Spiegel,* May 21, 1973, p. 138.

87. Paul Breitner, "Kein Handschlag für die Generale," in *Fussball und Folter: Argentinien '78,* p. 30.

88. Dieter Hochgesand, "Die Rolle des Paul Breitner," in *Fussball und Folter: Argentinien '78,* p. 33.

89. "Die Mannschaft kann etwas erreichen, indem sie fernbleibt," *Frankfurter Rundschau,* March 31, 1978; reprinted in *Fussball und Folter: Argentinien '78,* p. 38.

90. "Moscow Book Fair Poses Quandary for U.S. Houses Over Human Rights," *New York*

Times, July 2, 1977: "U.S. Publishers Press Cause of Soviet Writer," *New York Times*, February 18, 1979.

91. "Political science event in Moscow causes split," *Boston Globe*, May 11, 1979.

92. *New York Times*, April 18, 1978, p. 40.

93. "Dissidents and Olympics," *Manchester Guardian Weekly*, July 23, 1978.

94. Vadim Golovanov, "Who is Right?" *New York Times*, June 17, 1977.

95. Carl Diem, "The Olympic Idea," *Report of the Second Summer Session of the International Olympic Academy* (Athens: Hellenic Olympic Committee, 1962), p. 90.

96. Johan Huizinga, *Homo Ludens* (Boston: Beacon Press, 1955), pp. 197, 198.

97. Ibid., pp. 17-18.

98. Ibid., pp. 195-99.

99. Ibid., p. 206.

100. Johan Huizinga, *In the Shadow of Tomorrow* (New York: Norton, 1964), p. 170; for the quotation see *Homo Ludens*, p. 8.

101. *In the Shadow of Tomorrow*, p. 170.

102. "The Olympic Idea," p. 98.

103. Idem.

104. *Homo Ludens*, pp. 18, 19.

105. G.W.F. Hegel, *On Art, Religion, Philosophy* (New York: Harper Torchbooks, 1970), p. 73.

106. Quoted in Ginette Berthaud et al., eds. *Sport, culture et répression* (Paris: François Maspero, 1972), p. 34.

107. Dr. Henri Pouret, "Is Sport an Art?" *Report of the Tenth Session of the International Olympic Academy at Olympia* (Athens: Hellenic Olympic Committee, 1970), pp. 131-32.

108. Leo Lowenthal, "Knut Hamsun," in *Literature and the Image of Man* (Boston: The Beacon Press, 1966), p. 217.

109. Bertolt Brecht, "Mehr guten Sport," *Berliner Boersen-Courier*, February 6, 1926.

110. Jean-Paul Sartre, *Saint Genet: Actor and Martyr* (New York: New American Library, 1965), p. 52.

111. "Neue, höhere Ziele für Körperkultur und Sport," *Neues Deutschland*, March 15, 1978, p. 5.

112. Erhard Hohne, "Music and Sport," *Olympic Review*, No. 141-42 (July-August 1979), p. 438.

113. Andrzej Wohl, *Die gesellschaftlich-historischen Grundlagen des bürgerlichen Sports* (Köln: Pahl-Rugenstein, 1973), pp. 136, 137.

114. Yukio Mishima, *Sun and Steel* (New York: Grove Press, 1970), p. 45.

115. *Homo Ludens*, p. 7.

116. Susan Sontag, "Fascinating Fascism," *New York Review of Books*, February 6, 1975.

117. Winfried Joch, *Politische Leibeserziehung und ihre Theorie im Nationalsozialistischen Deutschland* (Frankfurt/M.: Peter Lang, 1976), pp. 215, 24.

118. "Russisk ishockeys ideologi," *Politiken* (Copenhagen), April 16, 1973.

119. "Bei uns ist immer Olympia," *Der Spiegel*, August 14, 1972, p. 92.

120. Olof Lagerkrantz, "The Playing Fields of Peking," *New York Times*, June 18, 1971.

II. "Playing the Chameleon: The Moral Bankruptcy of the Olympic Movement"

1. Carl Diem, *Weltgeschichte des Sports und der Leibeserziehung* (Stuttgart: Cotta Verlag, 1960), pp. 600-5.

2. Pierre de Coubertin, *Mémoires olympiques* (Lausanne: Bureau International de Pédagogie Sportive, 1931), p. 47.

3. Quoted in Richard D. Mandell, *The First Modern Olympics* (Berkeley: University of California Press, 1976), pp. 171-72.

4. *Mémoires olympiques*, p. 157.

5. *Olympic Rules, By-Laws and Instructions* (Lausanne: Comité International Olympique, 1975), p. 5.

6. "Lord Killanin at Brighton," *Olympic Review*, No. 134 (December 1978), p. 674.

7. Nadejda Lekarska, *Essays and Studies on Olympic Problems* (Sofia: Medicina and Fizcultura, 1973), p. 73.

8. *Weltgeschichte des Sports und der Leibeserziehung*, pp. 601-5.

9. "H.H. Paul VI: the educational factor of sport," *Olympic Review*, No. 125-26 (March-April 1978), p. 171.

10. *Essays and Studies on Olympic Problems*, p. 122.

11. *Olympic Rules*, pp. 5, 15.

12. "Lord Killanin in Algiers," *Olympic Review,* No. 131-32 (August-September 1978), p. 491.

13. "Lord Killanin at Brighton," p. 671.

14. Ibid., p. 675.

15. "Religion and sport," *Olympic Review,* No. 132-33 (October-November 1978), p. 588.

16. Pierre de Coubertin, *Pédagogie sportive* (Lausanne: Bureau International de Pédagogie Sportive, 1922), p. 53.

17. "Religion and sport," p. 591.

18. For an account of Diem's career in English see Richard D. Mandell, *The Nazi Olympics* (New York: Macmillan, 1971), pp. 84-88, 237-42, 283-85; for a chronology and a brief apologia by Diem's widow and a co-author, see Liselott Diem and Herbert Maag, "Carl Diem born 100 years ago (6/24 1882)—Life and Work," *International Journal of Physical Education,* Vol. XIX, issue 2 (1982), pp. 24-30.

19. Carl Diem, "The Olympic Idea," in the *Report of the Second Session of the International Olympic Academy* (Athens: The Hellenic Olympic Committee, 1962), pp. 95, 90, 89, 97.

20. In a memorial essay on Coubertin published in 1941, Diem reports that Coubertin had expressed his satisfaction regarding the Berlin Olympiad both to Diem personally and to "a French newspaper." See Carl Diem, "Pierre de Coubertin (1863-1937)," in *Olympische Flamme: Das Buch vom Sport* (Berlin: Deutscher Arkiv Verlag, 1942), p. 256. The allusion to Coubertin's published remarks may refer to a letter from André Lang to *L'Auto* which quotes an approving Coubertin at length. See Gaston Meyer, *Le phénomène olympique* (Paris: La Table Ronde, 1960), pp. 13-15.

21. "The Olympic Idea," p. 98.

22. Ibid., pp. 98-99.

23. See Ernest Seillière, *Un Artisan d'Energie Française: Pierre de Coubertin* (Paris: Henri Didier, 1917), pp. 141-43.

24. John J. MacAloon offers a more sympathetic account of Coubertin's reaction to religion in America: "But above all, he was happily surprised to discover the democratic sentiments of American Catholics, and he devoted a whole chapter of *Universités transatlantiques* to presenting the French public with the American example of a church passionately committed to democracy while backing the separation of church and state and the liberty of religious practice. These experiences hardly turned Coubertin to personal piety, but they ... softened his hostility to the Church and to his own Catholic heritage ... and set the stage for his later seeking of Vatican approval of the Olympic Games." See *This Great Symbol: Pierre de Coubertin and the Origins of the Modern Olympic Games* (Chicago: University of Chicago Press, 1981), p. 114.

25. *Mémoires olympiques,* p. 156.

26. Jean Meynaud, *Sport et politique* (Paris: Payot, 1966), p. 197.

27. "The Olympic Idea," p. 96.

28. Carl Diem, "Pierre de Coubertin (1863-1937)" [1941]; "Das Erbe Coubertins. Rundfunkansprache. [1938]"; "Das Festspiel Olympische Jugend" [1936]; in *Olympische Flamme,* pp. 249, 257, 279.

29. Allen Guttmann, "The Games Must Go On: On the origins of Avery Brundage's life-credo," *Stadion,* Vol. 5, No. 2 (1979), pp. 254, 261.

30. "The Olympic Idea," p. 95.

31. *Pédagogie sportive,* pp. 140, 145.

32. *Mémoires olympiques,* p. 213.

33. Idem.

34. See Pierre de Coubertin, *Pages d'histoire contemporaine* (Paris: Plon, 1909), pp. 83, 294; *Mémoires olympiques,* p. 212.

35. *Pédagogie sportive,* pp. 28-29.

36. Ibid., pp. 100, 134.

37. Eugen Weber, "Pierre de Coubertin and the introduction of organised sport in France," *Journal of Contemporary History,* Vol. 5, No. 2 (1970), p. 4.

38. Marie-Thérèse Eyquem, *Pierre de Coubertin: L'Epopée Olympique* (Paris: Calmann-Levy, 1966), p. 14.

39. For a sophisticated interpretation of Coubertin's relationship to his family see *This Great Symbol.*

40. "Pierre de Coubertin and the introduction of organised sport in France," p. 4.

41. Theodore Zeldin, *France 1848-1945: Politics and Anger* (New York: Oxford University Press, 1979), p. 43.

42. "Pierre de Coubertin and the introduction of organised sport in France," pp. 15, 19.

43. Jean Mabire, "Pierre de Coubertin et l'éducation 'totale'," *Défense de l'Occident* (January 1965), pp. 44, 51.

44. Paul Werrie, "Pierre de Coubertin: 'Rénovateur des Jeux Olympiques'," *Ecrits de Paris* (June 1963), p. 108.

45. Pierre de Coubertin, *Notes sur l'éducation publique* (Paris: Hachette, 1901), p. 199.

46. Andre Senay and Robert Hervet, *Monsieur de Coubertin* (Paris: Points & Contrepoints, 1960), p. 128.

47. *Pages d'histoire contemporaine*, p. 116.

48. *Mémoires olympiques*, p. 209.

49. *Notes sur l'éducation publique*, p. 268.

50. Ibid., p. 10.

51. *Pédagogie sportive*, p. 140.

52. Ibid., pp. 139-40.

53. *Notes sur l'éducation publique*, pp. 1, 217.

54. *Monsieur de Coubertin*, p. 127.

55. *Notes sur l'éducation publique*, p. 200.

56. "Pierre de Coubertin and the introduction of organised sport in France," p. 20.

57. Charles Maurras, "The Politics of Nature," in *The French Right: From de Maistre to Maurras*, ed. J.S. McClelland (New York: Harper Torchbooks, 1971) p. 284.

58. See *This Great Symbol*, pp. 262-63.

59. *Notes sur l'éducation publique*, p. 226.

60. *Monsieur de Coubertin*, p. 132.

61. Ibid., pp. 76, 9.

62. Ibid., p. 69.

63. Pierre de Coubertin, *Essais de psychologie sportive* (Lausanne et Paris: Libraire Payot & Cie, 1913), pp. 27, 32, 55, 105.

64. *Monsieur de Coubertin*, p. 155.

65. *Notes sur l'éducation publique*, pp. 213, 214.

66. *Pierre de Coubertin: L'Epopée olympique*, p. 79.

67. Albert Guerard, *France: A Modern History* (Ann Arbor: The University of Michigan Press, 1969), p. 330.

68. *Pages d'histoire contemporaine*, pp. 29-30.

69. Ibid., p. 28.

70. *Mémoires olympiques*, p. 132.

71. *Essais de psychologie sportive*, p. 230.

72. *France: A Modern History*, p. 340.

73. Ibid., pp. 341-42.

74. *Pédagogie sportive*, p. 53.

75. *Pierre de Coubertin: L'Epopée olympique*, pp. 178, 121.

76. His Holiness John Paul II, "Sport, a School for Human Virtue," *Olympic Review*, No. 144 (October 1979), p. 577.

77. *France 1848-1945: Politics and Anger*, pp. 260-61.

78. *Essais de psychologie sportive*, p. 166.

79. *Pages d'histoire contemporaine*, p. 4.

80. *Mémoires olympiques*, p. 73.

81. *Essais de psychologie sportive*, pp. 235-37.

82. *Pages d'histoire contemporaine*, pp. 31, 186.

83. Quoted in *France 1848-1945: Politics and Anger*, p. 252.

84. *Pédagogie sportive*, pp. 137-38.

85. Ibid., p. 138.

86. *Monsieur de Coubertin*, p. 85.

87. *Essais de psychologie sportive*, p. 263.

88. Ibid., p. 259.

89. *Mémoires olympiques*, p. 23.

90. Quoted in Ernest Nolte, *Three Faces of Fascism* (New York: Mentor Books, 1969), p. 516.

91. Quoted in *Pierre de Coubertin: L'Epopée olympique*, p. 117; see also p. 202.

92. *Pédagogie sportive*, p. 137.

93. Ibid., p. 136.

94. *Weltgeschichte des Sports und der Liebeserziehung*, p. 604.

95. *Pédagogie sportive*, pp. 7, 62.

96. *This Great Symbol*, pp. 141, 188.

97. *Mémoires olympiques*, p. 102.

98. *Notes sur l'éducation publique*, p. 140.

99. Quoted in *Pierre de Coubertin: L'Epopée olympique*, p. 122.

100. Ibid., p.105.

101. Ibid., p. 289.

102. Ibid., p. 122.

103. *Mémoires olympiques*, pp. 159-60; this translation appears in "The seventh Olympiad," *Olympic Review*, No. 124 (February 1978), p. 136.

104. *Pierre de Coubertin: L'Epopée olympique*, p. 122.

105. *Notes sur l'éducation publique*, p. 248.

106. *Pierre de Coubertin: L'Epopée olympique*, p. 280.

107. See, in particular, Richard Mandell, *The Nazi Olympics* (New York: Macmillan, 1971); Arnd Krüger, *Die olympischen Spiele 1936 und die Weltmeinung* (Berlin, Munchen, Frankfurt/M.: Verlag Bartels & Wernitz KG, 1972).

108. This interview, with one André Lang, appears in *Le phénomène olympique*, pp. 13-15. Arnd Krüger reproduces a pre-Olympic interview which has Coubertin responding disdainfully to the American boycott effort. These remarks, says Krüger, appear in the January 17, 1936, issue of the French sporting paper *L'Auto*. Krüger notes, however, that the editor of *L'Auto* had doubted their authenticity. See *Die olympischen Spiele 1936 und die Weltmeinung*, p. 177.

109. *Le phénomène olympique*, p. 15. It should be noted that Gaston Meyer says only that this letter was "addressed" to *L'Auto*; he does not say it was published.

110. Hans Joachim Teichler, "Coubertin und das Dritte Reich," *Sportwissenschaft*, Vol. 12, No. 1 (March 1982), pp. 18-55.

111. Richard D. Mandell, *The First Modern Olympics* (Berkeley: University of California Press, 1976), p. 173.

112. *Die olympischen Spiele und die Weltmeinung*, p. 62.

113. Idem.

114. "Er betrachtete mit grossem Vergnügen unsere Versuche der künstlerischen Gestaltung." See "Pierre de Coubertin (1863-1937)," p. 256.

115. *This Great Symbol*, p. 278.

116. *Le phénomène olympique*, pp. 12-13.

117. *Mémoires olympiques*, pp. 23, 59.

118. Ibid., pp. 132, 212.

119. *Notes sur l'éducation publique*, p. 226.

120. *Monsieur de Coubertin*, p. 95.

121. *This Great Symbol*, p. 96.

122. "Pierre de Coubertin (1863-1937)," p. 256.

123. *The Nazi Olympics*, p.241.

124. *This Great Symbol*, p. 181.

125. Carl Diem, "Vom deutschen Sinn der Deutschen Kampfspiele" [1926], in *Olympische Flamme*, p. 231.

126. Carl Diem, "Wehrhaftigkeit" [1931]; "Plato, du bist veraltet" [1924]; "Germanen" [1932]; "Sturmlauf durch Frankreich" [1940], in *Olympische Flamme*, pp. 86, 141; 37; 124.

127. *Die olympischen Spiele 1936 und die Weltmeinung*, p. 88.

128. *Pédagogie sportive*, pp. 133f., 63.

129. Carl Diem, "Germanen" [1932], in *Olympische Flamme*, p. 38.

130. *Pédagogie sportive*, p. 139.

131. Carl Diem, "Sport ist Zeitvertreib" [1924], in *Olympische Flamme*, p. 166.

132. Carl Diem, "Die Lücke" [1940], in *Olympische Flamme*, p. 133.

133. Carl Diem, "Der Erzieher" [1924], in *Olympische Flamme*, pp. 46-48.

134. Arnd Krüger, *Sport und Politik: Von Turnvater Jahn zum Staatsamateur* (Hannover: Fackelträger Verlag, 1975), p. 41. Coubertin also made study tours to the United States in 1889 and 1893 (see *This Great Symbol*, pp. 113-28, 164-66).

135. Carl Diem, "Grundsätze der Körpererziehung" [1936], "Wehrhaftigkeit" [1931], in *Olympische Flamme*, pp. 77, 95.

136. Carl Diem, "Der Professional" [1940], in *Olympische Flamme*, p. 185.

137. Some of the extensive evidence on this theme can be found in Carl Diem, "Persönlichkeit" [1923?], "Grundsätze der Körpererziehung" [1936], in *Olympische Flamme*, pp. 59, 78.

138. "Pierre de Coubertin (1863-1937)," p. 255.

139. Carl Diem, "Gut Deutsch im Sport" [1917], in *Olympische Flamme*, p. 226.

140. Carl Diem, "Sport für alle" [1932], in *Olympische Flamme*, p. 206.

141. Carl Diem, "Vorbemerkung" [1918], in *Olympische Flamme*, p. 241.

142. Carl Diem, "Weltspiele?" [1941], in *Olympische Flamme*, pp. 244-245.

143. "Vom deutschen Sinn der Deutschen Kampfspiele," p. 231.

144. George L. Mosse, *The Crisis of German Ideology: Intellectual Origins of the Third Reich* (New York: Schocken Books, 1981), p. 1. My account of Volkish thought is based primarily on Mosse.

145. Ibid., p. 4.

146. *The Nazi Olympics*, p. 239.

147. Carl Diem, *Der deutsche Sport in der Zeit des*

Nationalsozialismus (Köln: Carl-Diem-Institut, 1980), p. 34; *Weltgeschichte des Sports und der Leibeserziehung*, p. 996. It should be noted, however, that Diem's record in matters pertaining to the Jews is not entirely clean. In a letter dated October 17, 1940, Diem asks Otto Abetz, the German ambassador to occupied France, to confirm whether two French sport officials are "both Jews" who might constitute an obstacle to the "new order" (*Neuordnung*) Germany was about to bring to international sport. Diem was no doubt relieved to learn that both men in question were of "Aryan" descent. See "Coubertin und das Dritte Reich," pp. 50-51.

148. Carl Diem, "Sport und Geist" [1927], in *Olympische Flamme*, p. 150.

149. *The Crisis of German Ideology*, pp. 28-29.

150. "Persönlichkeit" [1923?], p. 59. A printing error makes it unclear whether this address was made in 1923 or 1932. I believe that 1923 is the more probable date.

151. "Philosophie der Leibesübungen," p. 66.

152. "Weltspiele?," p. 245.

153. Carl Diem, "Die Welt für Deutschland fordern" [1925], in *Olympische Flamme*, p. 44.

154. Carl Diem, "Sehnen nach einem Führer" [1923], in *Olympische Flamme*, p. 44.

155. Carl Diem, "Gegen den Schattenreiter!" [1915], in *Olympische Flamme*, p. 228.

156. *The Crisis of German Ideology*, p. viii.

157. "Sport für alle" [1932], p. 206.

158. Carl Diem, "Olympische Spiele sind..." [1936], in *Olympische Flamme*, p. 241. The German phrase is "Volkstum mit Weitblick und Weltsinn."

159. "Sport und Geist" [1927], p. 151.

160. Carl Diem, "Der Weg zum wahren Sport" [1928], in *Olympische Flamme*, p. 191.

161. "Sport und Geist" [1927], p. 142.

162. Carl Diem "Allerlei Formulierungen" [1938], in *Olympische Flamme*, p. 119.

163. "Philosophie der Leibesübungen" [1932], p. 63.

164. Carl Diem, "Wesen und Wert des Sports" [1933], in *Olympische Flamme*, p. 109. .

165. "Allerlei Formulierungen" [1941], p. 118.

166. *Weltgeschichte des Sports und der Leibeserziehung*, p. vii.

167. "Philosophie der Leibesübungen" [1932], p. 64.

168. Ibid., p. 68.

169. *The Crisis of German Ideology*, p. 116.

170. "Persönlichkeit" [1923?], p. 58.

171. "Sehnen nach einem Führer" [1923/24], in *Olympische Flamme*, pp. 45, 45; "Persönlichkeit" [1923?], p. 51; "Sport und Geist" [1927], p. 148.

172. "Sehnen nach einem Führer" [1923/24], pp. 46, 46; "Persönlichkeit" [1923?], p. 49.

173. *The Nazi Olympics*, p. 84.

174. *Sport und Politik*, p. 34.

175. Carl Diem, "Zum Amateurbegriff" [1926], in *Olympische Flamme*, p. 181.

176. Ibid., p. 182.

177. "Der Weg zum wahren Sport" [1928], p. 190.

178. "Der Professional" [1940], p. 183.

179. "Zum Amateurbegriff," p. 181.

180. "Sport und Geist" [1927], p. 152; "Der Professional" [1940], p. 184.

181. "Der Professional" [1940], p. 185.

182. Albert Speer, *Inside the Third Reich* (New York: Avon, 1971), p. 162. Speer went on to become Minister of Armaments in 1942.

183. *The Nazi Olympics*, p. 240.

184. *Die olympische Spiele 1936 und die Weltmeinung*, p. 88.

185. Ibid., p. 43.

186. *Sport und Politik*, pp. 42-43.

187. Hajo Bernett, *Sportpolitik im Dritten Reich* (Schorndorf bei Stuttgart: Verlag Karl Hofmann, 1971), pp. 85-89.

188. *Die olympischen Spiele 1936 und die Weltmeinung*, p. 45.

189. "Pierre de Coubertin (1863-1937)," p. 253.

190. *Die olympischen Spiele 1936 und die Weltmeinung*, p. 173.

191. *Der deutsche Sport in der Zeit des Nationalsozialismus*, pp. 36, 34.

192. Hajo Bernett, *Untersuchungen zur Zeitgeschichte de sports*, (Schorndorf bei Stuttgart: Verlag Karl Hofmann, 1973), p. 129.

193. Weltgeschicte des Sports und der Leibeserziehung, pp. 1017-18.

194. *Der deutsche Sport in der Zeit des National-*

sozialismus, pp. 1, 2.

195. See, for example, *Die olympischen Spiele 1936 und die Weltmeinung*, pp. 18-19. A centennial volume, including essays by two prominent sport scholars, Ommo Grupe and Hans Lenk, is *100 Jahre Carl Diem* (Köln: Carl-Diem-Institut an der Deutschen Sporthochschule Köln, 1882).

196. *Mémoires olympiques*, p. 108.

197. For a brief summary of Brundage's career see "Avery Brundage, Ex-Olympics Chairman, 87, Is Dead," *New York Times*, May 9, 1975; for an account of Brundage's role in the Berlin Olympiad see *The Nazi Olympics*, especially pp. 71-82; for a psychological study of Brundage see Allen Guttmann, "The Games Must Go On: On the Origins of Avery Brundage's life-credo," *Stadion*, Vol. 5, No. 2 (1979), pp. 253-62. Guttmann's biography is *The Games Must Go On: Avery Brundage and the Olympic Movement* (New York: Columbia University Press, 1983).

198. "Fair Play for American Athletes" (American Olympic Committee, 1935), pp. 2, 1.

199. *Mémoires olympiques*, pp. 102-4.

200. Red Smith, "The Noblest Badger of Them All," *New York Times*, May 12, 1975, p. 33.

201. Robert Shaplen, "Amateur," *New Yorker*, July 23, 1960, p. 62.

202. Idem.

203. "Fair Play for American Athletes," pp. 9, 2.

204. "Amateur," p. 38.

205. Quoted in Robert Creamer, "The Embattled World of Avery Brundage," *Sports Illustrated*, January 30, 1956, p. 58.

206. Avery Brundage, "The Fumbled Ball," *Vital Speeches of the Day*, Vol. 33 (April 15, 1967), p. 414.

207. "Amateur," p. 52.

208. "The Embattled World of Avery Brundage," p. 57.

209. "The Fumbled Ball," p. 414.

210. William Oscar Johnson, "Avery Brundage: The Man Behind the Mask," *Sports Illustrated*, August 4, 1980, p. 52.

211. "The Embattled World of Avery Brundage," p. 57.

212. "Amateur," p. 70.

213. Ibid., pp. 60, 47, 48.

214. "Avery Brundage: The Man Behind the Mask," p. 57.

215. Avery Brundage, "I Must Admit—Russian Athletes Are Great!", *Saturday Evening Post*, April 30, 1955, p. 35.

216. Roger Butterfield, "Avery Brundage," *Life*, June 14, 1948.

217. "Fair Play for American Athletes," p. 2.

218. *Die olympischen Spiele 1936 und die Weltmeinung*, p. 84.

219. "Fair Play for American Athletes," p. 2.

220. Robert Creamer, "Of Greeks—and Russians," *Sports Illustrated*, February 6, 1956, p. 32.

221. "I Must Admit—Russian Athletes Are Great!", p. 37.

222. Ibid., pp. 37, 36.

223. "The Fumbled Ball," p. 414.

224. "I Must Admit—Russian Athletes Are Great!", p. 38.

225. The best treatment of the subject is David Caute, *The Fellow-Travellers* (New York: Macmillan, 1973).

226. Ibid., p. 3.

227. "Amateur," p. 37; "Of Greeks—and Russians," p. 32.

228. Quoted in Robert Creamer, "The Embattled World of Avery Brundage," *Sports Illustrated*, January 30, 1956, p. 57.

229. "Amateur," p. 32.

230. William Johnson, "Defender of the Faith," *Sports Illustrated*, July 24, 1972, p. 40.

231. "Of Greeks—and Russians," p. 30.

232. "Defender of the Faith," p. 32.

233. "Killanin's Speech Altered in Czech Text," *New York Times*, June 16, 1977; see also "Lord Killanin censuré?" *L'Equipe*, June 16, 1977.

234. Quoted in S. Popov, *Socialism and Humanism* (Moscow: Progress Publishers, 1977), p. 146.

235. "Rings round them," *The Economist*, February 2, 1980, p. 14.

236. Henry Morton, *Soviet Sport* (New York: Collier Books, 1963), pp. 83, 70, 83, 84.

237. "Olympia dient der Erhaltung des Friedens," *Neues Deutschland*, Janaury 25, 1979, p. 5.

238. Avery Brundage, "I Must Admit—Russian Athletes Are Great," *Saturday Evening Post*, April 30, 1955, p. 36.

239. Robert Creamer, "Of Greeks—and Russians," *Sports Illustrated*, February 6, 1956, p. 32.

240. Idem.

241. "International Olympic Committee," *Great Soviet Encyclopedia*, Vol. 15 (New York: Macmillan, Inc., 1977), pp. 66-67.

242. Willi Knecht, "Moskaus zweiter Versuch: Olympia 1980 in der Sowjetunion?" *Deutschland Arkiv*, Vol. 4, No. 11 (November 1971), pp. 1152-54; see also Willi Knecht, "Moskaus ultimative Kandidatur," *Deutschland Arkiv*, Vol. 7, No. 5 (May 1974), pp. 464-67.

243. "Moskaus zweiter Versuch: Olympia 1980 in der Sowjetunion?," pp. 1154, 1151, 1156.

244. "Sportler aus 45 Ländern werden in Algier starten," *Neues Deutschland*, July 13, 1978, p. 5.

245. See Jean Meynaud, *Sport et politique* (Paris: Payot, 1966), p. 291.

246. Klaus Ullrich, "Olympia, Coubertin und wir," *Neues Deutschland*, July 10/11, 1976, p. 9.

247. "Zur Frage der Olympischen Spiele," *Theorie und Praxis der Körperkultur* (1953), pp. 79, 85.

248. Yves-Pierre Boulongne, "Pierre de Coubertin: Ein Beitrag zu einer wissenschaftlichen Untersuchung seines Lebens und seines Werkes," in Hans-Jürgen Schulke, *Die Zukunft der Olympischen Spiele* (Köln: Pahl-Rugenstein, 1976), p. 94.

249. Ibid., p. 93.

250. Pierre de Coubertin, *Mémoires olympiques*, (Lausanne: Bureau International de Pédagogie Sportive, 1931), p. 182.

251. Horst Ueberhorst, *Frisch, frei, stark und treu: Die Arbeitersportbewegung in Deutschland* (Düsseldorf: Droste Verlag, 1973), pp. 158-159.

252. See Robert F. Wheeler, "Organized Sport and Organized Labour: The Workers' Sports Movement," *Journal of Contemporary History*, Vol. 13 (1978), pp. 200-2; James Riordan, *Sport in Soviet Society* (New York: Cambridge University Press, 1977), p. 110.

253. *Mémoires olympiques*, pp. 212, 213.

254. Klaus Ullrich, "80 Jahre Olympische Spiele," in *Die Zukunft der Olympischen Spiele*, p. 32.

255. Nadeja Lekarska, *Essays and Studies on Olympic Problems* (Sofia: Medicina and Fizcultura, 1973), p. 16.

256. *Sport in Soviet Society*, p. 252.

257. "Gilkes Appeal Denied," *New York Times*, July 23, 1976, p. A13.

258. "Boycott threat to IOC bankroll," *Dallas Times Herald*, February 5, 1980, p. 4-D.

259. Mohamed Mzali, "Olympism and culture (II)," *Olympic Review*, No. 144 (October 1979), p. 574.

260. Czeslaw Milosz, *The Captive Mind* (New York: Vintage Books, n.d.), p. 223.

261. "Olympism and culture (II)," p. 574.

262. See, for example, Klaus Ullrich, "Wurde Angelo Jacopucci ein Opfer der Manager?", *Neues Deutschland*, August 4, 1978, p. 8.

263. "Olympism and culture (II)," p. 575.

264. Andrzej Wohl, "Fifty Years of Physical Culture in the U.S.S.R.: Reflections and Conclusions," *International Review of Sport Sociology*, Vol. 3 (1968), p. 186.

III. The Moscow Olympiad In Its Political Context

1. Willi Ph. Knecht, *Der Boykott: Moskaus missbrauchte Olympiade* (Köln: Verlag Wissenschaft und Politik, 1980), p. 67.

2. Christopher Booker, *The Games War: A Moscow Journal* (London: Faber and Faber, 1981), p. 77.

3. "Text of Carter's Letter to President of the U.S. Olympic Committee," *New York Times*, January 21, 1980, p. A4. It should be noted that the Carter letter represented a departure from his position enunciated a year and a half earlier. When asked during his press conference of July 20, 1978, whether he would support a boycott of the Moscow Olympics "as a protest of Soviet treatment of dissidents," the President replied: "This is a decision that will be made by the United States Olympic Committee. My own hope is that the American athletes will participate in the 1980 Olympics." (*New York Times*, July 21, 1978).

4. *Der Boykott: Moskaus misbrauchte Olympiade*, p. 88.

5. "President Proposes Deadline of Month for Olympics Move," *New York Times*, January 21, 1980, p. 1.

6. "Vance reiterates U.S. stance on Summer Games to IOC, no action taken," *Houston*

Chronicle, February 10, 1980, p. 30, § 1.

7. Dave Anderson, "What Olympic Movement?" *New York Times,* February 11, 1980.

8. "Olympic Committee Appears Set on Moscow as Site," *New York Times,* February 11, 1980.

9. The best account of the political and diplomatic maneuvers surrounding the Moscow Olympiad is Willi Ph. Knecht, *Der Boykott: Moskaus missbrauchte Olympiade.* A good description of the Moscow Games by a journalist who attended them is Christopher Booker, *The Games War: A Moscow Journal.* A useful analysis of political developments during 1980 prior to the Olympiad is David B. Kanin, *A Political History of the Olympic Games* (Boulder, Colorado: Westview Press, 1981), pp. 108-47.

10. *The Current Digest of the Soviet Press,* Vol. XXXII, No. 11, p. 8.

11. *The Current Digest of the Soviet Press,* Vol. XXXII, No. 5, p. 6.

12. "Soviet Charges Carter with Blackmail on Olympics," *New York Times,* January 14, 1980.

13. "Some Russians Feel U.S. Overreacts on Afghanistan," *New York Times,* January 27, 1980, p. 3.

14. *The Current Digest of the Soviet Press,* Vol. XXXII, No. 2, p. 9.

15. *The Current Digest of the Soviet Press,* Vol. XXXII, No. 15, p. 6.

16. "Tass Says Carter is Playing Politics With Olympics," *New York Times,* January 22, 1980, p. A9.

17. *The Current Digest of the Soviet Press,* Vol. XXXII, No. 5, p. 6.

18. "News of Olympic Boycott Move Puzzles Ordinary Soviet Citizens," *New York Times,* April 17, 1980, p. A16.

19. *The Current Digest of the Soviet Press,* Vol. XXXII, No. 30, p. 1.

20. "Some Russians Feel U.S. Overreacts on Afghanistan," *New York Times,* January 27, 1980, p. 3.

21. *The Current Digest of the Soviet Press,* Vol. XXXII, No. 10, p. 14.

22. "Soviets say U.S. plotting to ruin Games," *Dallas Times Herald,* April 20, 1980, p. 26-A.

23. Idem.

24. *The Games War,* p. 27.

25. *Der Boykott,* p. 40.

26. Ibid., p. 59.

27. "Sacharov släpps när OS är över," *Dagens Nyheter* (Stockholm), January 24, 1980. On April 17, 1980, the *New York Times,* reported (p. A16) that Sakharov had called participation in the Moscow Games "inadmissible."

28. *The Current Digest of the Soviet Press,* Vol. XXXII, No. 3, p. 1.

29. Ibid.. p. 1, 2.

30. "Les dissidents contre les J.O.," *L'Express.* February 2, 1980, p. 40.

31. *Der Boykott,* p. 68.

32. *The Games War,* p. 34.

33. "Soviets support boycott" [UPI], *The Daily Texan,* April 11, 1980, p. 15.

34. This account of Medvedev's career prior to the boycott controversy is based on Hedrick Smith, *The Russians* (New York: Ballantine Books, 1977), pp. 596-603.

35. Ibid., p. 596.

36. René Fuelopp-Miller, *The Mind and Face of Bolshevism* (New York: Harper Torchbooks, 1965), pp. 136-37.

37. Ibid., p. 151.

38. Ibid., p. 4.

39. Ibid., p. 2.

40. "Ritual movement is often organized in exactly the same precise and detailed way as military movement. The demonstration on mass political holidays, particularly from the thirties onwards, has been organized in every detail." Christel Lane, *The Rites of Rulers: Ritual in Industrial Society— The Soviet Case* (Cambridge: Cambridge University Press, 1981), p. 224.

41. Ibid., p. 20.

42. *The Mind and Face of Bolshevism,* p. 12.

43. Nigel Wade, "The Games: a triumph of Russian propaganda," *The Sunday Telegraph* (London), August 4, 1980.

44. "Grinding Out the Gold, *Newsweek,* August 4, 1980, p. 64.

45. Anthony Austin, "Games End on a Colorful Note," *New York Times,* August 4, 1980, p. C4.

46. Craig R. Whitney, "In Moscow, Icons and Smiles Materialize for Games," *New York Times,* August 2, 1980, p. 5.

47. *The Games War*, p. 172.

48. Nigel Wade, "All set for the Red Olympics," *The Sunday Telegraph*, July 13, 1980.

49. *The Games War*, p. 172.

50. " 'Wir haben dem Druck widerstanden'," *Der Spiegel*, August 4, 1980, p. 17.

51. Henry Morton, *Soviet Sport* (New York: Collier Books, 1963), p. 74.

52. James Riordan, "The USSR," in James Riordan, ed., *Sport under Communism* (London: C. Hurst & Company, 1978); p. 33.

53. James Riordan, *Sport in Soviet Society* (Cambridge: Cambridge University Press, 1977), p. 251.

54. From a statement published in *Sovetsky sport*, July 9, 1971, by Sergei Pavlov, Chairman of the Committee on Physical Culture and Sport, in *Sport in Soviet Society*, p. 250.

55. See, for example, the journalistic responses quoted in *Der Boykott*, p. 214.

56. *The Games War*, pp. 80-81.

57. *The Rites of Rulers*, p. 226.

58. Ibid., p. 225.

59. Susan Sontag, "Fascinating Fascism," in *Under the Sign of Saturn* (New York: Farrar Straus Giroux, 1980), pp. 91-92.

60. "Proposal Put Forward To Denationalize Games," *New York Times*, February 12, 1980.

61. "Britain Bars Special Olympic Leave for Civil Servants and the Military," *New York Times*, March 14, 1980.

62. "Kremlin fights to limit boycott," *Christian Science Monitor*, April 14, 1980.

63. The nations represented were: West Germany, Andorra, Austria, Belgium, Denmark, Finland, France, Great Britain, Greece, Ireland, Liechtenstein, Malta, The Netherlands, San Marino, Switzerland, Turkey, and Italy; the Swedish Olympic committee was represented by the Danish delegation; the national committees of Portugal and Spain had telephoned their support for the Rome resolutions. (From *Der Boykott*, p. 175.) Of these twenty countries, only West Germany, Liechtenstein, and Turkey withdrew from the Games.

64. Adapted from *Der Boykott*, pp. 174-175.

65. "European Olympic leaders call on world to resist Games boycott," *Dallas Times Herald*, May 4, 1980, p. 8-A.

66. Nigel Wade, "Ceremony boycott shows through Moscow pageantry," *The Daily Telegraph*, July 21, 1980, p. 15.

67. "Moscow Enjoys Games in Spite of Itself," *New York Times*, July 28, 1980.

68. *Sport in Soviet Society*, p. 252.

69. K. Zharov and I. Barchukov, "For the Olympic Ideals," *Soviet Military Review*, No. 10 (October 1981), p. 64.

70. Priscilla Johnson, *Khrushchev and the Arts: The Politics of Soviet Culture, 1962-1964* (Cambridge, Mass.: The M.I.T. Press, 1965), p. 217.

71. "All set for the Red Olympics," *The Sunday Telegraph*, July 13, 1980.

72. *Khrushchev and the Arts*, p. 102.

73. *The Current Digest of the Soviet Press*, Vol. XXXII, No. 3, p. 1. The date of the *Izvestia* article is January 24, 1980.

74. Paul Lendvai, *The Bureaucracy of Truth* (Boulder, Colorado: Westview Press, 1981), p. 183.

75. *The Current Digest of the Soviet Press*, Vol. XXXII, No. 10, p. 14.

76. Michael T. Harrington, "On an Olympic Boycott," *New York Times*, January 12, 1980.

77. Harrison E. Salisbury, "A Boon for the K.G.B." *New York Times*, January 31, 1980.

78. Interview with Nigel Wade, Moscow correspondent of *The Daily Telegraph* (London), Cambridge, Massachusetts, May 24, 1983.

79. Anthony Lewis, "Laurels for Moscow?" *New York Times*, February 11, 1980.

80. My account is based on "Moscow's Festival for Youth," *The New Republic*, July 15, 1957; and George Abrams, "Talking with Russians," *The New Republic*, October 14, 1957, pp. 13-16.

81. Interview with Nigel Wade.

82. *Khrushchev and the Arts*, p. 102.

83. "Moscow Enjoys Games in Spite of Itself," *New York Times*, July 28, 1980.

84. "Talking with Russians," p. 14.

85. "A Boon for the K.G.B."

86. See especially Christopher Booker, *The Games War: A Moscow Journal* (1981).

IV. The Critique of Olympia

1. John J. MacAloon, *This Great Symbol: Pierre*

de Coubertin and the Origins of the Modern Olympic Games (Chicago: University of Chicago Press, 1981), p. 176.

2. Richard D. Mandell, The First Modern Olympics (Berkeley: University of California Press, 1976), p. 92.

3. This Great Symbol, p. 269.

4. The First Modern Olympics, p. 169.

5. Pierre de Coubertin, Pédagogie sportive (Lausanne: Bureau International de Pédagogie Sportive, 1922), pp. 120, 137; Essais de psychologie sportive (Lausanne et Paris: Librairie Payot & Cie, 1913), p. 222.

6. Essais de psychologie sportive, p. 169.

7. Fritz Wildung, Arbeitersport (Berlin: Der Bücherkreis G.M.B.H., 1929), pp. 57-58.

8. Quoted in Henry Morton, Soviet Sport (New York: Collier Books, 1963), p. 73.

9. Friedrich Schiller, On the Aesthetic Education of Man (New York: Frederick Ungar, 1965), pp. 37-38, 79.

10. Fritz Stern, The Politics of Cultural Despair: A Study in the Rise of the Germanic Ideology (Berkeley: University of California Press, 1974), p. xvi.

11. Bruce Haley, The Healthy Body and Victorian Culture (Cambridge, Mass.: Harvard University Press, 1978), p. 124.

12 Ibid., p. 123.

13. José Ortega y Gasset, The Revolt of the Masses (New York: Norton, 1960), p. 43.

14. Ibid., p. 41.

15. The Healthy Body and Victorian Culture, p. 138.

16. Ibid., p. 129.

17. Ibid., p. 131.

18. The Revolt of the Masses, p. 39.

19. Richard Mandell, The Nazi Olympics (New York: Macmillan, 1971), p. 204. For an account of the evolution of the record performance, see Allen Guttmann, From Ritual to Record: The Nature of Modern Sports (New York: Columbia University Press), pp. 15-55.

20. Pierre de Coubertin, Mémoires olympiques, (Lausanne: Bureau International de Pédagogie Sportive, 1931), pp. 22-23.

21. Andre Senay and Robert Hervet, Monsieur de Coubertin (Paris: Points & Contrepoints, 1960), p. 133.

22. Ibid., p. 70.

23. Essais de psychologie sportive, pp. 126, 128.

24. Ibid., pp. 126, 127.

25. Ibid., p. 133.

26. Pédagogie sportive, pp. 23, 55, 56.

27. Mémoires olympiques, p. 210.

28. Ibid., p. 90.

29. Ibid., p. 215-216.

30. Ibid., p. 68.

31. Ibid., p. 49.

32. Ibid., p. 12.

33. Ibid., p. 102.

34. Ibid., p. 104.

35. Ibid., p. 216.

36. Gaston Meyer, Le phénomène olympique (Paris: La Table Ronde, 1960), p. 13. Coubertin's reference to "the true Olympic hero" is confirmed by Diem in "Olympia nur noch für Männer?" [1938], in Olympische Flamme (Berlin: Deutscher Arkiv Verlag, 1942), p. 400. Diem, however, attributes this phrase to a radio address, titled "Pax Olympica," broadcast a year before the Berlin Games.

37. Mémoires olympiques, p. 216.

38. "Olympia nur noch für Männer?" [1938], p. 400.

39. Mémoires olympiques, pp. 216-217.

40. Ibid., p. 217.

41. Ibid., p. 216.

42. Ibid., p. 196.

43. Adrian Lyttleton, "Introduction," in Adrian Lyttleton, ed. Italian Fascisms: From Pareto to Gentile (New York: Harper Torchbooks, 1975), pp. 12-13.

44. Benito Mussolini, "The Doctrine of Fascism," in Italian Fascisms, p. 52.

45. Ibid., p. 47.

46. Ernst Nolte, Three Faces of Fascism (New York: Mentor Books, 1969), pp. 215, 216.

47. Denis Mack Smith, Mussolini (New York: Knopf, 1982), pp. 18, 15.

48. "The Doctrine of Fascism," p. 42.

49. Ibid., p. 43.

50. Ibid., p. 57.

51. Ibid., p. 48.

52. "Introduction" to Italian Fascisms, p. 12.

53. Enrico Corradini, "Article from *Il Regno*," in *Italian Fascisms*, p. 139.

54. Giovanni Papini, "A Nationalist Programme," in *Italian Fascisms*, pp. 102, 106.

55. Ardengo Soffici, "Extract from *Lemmonio Boreo*," in *Italian Fascisms*, p. 256.

56. Alfredo Rocco, "The *Politica* Manifesto," in *Italian Fascisms*, p. 256.

57. "A Nationalist Programme," p. 102.

58. Vilfredo Pareto, "From *Les systèmes socialistes*" [1902], in *Italian Fascisms*, p. 81.

59. Ibid., p. 73.

60. "A Nationalist Programme," p. 101.

61. Curzio Malaparte, "Mussolini and National Syndicalism," in *Italian Fascisms*, p. 225.

62. See, for example, Denis Mack Smith, *Mussolini*, pp. 106, 107, 111, 113-14, 284.

63. See, for example, Hans Lenk, "Carl Diem— The Humanist," *International Journal of Physical Education*, No. 4 (1982), pp. 9-12. This uncritical encomium is, moreover, the work of a reputable sport scholar.

64. *Essais de psychologie sportive*, p. 259.

65. Ibid., p. 133.

66. *Mussolini*, p. 12.

67. Friedrich Nietzsche, *The Will to Power*, trans. Walter Kaufmann and R.J. Hollingdale (New York: Vintage Books, 1968), p. 359 (fragment 748).

68. *This Great Symbol*, p. 262.

69. *Mémoires olympiques*, p. 132.

70. *This Great Symbol*, p. 266.

71. See, for example,*Mémoires olympiques*, p. 89.

72. Mihajlo Mihajlov, "The Absurdity of Non-ideology," in *Underground Notes* (New Rochelle, New York: Caratzas Brothers, Publishers, 1982), p. 79.

73. *This Great Symbol*, pp. 167-168.

74. J. Astley Cooper, "An Anglo-Saxon Olympiad," *Nineteenth Century*, No. 187 (Sept. 1892), pp. 380-388; "The Pan-Britannic Gathering," *Nineteenth Century*, No. 197 (July 1893), pp. 81-93.

75. "The Pan-Britannic Gathering," pp. 84, 82.

76. J. Astley Cooper, "Olympic Games: What Has Been Done and What Remains to Be Done," *The Nineteenth Century*, No. 376 (June 1908), p. 1014.

77. Ibid., p. 1012.

78. "An Anglo-Saxon Olympiad," p. 381.

79. "Olympic Games," pp. 1011, 1018, 1020.

80. "An Anglo-Saxon Olympiad," p. 384.

81. "The Pan-Britannic Gathering," pp. 83-84, 84.

82. "An Anglo-Saxon Olympiad," p. 388.

83. "The Pan-Britannic Gathering," p. 81.

84. Ibid., p. 87.

85. "An Anglo-Saxon Olympiad," p. 385.

86. *Three Faces of Fascism*, p. 109.

87. William R. Tucker, *The Fascist Ego: A Political Biography of Robert Brasillach* (Berkeley: University of California Press, 1975), p. 78.

88. *Three Faces of Fascism*, p. 144.

89. *This Great Symbol*, p. 111.

90. See *Three Faces of Fascism*, pp. 94-95 and, especially, *This Great Symbol*, pp. 262-68.

91. Charles Maurras, "Les nations dans le stade et la course de Marathon," in *Le voyage d'Athènes* (Paris: Flammarion, 1929), pp. 56-57.

92. Ibid., p. 58.

93. Ibid., pp. 59, 66.

94. *Three Faces of Fascism*, p. 95.

95. Charles Maurras, "The Politics of Nature," in J.S. McClelland, ed. *The French Right from de Maistre to Maurras* (New York: Harper Torchbooks, 1971), p. 290.

96. Charles Maurras, "The Future of French Nationalism," in *The French Right*, p. 296.

97. Maurice Bardèche, "Les Ecrivains et la Politique," *Défense de l'Occident* (March 1954), p. 23.

98. *Three Faces of Fascism*, p. 144.

99. Charles Maurras, "Romanticism and Revolution," in *The French Right*, p. 255.

100. Ibid., p. 242.

101. *Three Faces of Fascism*, p. 142.

102. Ibid., p. 143.

103. Ibid., p. 123.

104. See, for example, J. Plumyène and R. Lasierra, *Les fascismes français 1923-1963* (Paris: Editions du Seuil, 1963), p. 208.

105. See *Les fascismes français*, p. 208; François Duprat, *Les mouvements d'extrême-droite en France depuis 1944* (Paris: Les Editions Al-

batros, 1972), p. 35.

106. Maurice Bardèche, "Réponse sur le fascisme," *Défense de l'Occident* (May 1962), p. 30; *Sparte et les sudistes* (Paris: Les Sept Couleurs, 1969), p. 11.

107. Adapted from John M. Hoberman, "The Mind of Maurice Bardèche," *Psychohistory Review*, Vol. V, No. 1 (June 1976), p. 11.

108. *Les temps modernes*, p. 61.

109. René Remond, *The Right Wing in France: From 1815 to de Gaulle* (Philadelphia: University of Pennsylvania Press, 1968), pp. 348-349.

110. René Chiroux, *L'Extrême-droite sous la Ve République* (Paris: Librarie Générale de Droit et de Jurisprudence, 1974), p. 247.

111. Serge Thomas, "Contre la trève olympique," *Défense de l'Occident* (Jan. 1973), p. 67; Maurice Bardèche, "Jeux olympiques, Maquisards et nantis," *Défense de l'Occident* (Aug.-Sept. 1973), pp. 3-4.

112. Paul Werrie, "De la pétanque à l'athlète d'Etat," *Ecrits de Paris* (Oct. 1961), p. 76.

113. Paul Werrie, "Pierre de Coubertin: 'Rénovateur' des Jeux Olympiques," *Ecrits de Paris* (June 1963), pp. 104-105.

114. Paul Werrie, " 'Tokio Olympiades' ou la mort des dieux," *Ecrits de Paris* (Nov. 1965), pp. 91, 94.

115. Ibid., p. 94. For a similar interpretation of the Berlin Olympiad see "Contre la trève olympique," p. 65.

116. "Jeux Olympiques, Maquisards et nantis," p. 4.

117. "De la pétanque à l'athlète d'Etat," p. 77.

118. "Pierre de Coubertin: 'Rénovateur' des Jeux Olympiques," p. 103.

119. "Jeux Olympiques, Maquisards et nantis," p. 4.

120. "Contre la trève olympique," p. 67.

121. "De la pétanque à l'athlète d'Etat," p. 76.

122. Paul Werrie, " 'Homo ludens, homo faber' ou l'évolution du sport," *Ecrits de Paris* (March 1970), p. 91.

123. Ibid., p. 89.

124. "Jeux Olympiques, Maquisards et nantis," p. 3.

125. "De la pétanque à l'athlète d'Etat," p. 83.

126. Ibid., p. 82.

127. Jean Mabire, "Pierre de Coubertin et l'éducation 'totale'," *Défense de l'Occident* (Jan. 1965), p. 48.

128. " 'Homo ludens, homo faber' ou l'évolution du sport," p. 91.

129. "Jeux Olympiques, Maquisards et nantis," p. 4.

130. "De la pétanque à l'athlète d'Etat," p. 79.

131. Maurice Bardèche, *Sparte et les sudistes* (Paris: Les Sept Couleurs, 1969), p. 19.

132. "Contre la trève olympique," p. 65.

133. "De la pétanque à l'athlète d'Etat," p. 78.

134. "Contre la trève olympique," pp. 66, 65.

135. Ibid., p. 69. John Akii-Bua of Uganda and Vince Matthews of the United States were Olympic champions in the 400-meter intermediate hurdles and the 400-meter dash, respectively, at the 1972 Munich Games.

136. Pierre de Coubertin, *Notes sur l'éducation publique* (Paris: Hachette, 1901), p. 132.

137. "Pierre de Coubertin et l'éducation 'totale'," pp. 50-51.

138. " 'Homo ludens, homo faber' ou l'évolution du sport," pp. 88, 90; "De la pétanque à l'athlète d'Etat," p. 77.

139. "Contre la trève olympique," p. 65.

140. " 'Tokio Olympiades' ou la mort des dieux," p. 95.

141. Under pressure from the Nazi regime, the German Gymnastics Association (DT) "dissolved itself" officially on September 30, 1936. For a detailed treatment of the relationship between the DT and the Nazis, see Hartmut Becker, "Die 'Arisierung' der Deutschen Turnerschaft," *Stadion*, Vol. II, No. 1 (1976), pp. 121-39.

142. George L. Mosse, *The Crisis of German Ideology: Intellectual Origins of the Third Reich* (New York: Schocken Books, 1981), p. 23.

143. Wolfgang Rothe, "When Sports Conquered the Republic: A Forgotten Chapter from the 'Roaring Twenties'," *Studies in Twentieth Century Literature*, Vol. 4, No. 1 (Fall 1980), p. 7.

144. Edmund Neuendorff, *Geschichte der neueren deutschen Leibesübung vom Beginn des 18. Jahrhunderts bis zur Gegenwart*, IV (Dresden: Wilhelm Limpert-Verlag, n.d.), pp. 174-75, 209, 493.

145. Ibid., p. 213.

149

146. Ibid., p. 498.

147. Arnd Krüger, *Die Olympischen Spiele 1936 und die Weltmeinung*, (Berlin, München, Frankfurt/M.: Verlag Bartels & Wernitz KG, 1972), p. 34.

148. Henning Eichberg, "Thing-, Fest- und Weihespiele in Nationalsozialismus, Arbeiterkultur und Olympismus," in Henning Eichberg et al., *Massenspiele: NS-Thingspiel, Arbeiterweihespiel und Olympisches Zeremoniell* (Stuttgart-Bad Cannstatt: frommann-holzboog, 1977), p. 152.

149. *Geschichte der neueren deutschen Leibesübung*, IV, pp. 481, 482, 482, 483, 498-99, 689,

150. Ibid., p. 480; Peter McIntosh, *Fair Play: Ethics in Sport and Education* (London: Heinemann, 1979), p. 51.

151. *Mémoires olympiques*, pp. 49-50.

152. " 'Homo ludens, homo faber' ou l'évolution du sport," p. 87.

153. *Geschichte der neueren deutschen Leibesübung*, IV, pp. 480, 486.

154. Ibid., p. 485.

155. Ibid., p. 486.

156. Ibid., p. 480.

157. Ibid., p. 499.

158. *Massenspiele*, p. 152.

159. Hajo Bernett, ed. *Nationalsozialistische Leibeserziehung* (Schorndorf bei Stuttgart: Verlag Karl Hofmann, 1966), p. 21.

160. Ibid., pp. 72, 141, 219, 94, 60.

161. Ibid., p. 37.

162. Arnd Krüger, *Die Olympischen Spiele 1936 und die Weltmeinung*, p. 42. Theodor Lewald, whose half-Jewish ancestry was known to his colleagues, was eventually forced to resign from this position. His replacement was Carl Diem. On the meeting of March 16, see also Hajo Bernett, *Sportpolitik im dritten Reich* (Schorndorf bei Stuttgart: Verlag Karl Hofmann, 1971), p. 40.

163. *Die Olympischen Spiele 1936 und die Weltmeinung*, p. 31.

164. Ibid., p. 38.

165. Hajo Bernett, *Untersuchungen zur Zeitgeschichte des Sports* (Schorndorf bei Stuttgart: Verlag Karl Hofmann, 1973), footnote p. 93.

166. Ibid., p. 16.

167. *Die Olympischen Spiele 1936 und die Weltmeinung*, p. 35.

168. Idem.

169. Ibid., p. 32.

170. *Untersuchungen*, p. 93.

171. Idem.

172. *Die Olympischen Spiele 1936 und die Weltmeinung*, p. 33.

173. *Essais de psychologie*, pp. 235-37.

174. Carl Diem, "Weltspiele?" [1941], in *Olympische Flamme: Das Buch vom Sport*, I (Berlin: Deutscher Archiv-Verlag, 1942), p. 245.

175. Albert Speer, *Inside the Third Reich* (New York: Avon Books, 1971), p. 114.

176. *Sportpolitik im dritten Reich*, pp. 52, 53.

177. *Untersuchungen*, p. 94.

178. *Die Olympischen Spiele 1936 und die Weltmeinung*, p. 91.

179. Idem.

180. Winfried Joch, *Politische Leibeserziehung und ihre Theorie im Nationalsozialistischen Deutschland* (Frankfurt/M.: Peter Lang, 1976), pp. 170, 225, 225.

181. *Untersuchungen*, p. 107.

182. *The Crisis of German Ideology*, p. vii.

183. *Sport und Politik*, p. 54.

184. *Untersuchungen*, p. 100.

185. Ibid., p. 44.

186. *Massenspiele*, pp. 152-53.

187. *Die Olympischen Spiele 1936 und die Weltmeinung*, p. 35.

188. *Massenspiele*, p. 36.

189. *Soviet Sport*, p. 70. Unfortunately, no date for this quotation is provided.

190. K. Zharov and I. Barchukov, "For the Olympic Ideals," *Soviet Military Review*, No. 10 (Oct. 1981), p. 63.

191. See *Soviet Sport*, pp. 78-84.

192. Ibid., p. 84.

193. Ibid., p. 83.

194. The RSI, founded in 1921, was a satellite organization of the Soviet-dominated Comintern, founded in 1919. The LSI was formed in 1920. See *Soviet Sport*, pp. 69-78; also, David A. Steinberg, "The Workers' Sport Internationals 1920-1928," *Journal of Contemporary History*, Vol. 13 (1978), pp. 233-51.

195. "The Workers' Sport Internationals 1920-1928," pp. 244, 247.

196. Ibid., p. 244.

197. Ibid., p. 245.

198. Ibid., p. 249.

199. *Arbeitersport*, p. 57.

200. Helmut Wagner, *Sport und Arbeitersport* [1931] (Köln: Pahl-Rugenstein, 1973), p. 181.

201. "The Workers' Sport Internationals 1920-1928," p. 245.

202. "Thing-, Fest- und Weihespiele in Nationalsozialismus, Arbeiterkultur und Olympismus," p. 89.

203. Ibid., p. 150.

204. *L'Humanité*, May 4, 1924, p. 2.

205. *L'Humanité*, May 22, 1924, p. 3.

206. *L'Humanité*, June 4, 1924, p. 2.

207. *L'Humanité*, May 26, 1924, p. 1.

208. *L'Humanité*, May 18, 1924, p. 2.

209. *L'Humanité*, May 29, 1924, p. 3.

210. This is a distortion of the facts; as we have seen, the Soviets excluded themselves from the "bourgeois" Olympiads they denounced (see *Soviet Sport*, p. 70).

211. *L'Humanité*, June 16, 1924, p. 1.

212. *L'Humanité*, May 26, 1924, p. 1.

213. *L'Humanité*, June 13, 1924, p. 3.

214. Paul Laurent, Robert Barran, Jean-Jacques Faure, *Les communistes et le sport: A l'heure de Munich* (Paris: Editions Sociales, 1972), p. 36.

215. *L'Humanité*, May 9, 1924, p. 3; May 26, 1924, p. 1.

216. *L'Humanité*, May 4, 1924.

217. Paul Werrie, " 'Tokio Olympiades' ou la mort des dieux," *Ecrits de Paris* (November 1965), p. 91.

218. For extended discussions of neo-Marxist sport theory see Allen Guttmann, "Translator's Introduction" to Bero Rigauer, *Sport and Work* (New York: Columbia University Press, 1981), pp. vii-xxxi; John M. Hoberman, *Sport and Political Ideology* (Austin: The University of Texas Press, 1984), chapter 11.

219. Gerhard Vinnai, "Vorwort," in Gerhard Vinnai, ed. *Sport in der Klassengesellschaft* (Frankfurt/M.: Fischer Taschenbuch Verlag, 1972), p. 7.

220. Pierre Laguillaumie, "Pour une critique fondamentale du sport," in Ginette Berthaud, Jean-Marie Brohm, François Gantheret, Pierre Laguillaumie, eds. *Sport, culture et répression* (Paris: François Maspero, 1972), p. 37.

221. *Sport and Work*, p. 10.

222. Ulrike Prokop, *Soziologie der Olympischen Spiele: Sport und Kapitalismus* (Munich: Carl Hanser Verlag, 1971), p. 21.

223. Jean-Marie Brohm, "Sociologie politique du sport," in *Sport, culture et répression*, p. 20.

224. Christine Kulke, "Emanzipation oder gleicher Recht auf 'Trimm Dich'?," in *Sport in der Klassengesellschaft*, p. 104.

225. Jean-Marie Brohm, *Critiques du sport* (Paris: Christian Bourgois, 1976), p. 148.

226. "Sociologie politique du sport," p. 22.

227. *Critiques du sport*, p. 226.

228. Johannes Gehrmann, "Der bundesdeutsche Sport und seine Führer," in *Sport in der Klassengesellschaft*, p. 50.

229. *Critiques du sport*, p. 228.

230. Gerhard Vinnai, "Leibeserziehung als Ideologie," in *Sport in der Klassengesellschaft*, p. 22.

231. *Soziologie der Olympischen Spiele*, p. 38.

232. Gerhard Vinnai, *Fussballsport als Ideologie* (Frankfurt/M.: Europäische Verlagsanstalt, 1970), p. 89.

233. "Leibeserziehung als Ideologie," pp. 11-12, Ginette Berthaud and Jean-Marie Brohm, "Présentation," in *Sport, culture et répression*, p. 13.

234. Eric Ertl, "Sport-Journalismus: Wie der Leistungssport auf seinen Begriff kommt," in *Sport in der Klassengesellschaft*, p. 146.

235. *Critiques du sport*, p. 144.

236. "Pour une critique fondamentale du sport," p. 48.

237. "Der bundesdeutsche Sport und seine Führer," p. 27.

238. "Présentation," p. 10.

239. Frank E. Manuel and Fritzie P. Manuel, *Utopian Thought in the Western World* (Cambridge, Mass.: The Belknap Press of Harvard University Press, 1979), p. 717.

240. *Soziologie der Olympischen Spiele*, pp. 15, 38, 73-74.

241. *Utopian Thought in the Western World*, p. 723.

242. *Soziologie der Olympischen Spiele*, p. 113.

243. "Présentation," p. 7.

244. The forerunners of the West German neo-Marxist sport critics are the German workers' sport theorists, whose most important manifestos appeared during 1928-1931. It should be noted, however, that the neo-Marxists refer to their socialist predecessors with surprising infrequency; it is rather the East Germans who, inappropriately, claim the *Arbeitersportler* as spiritual brethren.

245. *Geschichte der neueren deutschen Leibesübung*, IV, pp. 485, 480, 480.

246. *L'Humanité*, June 5, 1924, p. 1.

247. " 'Tokio Olympiades' ou la mort des dieux," p. 95.

248. Henning Eichberg, *Der Weg des Sports in die industrielle Zivilization* (Baden-Baden: Nomos Verlagsgesellschaft, 1973), p. 120.

249. *Geschichte der neueren deutschen Leibesübung*, IV, p. 482.

250. *L'Humanité*, June 6, 1924, p. 1.

251. " 'Homo ludens, homo faber' ou l'évolution du sport," p. 87.

252. " 'Tokio Olympiades' ou la mort des dieux," p. 95.

253. "Contre la trève olympique," p. 65.

254. *L'Humanité*, June 6, 1924, p. 2.

255. "Jeux Olympiques, Maquisards et nantis," p. 3.

256. Karl Jaspers, *Man in the Modern Age* (Garden City, N.Y.: Anchor Books, 1957), p. 57.

257. "Pour une critique fondamentale du sport," p. 35.

258. *Critiques du sport*, p. 137.

259. "Présentation," p. 15.

260. *Geschichte der neueren deutschen Leibesübung*, IV, pp. 484-85.

261. Ibid., p. 483.

262. Lothar Hack, "Alle haben doch die gleiche Chance," in *Sport in der Klassengesellschaft*, p. 119.

263. "Sociologie politique du sport," pp. 28, 29, 28.

264. *Critiques du sport*, p. 106.

265. *Geschichte der neueren deutschen Leibesübung*,

266. Ibid., p. 486.

267. Franz Dwertmann, "Sporthilfe: eine gemeinnützige Einrichtung?" in *Sport in der Klassengesellschaft*, p. 77.

268. "De la pétanque à l'athlète d'Etat," p. 82.

269. *Critiques du sport*, p. 140.

270. "Jeux Olympiques, Maquisards et nantis," p.5

271. Jean-Marie Brohm, 'vèrs l'analyse institutionnelle du sport de compétition," *L'Homme et la Société*, Nos. 29-30 (July-Dec. 1973), pp. 186-87.

272. See Jacques Ellul, *The Technological Society* (New York: Vintage Books, rev. ed. 1964, orig. ed. 1954).

273. Quoted in Klaus Ullrich, *Kreuzritter im Stadion: Bemerkungen zum Anti-kommunismus im Sport* (Berlin: Sportverlag, 1978), p. 15.

274. Quoted in Walter Sieger, "Zum Körperkultur in der sozialistischen Gesellschaft," *Deutsche Zeitschrift für Philosophie*, Vol. 12, No. 8 (1964), p. 934.

275. Idem.

276. Günter Witt, "Zu einigen Entwicklungstendenzen der Ästhetik des Sports in den sozialistischen Ländern," *Theorie und Praxis der Körperkultur*, Vol. 29, No. 2 (1980), p. 91.

277. Ilona Petzold, "Kunst und Sport in der DDR—Die Sammlung 'Sport in der bildenden Kunst der DDR' der DHfK Leipzig," *Theorie und Praxis der Körperkultur*, Vol. 29, No. 2 (1980), pp. 94, 101.

278. Andrzej Wohl, *Die gesellschaftlich-historischen Grundlagen des bürgerlichen Sports* (Köln: Pahl-Rugenstein, 1973), pp. 136-137.

279. N. Ponomaryov, *Sport and Society* (Moscow: Progress Publishers, 1981), p. 206.

280. Ibid., pp. 147, 148.

281. *Mémoires olympiques*, p. 81. Michael Poliakoff has pointed out to me that the Greek model of undifferentiated excellence is only valid within the boundaries of "non-wage" pursuit. The Greeks seemed to distinguish sharply between a *misthos* "wage" and a *doron* "gift." On this point see H. W. Pleket, "Games, Prizes, and Ideology," *Stadion*, Vol. 1 (1975), pp. 82ff.

282. *This Great Symbol*, p. 21.

283. *Pédagogie sportive*, p. 21.

IV, p. 481.

284. *Mémoires olympiques*, p. 64.

285. "Pierre de Coubertin (1863-1937)" [1941], in *Olympische Flamme*, p. 252.

286. "Grundsätze der Körpererziehung" [1936], in *Olympische Flamme*, p. 74.

287. "Höchstleistungen" [1923], in *Olympische Flamme*, p. 176.

288. "Olympische Kunst eng oder weit?" [1939], in *Olympische Flamme*, pp. 405, 406, 406, 406, 404.

289. Rufus W. Mathewson, *The Positive Hero in Russian Literature* (Stanford: Stanford University Press, 1975), p. 227.

290. Quoted in *The Positive Hero in Russian Literature*, p. 227.

291. Ibid., p. 230.

292. Priscilla Johnson, *Khrushchev and the Arts: The Politics of Soviet Culture, 1962-1964* (Cambridge, Mass.: The M.I.T. Press, 1965), p. 177.

293. A. Wohl, "Competitive Sport and its Social Functions," *International Review of Sport Sociology*, Vol. 5 (1970), pp. 119-120.

294. See Katerina Clark, "Utopian Anthropology as a Context for Stalinist Literature," in Robert C. Tucker, ed. *Stalinism: Essays in Historical Interpretation* (New York: Norton, 1977).

295. F. D. Gorbov and F. P. Kosmolinskiy, "From Aviation Psychology to Space Psychology," *The Soviet Review*. Vol. X, No. 2 (1969). p. 7.

296. E. Ozolin, "Science Helps Sport," *Soviet Military Review*, No. 5 (May 1981), p. 64.

297. Idem.

298. "Overcoming Weightlessness," *Soviet Military Review*, No. 6 (June 1981), p. 63.

299. Christopher Booker, *The Games War. A Moscow Journal* (London: Faber and Faber, 1981), p. 153.

300. Nina Tumarkin, *Lenin Lives!* (Cambridge, Mass.: Harvard University Press, 1983), p. 267.

301. "Overcoming Weightlessness," p. 63.

302. *The Technological Society*, p. xxv.

303. Ibid., pp. 4, 5, 12, 14, 97, 110.

304. Ibid., p. 384.

305. *The Technological Society*, pp. 78-79.

306. *This Great Symbol*, p. 267.

307. Ibid., p. 268.

308. H. Joachim Maître, *The 1980 Moscow Olympics: Politics and Policy* (Chicago: Intercollegiate Studies Institute - Philadelphia Society Conference, 1980), p. 23.

309. Ibid., p. 24.

310. John J. MacAloon, "Olympic Games and the Theory of Spectacle in Modern Societies," in J. MacAloon, ed. *Rite, Drama, Festival, Spectacle: Rehearsals Toward a Theory of Cultural Performance* (Philadelphia: Institute for the Study of Human Issues Press, 1984), p. 252.

311. *This Great Symbol*, p. 264.

312. Ibid., p. 262.

313. Thomas J. Schlereth, *The Cosmopolitan Ideal in Enlightenment Thought* (Notre Dame: The University of Notre Dame Press, 1977), pp. 127, 105, 59, 59, 38, 45.

314. Konrad Lorenz, *On Aggression* (New York: Harcourt, Brace & World, 1966), p. 281.

315. Ibid., p. 282.

316. *The Cosmopolitan Ideal in Enlightenment Thought*, p. 43.

317. *On Aggression*, pp. 287, 288.

318. Helmut Schelsky, *Friede auf Zeit: Die Zukunft der Olympischen Spiele* (Osnabrück: Verlag A. Fromm, 1973), p. 33.

319. Ibid., pp. 27, 7, 17, 36-37, 18, 16, 19.

320. Ibid., pp. 20-21.

321. Ibid., pp. 52-53, 48.

322. The first of these books to appear is Bero Rigauer, *Sport und Arbeit* (1969). See also Gerhard Vinnai, *Fussballsport als Ideologie* (1970) and Gerhard Vinnai, ed. *Sport in der Klassengesellschaft* (1972).

323. *Friede auf Zeit*, pp. 66, 55, 54, 59, 68-70.

324. Ibid., p. 17.

325. Maurice Druon, "L'Exposition avait-elle un sens?" *Le Figaro* (Paris), July 15, 1983.

326. *Friede auf Zeit*, p. 38.

327. "Olympic Games and the Theory of Spectacle in Modern Societies," pp. 242, 267.

328. Ibid., pp. 258, 259.

329. Ibid., pp. 269-270.

330. Ibid., pp. 270, 247, 274-275.

331. Ibid., pp. 241, 259.

332. Ibid., p. 260.

333. Ibid., pp. 249, 262.

334. "Sanfte Spiele statt Konkurrenz," *Der Spiegel*,

March 11, 1981, p. 228.

335. *Sport and Society,* p. 208.

336. "Olympic Games and the Theory of Spectacle in Modern Societies," p. 253.

337. Theodor W. Adorno, *Introduction to the Sociology of Music* (New York: The Seabury Press, 1976), p. 154.

338. "Olympic Games and the Theory of Spectacle in Modern Societies," p. 273.

339. Idem.

154 340. *The Cosmopolitan Ideal in Enlightenment Thought,* p. 135.

Epilogue

1. "Text of Soviet Statement on Olympic Games," *New York Times,* May 9, 1984, p. 4; "Comments in Last Month on Soviet Participation in Games," *New York Times,* May 9, 1984, p. 5.

2. "Soviet to Decide in May on Attending Games," *New York Times,* April 17, 1984, p. 47.

3. "Comments in Last Month on Soviet Participation in Games," p. 5.

4. "U.S. Calls the Soviet Complaints a 'Classic Case' of Distortion," *New York Times,* May 15, 1984, p. A13.

5. "Soviets maintain Olympic boycott stance despite criticism," *Austin American-Statesman,* May 16, 1984, p. E8.

6. "Europeans Regret Soviet Olympic Boycott," *Washington Post,* May 10, 1984, p. A28.

7. "U.S. Misread Soviets on Withdrawal From Games, Officials Say," *Washington Post,* May 10, 1984, p. A30.

8. "Olympics Decision Final, Soviet Says," (New York: May 15, 1984, p. A12.

9. Seweryn Bialer, "Danger in Moscow," *New York Review of Books,* February 16, 1984, p. 6.

10. On the decline of Soviet Olympic performance see "Die Sieger sind müde," *Der Spiegel,* May 14, 1984, p. 125.

11. "Organizers Respond to Criticism by Soviet," *New York Times* (nat. ed.), April 10, 1984, p. 24.

12. Stephen S. Rosenfeld, "Olympian Detachment," *Washington Post,* May 11, 1984, p. A23.

13. "Game Point for Olympics," *Washington Post,* May 13, 1984, p. F10.

14. "Moscow Charges Anti-Soviet Bias at Olympic Games," *New York Times,* (nat. ed.), April 10, 1984, p. 24.

15. "Moscow Adamant on Olympics Issue," *New York Times,* May 13, 1984, p. 4.

16. "Comments in Last Month on Soviet Participation in Games," *New York Times,* May 9, 1984, p. 9.

17. Kevin Klose, "What Are the Soviets Afraid of?" *Washington Post,* May 20, 1984, p. B5.

18. "Western Athletes May Be Invited to Soviet 'Counter' Games," *Washington Post,* May 20, 1984, p. F11.

19. " 'Wir werden immer erpressbar sein'," *Der Spiegel,* May 14, 1984, p. 128.

20. "Olympic Group Fails to Sway Soviet," *New York Times,* May 19, 1984, p. 3.

21. "Game Point for Olympics," *Washington Post,* May 13, 1984, p. F1.

22. *Washington Post,* May 26, 1984, p. D2.

23. "Samaranch Will Extend Deadline If Soviets Show Positive Signs," *Washington Post,* May 30, 1984, p. D4.

24. See "Questions Run Deep for Budd and Britain," *Washington Post,* April 11, 1984, pp. D1, D3.

25. Peter Hawthorne and Kenny Moore, "A Flight to a Stormy Haven," *Sports Illustrated,* April 9, 1984, p. 33.

26. "Questions Run Deep for Budd and Britain," *Washington Post,* April 11, 1984, p. D1.

27. Quoted in "A Flight to a Stormy Haven," p. 33.

28. "No Action in Budd Case," *New York Times,* April 29, 1984.

29. "Hells Angels pay for privilege to carry Olympic torch," *Dallas Times Herald,* April 21, 1984, p. A23.

30. This account is taken from "A Question of Independence," *Sports Illustrated,* April 11, 1984, p. 11.

31. "Nasty Games," *The New Republic,* March 19, 1984, p. 12.

32. *Olympic Rules, By-Laws and Instructions* (Lausanne: Comité International Olympique, 1975), p. 8.

33. "A Question of Independence," *Sports Illustrated,* April 11, 1984, p. 11.

34. "U.S., Soviets Agree to Back Future Games," *Washington Post,* May 21, 1984, p. A1.

35. "Olympics Decision Final, Soviet Says," *New York Times,* May 15, 1984, p. A12.

36. "U.S. Olympic Aides Expect Soviet to Stick to Decision," *New York Times,* May 9, 1984, p. 5.

37. See "Seoul Setting a Quick Pace on '88 Games," *New York Times,* September 18, 1983, p. 9; "Olympic Boycott Raises Doubt in Seoul on '88," *New York Times,* May 22, 1984.

38. "Ol til Kina i år 2000?" *Ukens Nytt* (Oslo), March 20, 1984, p. 14.

Bibliography

ADORNO, Theodor W. *Introduction to the Sociology of Music.* New York: The Seabury Press, 1976.

ANDERSON, Dave. "What Olympic Movement." *New York Times,* February 11, 1980.

AUSTIN, Anthony. "Games End on a Colorful Note." *New York Times,* August 4, 1980.

BARDÈCHE, Maurice. "Les Ecrivains et la Politique." *Défense de l'Occident* (March 1954).

_____ . "Jeux Olympiques, Maquisards et nantis." *Défense de l'Occident* (August-September 1972).

_____ . "Réponse sur le fascisme." *Défense de l'Occident* (May 1962).

_____ . *Sparte et les sudistes.* Paris: Les Sept Couleurs, 1969.

BAZUNOV, B. "Olympic Horizons." *Sport in the USSR* (1974: 12).

BECKER, Hartmut. "Die 'Arisierung' der Deutschen Turnerschaft." *Stadion* II, no. 1 (1976).

BERNETT, Hajo, ed. *Nationalsozialistische Leibeserziehung.* Schorndorf bei Stuttgart: Verlag Karl Hofmann, 1966.

_____ . *Sportpolitik im dritten Reich.* Schorndorf bei Stuttgart: Verlag Karl Hofmann, 1971.

_____ . *Untersuchungen zur Zeitgeschichte des Sports.* Schorndorf bei Stuttgart: Verlag Karl Hofmann, 1973.

BERTHAUD, Ginette, et al., eds. *Sport, culture et répression.* Paris: François Maspero, 1972.

BIALER, Seweryn. "Danger in Moscow." *New York Review of Books,* February 16, 1984.

BOOKER, Christopher. *The Games War: A Moscow Journal.* London: Faber and Faber, 1981.

BOULONGNE, Yves-Pierre. "Pierre de Coubertin: Ein Beitrag zu einer wissenschaftlichen Untersuchung seines Lebens und seines Werkes." In *Die Zukunft der Olympischen Spiele,* by Hans-Jürgen Schulke. Köln: Pahl-Rugenstein, 1976.

BRECHT, Bertolt. "Mehr guten Sport." *Berliner Boersen-Courier,* February 6, 1926.

BREITNER, Paul. "Kein Handschlag für die Generale." In *Fussball und Folter: Argentinien '78,* edited by U. Pramann et al. Reinbek bei Hamburg: Rowohlt, 1978.

BROHM, Jean-Marie. *Critiques du sport.* Paris: Christian Bourgois, 1976.

_____ . "Vers l'analyse institutionnelle du sport de competition." *L'Homme et la Société,* nos. 29-30 (July-December 1973).

BRUNDAGE, Avery. "The Fumbled Ball." *Vital Speeches of the Day* 33 (April 15, 1967).

_____ . "I Must Admit—Russian Athletes are Great." *Saturday Evening Post,* April 30, 1955.

BUTTERFIELD, Roger. "Avery Brundage." *Life,* June 14, 1948.

CAUTE, David. *The Fellow-Travellers.* New York: Macmillan, 1973.

CHIROUX, René. *L'Extrême-droite sous la Vᵉ Republique.* Paris: Librarie Generale de Droit et de Jurisprudence, 1974.

CLARK, Katerina. "Utopian Anthropology as a Context for Stalinist Literature." In *Stalinism: Essays in Historical Interpretation* edited by Robert C. Tucker. New York: Norton, 1977.

CLERC, Jean-Pierre. "Argentina in a state of shock." *Manchester Guardian Weekly,* June 18, 1978.

COOPER, J. Astley. "An Anglo-Saxon Olympiad." *Nineteenth Century* 187 (September 1892).

_____ . "Olympic Games: What Has Been Done and What Remains to Be Done." *Nineteenth Century* 376 (June 1908).

_____ . "The Pan-Britannic Gathering." *Nineteenth Century* 197 (July 1893).

COUBERTIN, Pierre de. *Essais de psychologie sportive.* Lausanne et Paris: Librarie Payot & Cie, 1914.

_____ . *Mémoires olympiques.* Lausanne: Bureau International de Pédagogie Sportive, 1931.

_____ . *Notes sur l'éducation publique.* Paris: Hachette, 1901.

_____ . *Pages d'histoire contemporaine.* Paris: Plon, 1909.

_____ . *Pédagogie sportive.* Lausanne: Bureau International de Pédagogie Sportive, 1922.

CREAMER, Robert. "Of Greeks—and Russians." *Sports Illustrated,* February 6, 1956.

_____ . "The Embattled World of Avery Brundage." *Sports Illustrated*, January 30, 1956.

The Current Digest of the Soviet Press, XXXII (nos. 2, 3, 5, 10, 11, 15, 30).

DEUTSCH, Julius. *Sport und Politik*. Berlin: Verlag J.H.W. Dietz Nachfolger, 1928.

DIEM, Carl. "The Olympic Idea." In the *Report of the Second Session of the International Olympic Academy*. Athens: The Hellenic Olympic Committee, 1962.

———. *Olympische Flamme: Das Buch vom Sport*. Berlin: Deutscher Arkiv Verlag, 1942.

———. *Weltgeschichte des Sports und der Leibeserziehung*. Stuttgart: Cotta Verlag, 1960.

DIEM, Liselott and Herbert Maag. "Carl Diem born 100 years ago (6/24/1882)—Life and Work." *International Journal of Physical Education* XIX (Issue 2 1982).

DRUON, Maurice. "L'Exposition avait-elle un sens." *Le Figaro* (Paris), July 15, 1983.

DUPRAT, François. *Les Mouvements d'extrême-droite en France depuis 1944*. Paris: Les Editions Albatros, 1972.

EICHBERG, Henning. "Thing-, Fest- und Weihespiele in Nationalsozialismus, Arbeiterkultur und Olympismus." In *Massenspiele: NS-Thingspiel, Arbeiterweihespiel und Olympisches Zeremoniell*, by Henning Eichberg, et al. Stuttgart-Bad Cannstatt: frommann-holzboog, 1977.

———. *Der Weg des Sports in die industrielle Zivilization*. Baden-Baden: Nomos Verlagsgesellschaft, 1973.

ELLUL, Jacques. *The Technological Society*. New York: Vintage Books, 1964.

ESPY, Richard. *The Politics of the Olympic Games*. Berkeley: University of California Press, 1981.

EYQUEM, Marie-Thérèse. *Pierre de Coubertin: L'Epopée Olympique*. Paris: Calmann-Levy, 1966.

FISCHER, Jürgen. "Die Olympiade der Sozialistischen Arbeitersportinternationale in Frankfurt 1925. In *Die Zukunft der Olympischen Spiele*, edited by Hans-Jürgen Schulke. Köln: Pahl-Rugenstein, 1976.

FRANKEN, Paul. *Vom Werden einer neuen Kultur*. Berlin: E. Laubsche Verlagsbuchhandlung, 1930.

FREUD, Sigmund. *Totem and Taboo*. New York: Vintage Books, n.d.

From Helsinki to Belgrade: The Soviet Union and the Implementation of the Final Act of the European Conference. Moscow: Progress Publishers, 1977.

FUELOPP-MILLER, René. *The Mind and Face of Bolshevism*. New York: Harper Torchbooks, 1965.

GOLOVANOV, Vadim. "Who is Right." *New York Times*, June 17, 1977.

GORBCV, F.D. and F.P. Kosmolinskiy. "From Aviation Psychology to Space Psychology." *The Soviet Review* X, no. 2 (1969).

Great Soviet Encyclopedia. "International Olympic Committee." New York: Macmillan, Inc., 1977.

GUERARD, Albert. *France: A Modern History*. Ann Arbor: The University of Michigan Press, 1969.

GUTTMANN, Allen. *From Ritual to Record: The Nature of Modern Sports*. New York: Columbia University Press.

———. "The Games Must Go On: On the Origins of Avery Brundage's Life-credo." *Stadion* 5, no. 2. (1979).

HALEY, Bruce. *The Healthy Body and Victorian Culture*. Cambridge, Mass.: Harvard University Press, 1978.

HARRINGTON, Michael T. "On an Olympic Boycott." *New York Times*, January 12, 1980.

HAWTHORNE, P. and K. Moore. "A Flight to a Stormy Haven." *Sports Illustrated*, April 9, 1984.

HEGEL, G.W.F. *On Art, Religion, Philosophy*. New York: Harper Torchbooks, 1970.

HOBERMAN, John M. "The Mind of Maurice Bardèche." *Psychohistory Review* V, no. 1 (June 1976).

———. *Sport and Political Ideology*. Austin: The University of Texas Press, 1984.

HOCHGESAND, Dieter. "Die Rolle des Paul Breitner." In *Fussball und Folter: Argentinien '78*.

HOHNE, Erhard. "Music and Sport." *Olympic Review* 141-142 (July-August 1979).

HUIZINGA, Johan. *Homo Ludens*. Boston: Beacon Press, 1955.

———. *In the Shadow of Tomorrow*. New York: Norton, 1964.

HYDE, Charles Cheney. "The Boycott as a Sanction of International Law." *Political Science Quarterly* 48 (1933).

JASPERS, Karl. *Man in the Modern Age*. Garden City, N.Y.: Anchor Books, 1957.

JOCH, Winfried. *Politische Leibeserziehung und ihre Theorie im Nationalsozialistischen Deutschland*. Frankfurt/M.: Peter Lang, 1976.

John Paul II. "Sport, a School for Human Virtue." *Olympic Review* 144 (October 1979).

JOHNSON, Priscilla. *Khrushchev and the Arts: The Politics of Soviet Culture, 1962-1964*. Cambridge, Mass.: The M.I.T. Press, 1965.

JOHNSON, William Oscar. "Avery Brundage: The Man Behind the Mask." *Sports Illustrated*, August 4, 1980.

———. "Defender of the Faith." *Sports Illustrated*, July 24, 1972.

KANIN, David B. *A Political History of the Olympic Games*. Boulder, Colorado: Westview Press, 1981.

KAROL, K.S. *Guerillas in Power*. New York: Hill

and Wang, 1970.

Keesing's Contemporary Archives (London). September 1-7, 1975.

KLOSE, Kevin. "What Are the Soviets Afraid Of." Washington Post, May 20, 1984.

KNECHT, Willi. Der Boykott: Moskaus missbrauchte Olympiade. Köln: Verlag Wissenschaft und Politik, 1980.

_____ . "Moskaus ultimative Kandidatur." Deutschland Arkiv 7, no. 5 (May 1974).

_____ . "Moskaus zweiter Versuch: Olympia 1980 in der Sowjetunion." Deutsche Arkiv 4, no. 11 (November 1971).

KRÜGER, Arnd. Die olympischen Spiele 1936 und die Weltmeinung. Berlin, Munchen, Frankfurt/ M.: Verlag Bartels & Wernitz KG, 1972.

LAGERKRANTZ, Olof. "The Playing Fields of Peking." New York Times, June 18, 1971.

LAGUILLAUMIE, Pierre. "Pour une critique fondamentale du sport." In Sport, culture et répression, edited by Ginette Berthaud et al. Paris: François Maspero, 1972.

LANE, Christel. The Rites of Rulers: Ritual in Industrial Society—The Soviet Case. Cambridge: Cambridge University Press, 1981.

LAPCHICK, Richard Edward. The Politics of Race and International Sport: The Case of South Africa. Westport, Conn.: The Greenwood Press, 1975.

LAURENT, Paul, Robert Barran, and Jean-Jacques Faure. Les communistes et le sport: A l'heure de Munich. Paris: Editions Sociales, 1972.

LEKARSKA, Nadeja. Essays and Studies on Olympic Problems. Sofia: Medicina and Fizcultura, 1973.

LENDVAI, Paul. The Bureaucracy of Truth. Boulder, Colorado: Westview Press, 1981.

LENK, Hans. "Carl Diem—The Humanist." International Journal of Physical Education 4 (1982).

LEWIS, Anthony. "Laurels for Moscow." New York Times, February 11, 1980.

LORENZ, Konrad. On Aggression. New York: Harcourt, Brace & World, 1966.

LOWENTHAL, Leo. "Knut Hamsun." In Literature and the Image of Man. Boston: The Beacon Press, 1966.

LYTTLETON, Adrian, ed. Italian Fascisms: From Pareto to Gentile. New York: Harper Torchbooks, 1975.

McINTOSH, Peter. Fair Play: Ethics in Sport and Education. London: Heinemann, 1979.

McCLELLAND, J.S., ed. The French Right from de Maistre to Maurras. New York: Harper Torchbooks, 1971.

MABIRE, Jean. "Pierre de Coubertin et l'éducation 'totale'." Défense de l'Occident (January 1965).

MACALOON, John J. "Olympic Games and the Theory of Spectacle in Modern Societies." In Rite, Drama, Festival, Spectacle: Rehearsals Toward a Theory of Cultural Performance, edited by J. MacAloon. Philadelphia: Institute for the Study of Human Issues Press, 1984.

_____ . This Great Symbol: Pierre de Coubertin and the Origins of the Modern Olympic Games. Chicago: The Universitgy of Chicago Press, 1981.

MAÎTRE, H. Joachim. The 1980 Moscow Olympics: Politics and Policy. Chicago: Intercollegiate Studies Institute—Philadelphia Society Conference, 1980.

MANDELL, Richard D. The First Modern Olympics. Berkeley: University of California Press, 1976.

_____ . The Nazi Olympics. New York: Macmillan, 1971.

MANUEL, Frank E., and Fritzie P. Manuel. Utopian Thought in The Western World. Cambridge, Mass.: The Belknap Press of Harvard University Press, 1979.

MATHEWSON, Rufus W. The Positive Hero in Russian Literature. Stanford: Stanford University Press, 1975.

MAURRAS, Charles. "Les nations dans le stade et la course de Marathon." In Le voyage d'Athènes. Paris: Flammarion, 1929.

_____ . "The Politics of Nature." In The French Right: From de Maistre to Maurras.

MEYER, Gaston. Le phénomène olympique. Paris: La Table Ronde, 1960.

MEYNAUD, Jean. Sport et politique. Paris: Payot, 1966.

MIHAJLOV, Mihajlo. "The Absurdity of Nonideology." In Underground Notes. New Rochelle, New York: Caratzas Brothers, Publishers, 1982.

MILOSZ, Czeslaw. The Captive Mind. New York: Vintage Books, n.d.

MISHIMA, Yukio. Sun and Steel. New York: Grove Press, 1970.

MORTON, Henry. Soviet Sport. New York: Collier Books, 1963.

MOSSE, George L. The Crisis of German Ideology: Intellectual Origins of the Third Reich. New York: Schocken Books, 1981.

MZALI, Mohamed. "Olympism and culture (II)." Olympic Review 144 (October 1979).

NEUENDORFF, Edmund. Geschichte der neueren deutschen Leibesübung vom Beginn des 18. Jahrhunderts bis zur Gegenwart, IV. Dresden: Wilhelm Limpert-Verlag, n.d.

NIETZSCHE, Friedrich. The Will to Power. Trans. by Walter Kaufmann and R.J. Hollingdale. New York: Vintage Books, 1968.

NOLTE, Ernst. Three Faces of Fascism. New York: Mentor Books, 1969.

Olympic Rules, By-Laws and Instructions. Lausanne:

Comité International Olympique, 1975.

ORTEGA Y GASSET, José. *The Revolt of the Masses.* New York: Norton, 1960.

OZOLIN, E. "Science Helps Sport." *Soviet Military Review* 5 (May 1981).

PAZ, Octavio. *The Other Mexico: Critique of the Pyramid.* New York: Grove Press, 1972.

PETZOLD, Ilona. "Kunst und Sport in der DDR— Die Sammlung 'Sport in der bildenden Kunst der DDR' der DHfK Leipzig." *Theorie und Praxis der Körperkultur* 29, no. 2 (1980).

PLUMYÈNE, J. and R. Lasierra. *Les fascismes français 1923-1963.* Paris: Editions du Seuil, 1963.

160 POWELL, David E. *Antireligious Propaganda in the Soviet Union.* Cambridge, Mass.: The MIT Press, 1978.

PONOMARYOV, N. *Sport and Society.* Moscow: Progress Publishers, 1981.

POPOV, S. *Socialism and Humanism.* Moscow: Progress Publishers, 1977.

POURET, Henri. "Is Sport an Art?" *Report of the Tenth Session of the International Olympic Academy at Olympia.* Athens: Hellenic Olympic Committee, 1970.

PRAMANN, Ulrich et al., eds. *Fussball und Folter: Argentinien '78.* Reinbek bei Hamburg: Rowohlt, 1978.

PROKOP, Ulrike. *Soziologie der Olympischen Spiele: Sport und Kapitalismus.* Munich: Carl Hanser Verlag, 1971.

REMOND, René. *The Right Wing in France: From 1815 to de Gaulle.* Philadelphia: University of Pennsylvania Press, 1968.

RIGAUER, Bero. *Sport and Work.* New York: Columbia University Press, 1981.

RIORDAN, James. *Sport in Soviet Society.* Cambridge: Cambridge University Press, 1977.

———. "The USSR." In *Sport under Communism,* edited by James Riordan. London: C. Hurst & Company, 1978.

RITTER, Gerhard A. "Workers' Culture in Imperial Germany." *Journal of Contemporary History* 13 (1978).

ROSENFELD, S.S. "Olympian Detachment." *Washington Post,* May 11, 1984.

ROTHE, Wolfgang. "When Sports Conquered the Republic: A Forgotten Chapter from the 'Roaring Twenties'." *Studies in Twentieth Century Literature* 4, no. 1 (Fall 1980).

SALISBURY, Harrison E. "A Boon for the K.G.B." *New York Times,* January 31, 1980.

SARTRE, Jean-Paul. *Saint Genet: Actor and Martyr.* New York: New American Library, 1965.

SCHELSKY, Helmut. *Friede auf Zeit: Die Zukunft der Olympischen Spiele.* Osnabrück: Verlag . A. Fromm, 1973.

SCHERER, Karl Adolf. *Der Männerorden: Die Geschichte des Internationalen Olympischen Komitees.* Frankfurt/M: Limpert, 1974.

SCHILLER, Friedrich. *On the Aesthetic Education of Man.* New York: Frederick Ungar, 1965.

SCHLERETH, Thomas J. *The Cosmopolitan Ideal in Enlightenment Thought.* Notre Dame: The University of Notre Dame Press, 1977.

SCHULKE, H.J., ed. *Die Zukunft der Olympischen Spiele.* Köln: Pahl-Rugenstein, 1976.

SEILLIÈRE, Ernest. *Un Artisan d'Energie Française Pierre de Coubertin.* Paris: Henri Didier, 1917.

SENAY, Andre and Robert Hervet. *Monsieur de Coubertin.* Paris: Points & Contrepoints, 1960.

SHAPLEN, Robert. "Amateur." *The New Yorker,* July 23, 1960.

SIEGER, Walter. "Zum Körperkultur in der socialistischen Gesellschaft." *Deutsche Zeitschrift für Philosophie* 12, no. 8 (1964).

SMITH, Denis Mack. *Mussolini.* New York: Knopf, 1982.

SMITH, Hedrick. *The Russians.* New York: Ballantine Books, 1977.

SMITH, Red. "The Noblest Badger of Them All." *New York Times,* May 12, 1975.

———. "The Games We Need Not Play." *New York Times,* January 16, 1980.

SONTAG, Susan. "Fascinating Fascism." *New York Review of Books,* February 6, 1975.

SPEER, Albert. *Inside the Third Reich.* New York: Avon Books, 1971.

STEINBERG, David A. "The Workers' Sport Internationals 1920-1928." *Journal of Contemporary History* 13 (1978).

STERN, Fritz. *The Politics of Cultural Despair: A Study in the Rise of the Germanic Ideology.* Berkeley: University of California Press, 1974.

THOMAS, Serge. "Contre la trève olympique." *Défense de l'Occident* (January 1973).

TIMMERMANN, Heinz. *Geschichte und Struktur der Arbeitersportbewegung 1893-1933.* Ahrensburg bei Hamburg: Verlag Ingrid Czwalina, 1973.

TUCKER, William R. *The Fascist Ego: A Political Biography of Robert Brasillach.* Berkeley: University of California Press, 1975.

TUMARKIN, Nina. *Lenin Lives.* Cambridge, Mass.: Harvard University Press, 1983.

UEBERHORST, Horst. *Frisch, frei, stark und treu: Die Arbeitersportbewegung in Deutschland.* Düsseldorf: Droste Verlag, 1973.

ULLRICH, Klaus. "Olympia, Coubertin und wir." *Neues Deutschland,* July 10-11, 1976.

———. "80 Jahre Olympische Spiele." In *Die Zukunft der Olympischen Spiele,* edited by H.J. Schulke. Köln: Pahl-Rugenstgein, 1976.

———. *Kreuzritter im Stadion: Bemerkungen zum*

Antikommunismus im Sport. Berlin: Sportverlag, 1978.

_____ . "Wurde Angelo Jacopucci ein Opfer der Manager." *Neues Deutschland*, August 4, 1978.

UNGER, Leopold. "Soviet Tourniquet Tightens." *International Herald Tribune*, July 5, 1978.

UNTERMEYER, Samuel. "The Boycott is Our Only Weapon Against Nazi Germany." New York: American League for the Defense of Jewish Rights, 1933.

VAN DER WILL, Wilfried, and Rob Burns. *Arbeiterkulturbewegung in der Weimarer Republik*. Frankfurt/M.: Ullstein, 1982.

VINNAI, Gerhard. *Fussballsport als Ideologie*. Frankfurt/M.: Europäische Verlagsanstalt, 1970.

_____ . "Vorwort." In *Sport in der Klassengesellschaft*, edited by G. Vinnai. Frankfurt/M.: Fischer Taschenbuch Verlag, 1972.

WADE, Nigel. "All set for the Red Olympics." *The Sunday Telegraph*, July 13, 1980.

_____ . "Ceremony boycott shows through Moscow pageantry." *The Daily Telegraph*, July 21, 1980.

_____ . "The Games: a triumph of Russian propaganda." *The Sunday Telegraph*, August 4, 1980.

WAGNER, Helmut. *Sport und Arbeitersport* [1931]. Köln: Pahl-Rugenstein, 1973.

WEBER, Eugen. "Pierre de Coubertin and the introduction of organised sport in France." *Journal of Contemporary History* 5, no. 2 (1970).

VERRIE, Paul. "De la pétanque à l'athlète d'Etat." *Écrits de Paris* (October 1961).

_____ . " 'Homo ludens, homo faber' ou l'évolution du sport." *Écrits de Paris* (March 1970).

_____ . "Pierre de Coubertin: 'Rénovateur des Jeux Olympiques'." *Écrits de Paris* (June 1963).

_____ . " 'Tokio Olympiades' ou la mort des dieux." *Écrits de Paris* (November 1965).

WHEELER, Robert F. "Organized Sport and Organized Labour: The Workers' Sports Movement." *Journal of Contemporary History* 13 (1978).

WHITNEY, Craig R. "In Moscow, Icons and Smiles Materialize for Games." *New York Times*, August 2, 1980.

WILDUNG, Fritz. *Arbeitersport*. Berlin: Der Bücherkreis GmbH., 1929.

WITT, Günter. "Zu einigen Entwicklungstendenzen der Ästhetik des Sports in den sozialistischen Ländern." *Theorie und Praxis der Körperkultur* 29, no. 2 (1980).

WOHL, Andrzej. "Competitive Sport and its Social Functions." *International Review of Sport Sociology* 5 (1970).

_____ . "Fifty Years of Physical Culture in the U.S.S.R.: Reflections and Conclusions." *International Review of Sport Sociology* 3 (1968).

_____ . *Die gesellschaftlich-historischen Grundlagen des bürgerlichen Sports*. Köln: Pahl-Rugenstein, 1973.

ZELDIN, Theodore. *France 1848-1945: Politics and Anger*. New York: Oxford University Press, 1979.

ZHAROV, K. and I. Barchukov. "For the Olympic Ideals." *Soviet Military Review* 10 (October 1981).

Index

ABC-TV, 13, 70
abstract expressionism, 77
Action Française, 93
Adorno, Theodor W., 125
advertising, 81,102
aesthetics, 111, 112, 113, 124; fascist, 74; Marxist, 26, 114, 116
Afghanistan, 7, 13, 65, 66, 67, 68, 70, 71, 79, 127, 128
African Games (Algiers, 1978), 61
Akii-Bua, John, 99
Albania, 27
Ali, Muhammad, 8
Allende, Salvador, 19
Amalrik, Andrei, 70, 71
amateurism, 11, 49, 51, 59, 63, 87, 93
America First Committee, 52
American President's Commission on Olympic Sports, 78
Amnesty International, 16
amoral universalism, 2, 29-32, 122
Amsterdam (Holland), 60, 133
Andorra, 76
Andrianov, Konstantin, 59-60; Great Soviet Encylcopedia, 59
Angola, 127
anti-intellectualism, 27, 48, 87, 88, 100, 102, 110
anti-modernism, 100, 102, 111, 113
anti-Semitism, 100, 102, 105
apartheid, 130
Arabs, 121
Argentina, 15, 16, 20, 21, 22
artists, 26, 114, 121
asceticism, 53, 110, 111
Asian Games (New Delhi, November 1982), 2
Associated Press, 70
Astley, Sir John, 91, 92, 93, 101
Athletic Society of Great Britain, 84

Australia, 76
authenticity, 111, 112, 113
Auto, L', 43

Baeumler, Alfred, 105
Bagehot, Walter, 58
Baltic American Freedom League, 129
"Ban the Soviets Coalition," 128-129
Barcelona (Spain), 133
Bardèche, Maurice, 95, 96, 97, 98, 112; Nuremberg or the Promised Land (1948), 96; Les temps modernes (1956), 96; What is Fascism? (1960), 96
Barthes, Roland, 71
Bayreuth (West Germany), 115
Bazunov, B., 7
Beaumont, Count de, 75
Belgium, 75
Berchtesgaden (West Germany), 10
Bergson, Henri, 111
Berlin, East, 10, 20
Berlin, West, 10, 20
Berlin Wall, 10
Berlioux, Monique, 67, 75, 130, 131
Bernett, Hajo, 106
Biafra, 15
Bialer, Seweryn, 128
body, the, 75, 100, 102, 111, 112, 117, 124; cult of, 24-25, 31, 48, 106; Huizinga on, 26; sportive, 90, 113
body politic, 27, 33
Bolshevik political theater, 72
Borgia, Cesare, 44
Boulongne, Yves-Pierre, 62
boxing, 8, 64, 106
"Boxing and Storm Troop" (SS), 106
boycott, defined, 6

Boy Scouts, 24, 88
Brandt, Willy, 10, 128
Brauchitsch, Manfred von, 18
Brecht, Bertolt, 26
Breitner, Paul, 21, 22
Brezhnev, Leonid, 12, 67, 77
Brisbane (Australia), 133
Brundage, Avery, 18, 32, 44, 50-59, 60, 61, 63, 102, 118, 121
Brussels (Belgium), 65
Brzezinski, Zbigniew, 69
Bucharest (Rumania), 101
Buckley, James L., 70, 132
Budapest (Hungary), 101
Budd, Zola, 130-131
Buenos Aires (Argentina), 11, 15, 20, 21, 22
Bukovsky, Vladimir, 70, 71
Bulgaria, 54, 125, 127

Caramanlis, Constantin, 130
card-playing, 101
Carlyle, Thomas, 83-84
Carter, Jimmy, 13, 65, 66, 67, 68, 70, 79
Castro, Fidel, 17, 56
Catholic Church, 29, 31, 38, 41, 93
Caute, David, 56
Central Intelligence Agency (CIA), 67, 69, 129
Charter 77 human rights group, 12
chess, 101
Chile, 19, 20
China, People's Republic of, 65, 133
Chiroux, René, 96, 97, 98
chivalry, 41
chronometric sport, 85
Chun Doo Hwan, General, 2
cinema, 25
Citizens' Keep America Out of War Committee, 52

"Collective for the Boycott of the Moscow Olympic Games," 70
"collective man," 72
"collective record," 86
Colorado Springs (Colorado), 71
commercialism, 63, 81, 82, 83, 100, 108, 129
Commonwealth Games (Brisbane, 1982), 2
Commonwealth Games Act, 2
"competition of ideas," 22
Comte, August, 110
Condorcet, Marie-Jean, 120
Constantinople (Turkey), 101
Coolidge, Calvin, 52, 59
Corradini, Enrico, 89, 90
cosmonaut, 116, 117
cosmopolitan festival, 11, 122
cosmopolitanism, 49, 51, 53, 55, 94, 95, 118, 119, 120, 122
Coubertin, Pierre de, 2, 9, 10, 13, 30-44, 50, 53, 55, 57, 59-63, 76, 81, 83, 89-94, 97, 98, 101, 102, 104, 107, 108, 110, 115, 116, 118, 119; and critique of Olympia, 85-88; on mob, 44, 45; "Can Sport Stem the Universal Neurosis?" (1913), 39; "La limite du record" (1909), 85-86; Notes on Public Education (1901), 44, 99; Olympic Memoirs (1931)/ Mémoires olympiques (1931), 29, 32, 33, 44, 51, 62, 86, 87, 91, 93; Pages d'histoire contemporaine (1909), 45; "Le sport et la morale" (1910), 86; Sport Pedagogy (1922) / Pédagogie sportive (1922), 33, 40, 86
Cuba, 16, 19, 127
cultural exchange, 77
Czechoslovakia, 12, 127
Czechoslovak Psychiatric Society, 3

Dagens Nyheter (Stockholm), 12, 13
Daily Mail (London), 130
Daume, Willi, 68, 129, 130
Défense de l'Occident, 96
de Gaulle, Charles, 25
denationalization, 76, 91, 120, 124, 131
Denmark, 76
Devliger, Jules, 62
Diaz Ordaz, Gustavo, 17
Diem, Carl, 23, 31, 32, 33, 42, 43-50, 83, 85, 87, 90, 104, 115; pa-

ganism of, 24; "The Olympic Idea," 24, 31; World History of Sport and Physical Culture (1960), 50
discourse, 2, 3
Donald Duck, 21
Druon, Maurice, 122
Dubcek, Alexander, 12
Dulles, John Foster, 79
Duras, Marguerite, 71

East Germany (GDR), 9, 11, 15, 18, 20, 26, 27, 61, 62, 112, 114, 116, 121, 127
Eastwood, Clint, 131
Economist, The (London), 58
education, 38
Eichberg, Henning, 102, 106, 107-108
Ellul, Jacques, 113, 117; The Technological Society (1953), 117
El Salvador, 15
England, 19, 46, 75, 83, 98
Ethiopia, 127
European Sport Conference (Berchtesgaden, 1979), 10
Ewald, Manfred, 10, 11
Eyquem, Marie-Thérèse, 42

fascism, defined, 89
Feinberg, Viktor, 70
fellow-traveling, 56
Ferry, Jules, 37, 38-39
festival, 13, 87, 101, 123, 124, 125, 131
fine arts, 53
Florence (Italy), 95
Foreman, George, 8
Forum, 81
France, 21, 34, 39, 42, 75, 88, 94, 95, 96, 104, 108, 109, 128
Franco, Francisco, 18, 22
Franco-Prussian war, 33
Frankfurt (West Germany), 101
Frankfurter Rundschau, 16, 22
Franklin, Benjamin, 119
"free flow of information," 22
Freud, Sigmund, 11, 13, 11; Totem and Taboo (1913), 11
Fuelopp-Miller, René, 71, 72, 73

Gambetta, Leon, 39
Gandhi, Indira, 2
Gantry, Elmer, 32
Garmisch-Partenkirchen (West Germany), 45
Gazette de France, La, 94
GDR Review (East Berlin), 118

Genet, Jean, 26
German Commission for Physical Culture, 45
German Gymnastic Association (DT), 50, 101, 102, 105
German University for Physical Culture (Cologne), 45
Germany, 6, 32, 47, 54, 55, 56, 88, 98, 108. See also East Germany, West Germany
Gilkes, James, 63, 130
Ginzburg, Alexander, 67, 69, 70, 71
Giraudoux, Jean, 118
Goebbels, Joseph, 42, 103
Goldwater, Barry, 68
Goncharov, G.P., 71
Gorbanevskaya, Natalya, 70
Gorky, Maxim, 116
Gorky (Soviet Union), 7, 13, 70
Gramov, Marat V., 127, 128, 133
Gresko, Alexander, 71
Guerard, Albert, 37, 38
Gummel, Margitta, 114
Guyana, 63
gymnastics, 100

Haley, Bruce, 83; The Healthy Body and Victorian Culture (1978), 83
Halt, Karl Ritter von, 18, 49
Hamburg (West Germany), 49
Hammarskjöld, Dag, 29
Harvard University, 69
Havana (Cuba), 14
Haymann, Ludwig, 106
Hébert, Georges, 81
Hegel, G. W. F., 25
Heine, Heinrich, 47
Hellenic Olympic Committee, 25
Hell's Angels motorcycle club, 131
Helsinki Conference on European Security (1975), 7-8, 10, 12, 58, 68, 69, 77
"Helsinki Group," 70
Hervé, Gustave, 95
Hess, Rudolf, 29
Hitler, Adolf, 6, 10, 16, 17, 18, 20, 40, 43, 44, 45, 49, 50, 54, 55, 56, 88, 97, 100, 101, 102, 104, 106, 125; Mein Kampf, 103
Ho Chi Minh, 56
Holland, 15, 16, 22, 75
Honduras, 15
Hoover, Herbert, 52, 59
House of Delegates (USOC), 71

164

Hoxha, Enver, 27
Huizinga, Johan, 23-24, 26, 27; *Homo Ludens* (1938), 23-24
human image, 111, 113
humanism, 6, 8, 9, 17, 90, 113
Humanité, L' (Paris), 76, 108, 111, 112
human rights, 7, 8-9, 16, 22, 129
Hungary, 16, 79, 127
hunting, 101
Hyde, Charles Cheney, 6

ice hockey, 27
ice skating, 124
ideological coexistence," 77
India, 39, 104
industrialization, 48
International Football Association (FIFA), 19, 20
International Olympic Committee (IOC), 1, 2, 3, 10, 18, 29, 30, 32, 33, 51, 53, 55, 57, 58-63 passim, 66, 67, 68, 70, 75, 76, 82, 89, 91, 104, 106, 108, 113, 119, 121, 122, 129, 130, 131, 132, 133
International Political Science Association, 22
international sports festival, 3
internationalism, 23, 46, 51, 52-53, 54, 55, 88, 89, 90, 94, 95, 102, 103, 105, 126, 131, 132
Ionesco, Eugene, 22
Ireland, 75
isolationism, 51, 52
Israel, 121
Isthmian Games, 6
Italy, 75, 95, 103, 127
Izvestia, 67, 68, 70, 77, 129

Jahn, Friedrich Ludwig, 101
Jamaica, 16
Japan, 32
Jaspers, Karl, 112; *Man in the Modern Age* (1931), 112
jazz, 79
Judas, 70
Jungk, Robert, 124, 125

Kane, Robert J., 66
Karol, K.S., 14; *Guerillas in Power* (1970), 14
Käser, Dr. Helmut, 19, 20
Kennedy, Edward, 10
Khruschchev, Nikita, 77, 79, 116
Kiev (Soviet Union), 15
Killanin, Lord, 30, 57, 66, 67, 68
kitsch, 26
Klose, Kevin, 129

Kohl, Helmut, 128
Komsomolskaya Pravda, 129
Kosygin, Alexei, 17
Krüger, Arnd, 43, 45, 103
Kuznetsov, Eduard, 70

Labor Sport Federation (FST), 108
Lamine Ba, Amadou, 127
Laos, 127
Lausanne (Switzerland), 44, 67, 75, 130, 132
Le Bon, Gustave, 38; *The Crowd* (1895), 38
Lee, Bruce, 131
Leistritz, Hans Karl, 104
Lekarska, Nadejda, 30; *Essays and Studies on Olympic Problems* (1973), 30
Lenin, V. I., 56, 58, 76, 117
Leningrad (Soviet Union), 72
Lenin Stadium (Moscow), 19, 74
Leonov, A.A., 117
Leopold II, King (Belgium), 39
Lévi-Strauss, Claude, 99
Lévy, Bernard-Henri, 21
Lévy-Bruhl, L., 99
Lewald, Theodor, 103
Lewis, Anthony, 78
London (England), 91, 101, 130
Lorenz, Konrad, 119, 120, 123, 124; *On Aggression* (1963), 119
Los Angeles Olympic Organizing Committee (LAOOC), 130
Lowenthal, Leo, 26
Lucerne Sport International (LSI), 106-107
Luxembourg, 75
Lyttleton, Adrian, 89

MacAloon, John J., 45, 91, 115, 118, 122-123, 124, 125
Macaulay, Thomas, 96
Madrid (Spain), 12
Malaparte, Curzio, 90
Malitz, Bruno, 103
Manchester (England), 101
Manchester Guardian, 22
Mandell, Richard, 49, 85
Manley, Michael, 16
Mao Zedong, 27, 56, 109, 125
Marchais, Georges, 128
Marcuse, Herbert, 111
Marx, Karl, 35, 62
Marxism-Leninism, 75, 83, 106, 109, 113
mass psychology, 38

Matin, Le, 70
Matthews, Vince, 99
Maurras, Charles, 35, 88, 93-96, 97, 99, 100, 101
Maximov, Vladimir, 70
Mayakovsky, V., 72
mechanization, 48
Medvedev, Roy, 71, 78; *Let History Judge* (1968), 71; *On Socialist Democracy* (1975), 71
Melbourne (Australia), 101
Mexico, 1
Meyerhold, V. E., 72
Meynaud, Jean, 32
Miller, F. Don, 132
Milosz, Czeslaw, 63; *The Captive Mind* (1951), 64
Mishima, Yukio, 26
Mitterand, François, 21
Mobuto Sese Seko, Joseph, 8
modernity, 48, 51, 83, 85, 122
Mongolia, 127
Montoneros, 20-21
Montreal (Canada), 66
Morton, Henry, 1, 58
Moscow (Soviet Union), 7, 12, 44, 54, 55, 62, 63, 66, 67, 69, 72, 73, 78, 79, 101, 122
"Moscow '80 Committee on Human Rights," 70
Moscow International Book Fairs, 22
Moscow Olympic Organizing Committee, 65
Moscow Radio, 77
Moscow World Youth Festival, 79
Moskovskaya Pravda, 69
Mosse, George, 46, 47, 100, 105
motor skills, 116
movements, athletic and dance, 26
music, 114, 115, 125
Mussolini, Benito, 23, 37, 44, 56, 89, 90, 91, 95

narcissism, culture of, 79
National Stadium (Santiago de Chile), 19
NATO, 65
Nazi critique of sport, 102-103
NBC-TV, 69
Netherlands. See Holland
Neuendorff, Edmund, 50, 105
Neues Deutschland, 62
New Delhi (India), 2, 133
News of the World (London), 71
Newsweek, 66

New Yorker, The, 51
New York Review of Books, 128
New York Times, 6, 10, 14, 21, 78
New Zealand, 63, 76
Nicaragua, 16-17
Nietzsche, Friedrich, 90, 91; The Will to Power, 90
Nixon, Richard, 57
Nobel Peace Prize (1936), 50
Nolte, Ernst, 94, 95, 96
Northern Ireland, 19
North Korea, 9, 127
Norton, Ray, 98
Novosti, 22
Nuremberg (West Germany), 49, 97
Nurmi, Paavo, 108

Olympia (Greece), 5, 45, 83, 130
Olympic citizenship, 131, 132
"Olympic ethical principles," 30
Olympic festival, 3
Olympic flag, 75, 131
Olympic Games: as sport holidays, 11; Athens (1896), 35-36, 92, 94, 95, 99, 100, 101; Paris (1900), 87; St. Louis (1904), 87; Stockholm (1912), 56; Antwerp (1920), 17, 32, 42; Paris (1924), 17, 44, 62, 108; Lake Placid (1932), 17; Los Angeles (1932), 17, 54; Berlin (1936), 5, 16, 18, 19, 20, 23, 24, 31, 36, 42-45, 50, 51, 52, 54, 55, 66, 71, 85, 87, 88, 97, 103, 104, 105, 108, 131; London (1948), 32; Oslo (1952), 18; Helsinki (1952), 106; Melbourne (1956), 16; Rome (1960), 98, 130; Tokyo (1964), 53, 70, 99, 112; Mexico City (1968), 5, 13, 14, 17, 18, 19 20, 121; Munich (1972), 14, 76, 112, 113, 120-121; Montreal (1976), 57, 60, 61, 63, 70, 71, 121, 123; Lake Placid (1980), 66; Moscow (1980), 1, 5, 6, 7-8, 11, 12, 20, 22, 58, 61, 63. 65-80, 120, 121, 122, 128, 129; Sarajevo (1984), 132; Los Angeles (1984), 1, 5, 75, 127-130, 131, 132; Seoul (1988), 2, 133
Olympic hymn, 75
Olympic ideology, 9, 24, 46, 85, 91, 112
Olympic internationalism, 6, 76, 82, 91
Olympic jargon, 7
Olympic motto, 10

Olympic oath, 76
Olympic Review, 38
Olympic ritual, 76
"Olympic spirit," 7
Olympic truce, 5
Olympism, 24, 29, 31, 32, 33, 40, 58, 62, 64, 66, 81, 82, 89, 90, 91, 94, 97, 98, 113, 119, 122, 124,129
Olympus, Mount, 73
Ongania, Juan, 15
Onischenko, Boris, 71
Orlov, Yuri, 69
Ortega y Gasset, José, 84, 85; The Revolt of the Masses (1930), 84
Ossietsky, Carl von, 50
Ouroussoff, Prince Leo, 62
Owen, David, 69
Owens, Jesse, 104
Ozolin, Major E., 116, 117

paganism, 31, 42
pageantry, 73, 74, 90
Palestine Liberation Organization (PLO), 113
Palme, Olof, 21
Papini, Giovanni, 89, 90
Pareto, Vilfredo, 90
Paris (France), 70, 71, 91, 101, 133
Paul VI, Pope, 30
Pauls, Rolf, 16
Pavlov, Sergei, 60
Paz, Octavio, 13; The Other Mexico: Critique of the Pyramid (1972), 13
"peaceful coexistence," 58, 78, 106
Péguy, Charles, 95
Peking (China), 27
performance, intellectual, 121
performance principle, 10, 17, 103, 105, 106, 109, 111, 112, 113, 131
Physical Culture in Germany (Berlin, 1973), 61
physical dexterity, 25
Pius XII, Pope, 9, 41
Plato, 24
play, 27, 49, 98, 109, 115
Plyutsch, Leonard, 70
Poland, 15, 127
Politburo (Soviet), 77, 116
Ponomaryov, Nikolai, 114-115, 125
Popov, Vladimir, 73, 76
Portugal, 75
"positive thinking," 32, 64
Pound, Richard, 129
Pouret, Henri, 25-26; "Is Sport an Art?" 25

Prague (Czechoslovakia), 12, 5
Pravda (Moscow), 19, 67, 69, 77
professionalism, 49, 124
Prokop, Ulrike, 109, 110; Sociology of the Olympic Games Sport and Capitalism (1971) 110
"psychological warfare," 77, 78, 12
publicity, 131
Puerto Rico, 76

Quarrie, Donald, 16
Quisling, Vidkun, 52

radical critique of Olympia, 98 99
radio, 25
Radio Free Europe (RFE), 129 132
Radio Liberty (RL), 129, 132
record performance, 25, 81, 85 86, 98, 102, 103, 116, 117
Red Cross, 120
"Red Olympics," 133
Red Sport International (RSI) 106-107
Reich, Walter, 3
Reichstag fire, 50
religion, 9, 23-25, 38-39, 40-42, 53
Remond, René, 96
Renan, Ernest, 96
Rhodesia, 121
riddle-solving, 101
Riefenstahl, Leni, 97
Riehl, Wilhelm, 101
Rio de Janeiro (Brazil), 101
Riordan, James, 63
ritual, 123
Rocco, Alfredo, 90
Romanov, Sergei, 127
Rome (Italy), 75
Roosevelt, Julian K., 132
Rosenberg, Alfred, 103
Rothe, Wolfgang, 101
Rotterdam (Holland), 133
Royal College of Psychiatry, 3
Royal Dutch Football Association, 22
Rudolph, Wilma, 98
Russell, Bertrand, 14

Sakharov, Andrei, 7, 13, 70, 71, 77 122
Salisbury, Harrison E., 78, 79
Samaranch, Juan Antonio, 67 129, 133
San Marino, 75
Santiago de Chile (Chile), 20

166

Sartre, Jean-Paul, 14, 21
Saturday Review (London), 85
Schelsky, Helmut, 120, 121, 122, 123, 124; *Peace in Time: The Future of the Olympic Games* (1973), 120
Schiller, Friedrich, 83; *Letter on the Aesthetic Education of Man* (1795), 83
Schlereth, Thomas J., 119
Seelenbinder, Werner, 20
Seoul (Korea), 2, 133
Shaplen, Robert, 52, 57
Shaw, George Bernard, 56
Shcharansky, Anatoly B., 67, 69
Simon, William E., 130, 132, 133
Smith, Red, 51
Socialist Realism, 113, 115-116
Socialist Unity Party (SUP, East Germany), 18, 114
Socialist Workers' Sport International (SASI), 17, 62, 106
"Society for the Promotion of the Olympic Idea in the GDR," 18
Soffici, Ardengo, 90
Solzhenitsyn, Alexander, 71
Sontag, Susan, 27, 74
South Africa, Republic of, 5, 18, 19, 20, 30, 99, 121, 130
South Korea, 2, 128
South Yemen, 127
Soviet Football Association, 20
Soviet Military Review (Moscow), 76
Soviet Olympic Organizing Committee, 71, 73, 127
Sovietskaya Rossia, 68
Sovietski Sport, 63, 65, 67, 76, 106
Soviet Union, 3, 7, 8, 9-10, 12, 15, 18, 19, 20, 22, 55, 56, 58, 60, 64, 66, 67, 72, 82, 114, 127, 128, 132
Spain, 16, 18, 22, 59, 67, 76
Spanish-American War, 40
Sparta (Greece), 5, 86
Spartakiad, 61, 62, 74; (1928), 73, 82, 107; (1956), 73
spectacle, 123
Spectator (London), 81
speed, 85
Speer, Albert, 18, 49, 104, 106
Spiegel, Der, 10, 14, 20, 73, 129
Spinoza, Baruch, 47
spontaneity, 73, 110, 111, 117
sporting press, 81, 88, 102, 118
sportive drama, 26
sport jargon, 10
sport robot, 112
Stakhanovite super-worker, 116

Stalin, Joseph, 6, 11, 18, 56, 58, 71, 73, 106, 116
"star syndrome," 110
"state amateurism," 63
State Dept. (U.S.), 78, 128, 129
Steffens, Lincoln, 56
Stern, Fritz, 83
Stockholm (Sweden), 101, 133
"struggle of ideas," 78
Supreme Council for Sport in Africa, 127
Sweden, 21
Switzerland, 16, 75

Taoism, 52
technique, 117
technology, 48, 83, 105, 106, 109, 111, 112, 113, 115, 116, 117, 122, 124
technophobia, 109
Teichler, Hans Joachim, 42
television, 25, 82, 128
theater, 114
Theory and Practice of Physical Culture (East Berlin), 61
Third Republic (France), 33, 37-39, 45, 91, 110
Time, 66
Tlatelolco massacre (October 2, 1968), 1, 13-14, 17, 30, 118
Tolstoi, Leo, 25
totalitarian state, 9, 56
treason, 52, 57, 69, 70, 93
Trinquet, Pascale, 76
Tschammer und Osten, Hans von, 50
Tunisia, 64

Ueberroth, Peter, 130
Ulbricht, Walter, 10, 15, 18, 61
Unita, L', 128
United Nations, 5, 54, 82
United Nations Human Rights Commision, 16
United States House of Representatives, 66
United States Senate, 66
universal exposition, 122
universal intelligibility, 54
universalism, 2, 9, 10
Upper Volta, 127
Uruguay, 15
utopianism, 5, 39, 53, 58, 59, 86, 110, 118, 131

van Agt, Andreis, 16
Vance, Cyrus R., 66, 67, 79
Vatican, 3, 31, 38, 93
Venus de Milo, 114

Verne, Jules, 122
Verona (Italy), 101
Versailles Treaty, 103
Vichy regime (1940-44), 93
Videla, Lieutenant General Jorge, 12, 21
Vienna (Austria), 58, 70
Vietnam, 21, 65, 127
virility, cult of, 90, 98, 110
Visotsky, Harold M., 3
Vladimov, Georgi, 79
Völkischer Beobachter, 50, 103, 104, 106
Volkish critique of Olympia, 100-106, 111
Volkish doctrine, 45, 46-49, 83, 88, 112, 124
Voltaire, François Marie de, 118

Wagner, Helmut, 107; *Sport and Workers' Sport* (1931), 107
Wagner, Richard, 97
Walker, John, 11
Washington, George, 52, 53
Washington, D.C., 78
Weber, Eugen, 34, 35
Weimar Republic, 101, 103
Werrie, Paul, 34, 35, 97, 98, 99
West Germany, 15, 18, 20, 65, 76, 109, 121, 122, 127, 128
Wildung, Fritz, 17, 82, 107
Wohl, Andrzej, 26, 64, 114, 116; *Social-Historical Foundations of Bourgeois Sport* (1973), 114
work, 109, 116
Workers' Gymnastics League 102
Workers' Olympiads, 17, 18, 44, 62, 63, 82, 107, 108; Prague (1921), 17, 62; Frankfurt (1925), 62, 107, 108; Vienna (1931), 17, 62, 82, 107, 108; Antwerp (1937), 62
workers' sport, 17, 82, 107
world conscience, 14, 16
World Cup soccer tournament, 11, 14, 15, 16, 20, 21, 22
World Psychiatric Association 2, 3
World Youth Festivals, 18

xenophobia, 67, 68, 77, 79, 95, 97, 98, 100, 129

Yakir, Pyotr, 71
Yugoslavia, 128

Zaire, 8
Zeit, Die, 1
Zeldin, Theodore, 34, 38-39
Zhdanov, A.A., 116

167